M

KV-374-295

ffice

LIVERPOOL LIBRARIES & INFORMATION SERVICES

Renewals
www.liverpool.gov.uk/libraries
0151 233 3000

R.267

Que®

Que Publishing
800 East 96th Street
Indianapolis, IN 46240 USA

LV 20803508

Liverpool Libraries

Show Me Microsoft® Office Word 2003

Copyright © 2003 by Perspection, Inc.
All rights reserved. No part of this book shall be reproduced, stored in a retrieval system, or transmitted by any means, electronic, mechanical, photocopying, recording, or otherwise, without written permission from the publisher. No patent liability is assumed with respect to the use of the information contained herein. Although every precaution has been taken in the preparation of this book, the publisher and author assume no responsibility for errors or omissions. Nor is any liability assumed for damages resulting from the use of the information contained herein.

International Standard Book Number: 0-7897-3010-3

Library of Congress Catalog Card Number: 2003108682

Printed in the United States of America

First Printing: September 2003

06 05 04 03   4 3 2 1

Que Publishing offers excellent discounts on this book when ordered in quantity for bulk purchases or special sales. For information, please contact:

U.S. Corporate and Government Sales

1-800-382-3419

corpsales@pearsontechgroup.com

For sales outside the U.S., please contact:

International Sales

1-317-428-3341

International@pearsontechgroup.com

Trademarks

All terms mentioned in this book that are known to be trademarks or service marks have been appropriately capitalized. Que cannot attest to the accuracy of this information. Use of a term in this book should not be regarded as affecting the validity of any trademark or service mark.

Microsoft and the Microsoft Office logo are a registered trademarks of Microsoft Corporation in the United States and/or other countries.

Warning and Disclaimer

Every effort has been made to make this book as complete and as acc as possible, but no warranty or fitness is implied. The authors and the lishers shall have neither liability nor responsibility to any person or e with respect to any loss or damage arising from the information conta this book.

Publisher
Paul Boger

Associate Publisher
Greg Wiegand

Managing Editor
Steve Johnson

Author
Steve Johnson

Project Editor
Holly Johnson

Technical Editor
Melinda Lankford

Production Editor
Beth Teyler

Page Layout
Kate Lyerla
Joe Kalsbeek
Ryan Suzuki
Matt West

Interior Designers
Steve Johnson
Marian Hartsough

Indexer
Michael Brackney

Proofreaders
Beth Teyler
Melinda Lankford

Team Coordinator
Sharry Lee Gregory

LIVERPOOL LIBRARIES & INFORMATION SERV	
LV20803508	
Cypher	23.11.03
652.55369JOH	£14.50
KA	

Acknowledgements

Perspection, Inc.

Show Me Microsoft Office Word 2003 has been created by the professional trainers and writers at Perspection, Inc. to the standards you've come to expect from Que publishing. Together, we are pleased to present this training book.

Perspection, Inc. is a software training company committed to providing information and training to help people use software more effectively in order to communicate, make decisions, and solve problems. Perspection writes and produces software training books, and develops multimedia and Web-based training. Since 1991, we have written more than 60 computer books, with several bestsellers to our credit, and sold over 4.5 million books.

This book incorporates Perspection's training expertise to ensure that you'll receive the maximum return on your time. You'll focus on the tasks and skills that increase productivity while working at your own pace and convenience.

We invite you to visit the Perspection Web site at:

www.perspection.com

Acknowledgements

The task of creating any book requires the talents of many hard-working people pulling together to meet impossible deadlines and untold stresses. We'd like to thank the outstanding team responsible for making this book possible: the writer, Steve Johnson; the project editor, Holly Johnson; the technical editor, Melinda Lankford; the production team, Kate Lyerla, Joe Kalsbeek, Ryan Suzuki, and Matt West; the proofreaders, Beth Teyler and Melinda Lankford; and the indexer, Michael Brackney.

At Que publishing, we'd like to thank Greg Wiegand for the opportunity to undertake this project, Sharry Gregory for administrative support, and Sandra Schroeder for your production expertise and support.

Perspection

Dedication

Most importantly, I would like to thank my wife Holly, and my three children, JP, Brett, and Hannah, for their support and encouragement during the project. I would also like to thank Sarah Bartholomaei for her tender loving care and dedication towards our children during the deadline times.

About The Author

Steve Johnson has written more than twenty books on a variety of computer software, including Microsoft Office XP, Microsoft Windows XP, Macromedia Director MX and Macromedia Fireworks, and Web publishing. In 1991, after working for Apple Computer and Microsoft, Steve founded Perspection, Inc., which writes and produces software training. When he is not staying up late writing, he enjoys playing golf, gardening, and spending time with his wife, Holly, and three children, JP, Brett, and Hannah. When time permits, he likes to travel to such places as New Hampshire in October, and Hawaii. Steve and his family live in Pleasanton, California, but can also be found visiting family all over the western United States.

We Want To Hear From You!

As the reader of this book, *you* are our most important critic and commentator. We value your opinion and want to know what we're doing right, what we could do better, what areas you'd like to see us publish in, and any other words of wisdom you're willing to pass our way.

As an associate publisher for Que, I welcome your comments. You can email or write me directly to let me know what you did or didn't like about this book—as well as what we can do to make our books better.

Please note that I cannot help you with technical problems related to the topic of this book. We do have a User Services group, however, where I will forward specific technical questions related to the book.

When you write, please be sure to include this book's title and author as well as your name, email address, and phone number. I will carefully review your comments and share them with the author and editors who worked on the book.

Email: feedback@quepublishing.com

Mail: Greg Wiegand
         Que Publishing
         800 East 96th Street
         Indianapolis, IN 46240 USA

For more information about this book or another Que title, visit our Web site at *www.quepublishing.com*. Type the ISBN (excluding hyphens) or the title of a book in the Search field to find the page you're looking for.

Contents

LIVERPOOL LIBRARIES & INFORMATION SERVICES

LIVERPOOL LIBRARIES & INFORMATION SERVICES

C

Upgrade

A B C

Introduction

Welcome to *Show Me Microsoft Office Word 2003*, a visual quick reference book that shows you how to work efficiently with Microsoft Office Word 2003. This book provides complete coverage of basic and intermediate Word 2003 skills.

Find the Best Place to Start

You don't have to read this book in any particular order. We've designed the book so that you can jump in, get the information you need, and jump out. However, the book does follow a logical progression from simple tasks to more complex ones. Each task is no more than two pages long. To find the information that you need, just look up the task in the table of contents, index, or troubleshooting guide, and turn to the page listed. Read the task introduction, follow the step-by-step instructions along with the illustration, and you're done.

What's New

If you're searching for what's new in Word 2003, just look for the icon: New!. The new icon appears in the table of contents so you can quickly and easily identify a new or improved feature in Word 2003. A complete description of each new feature appears in the New Features guide in the back of this book.

How This Book Works

Each task is presented on no more than two facing pages, with step-by-step instructions in the left column and screen illustrations in the right column. This arrangement lets you focus on a single task without having to turn the page.

How You'll Learn

Find the Best Place to Start

What's New

How This Book Works

Step-by-Step Instructions

Real World Examples

Troubleshooting Guide

Show Me Live Software

Microsoft Office Specialist

Step-by-Step Instructions

This book provides concise step-by-step instructions that show you "how" to accomplish a task. Each set of instructions include illustrations that directly correspond to the easy-to-read steps. Also included in the text are timesavers, tables, and sidebars to help you work more efficiently or to teach you more in-depth information. A "Did You Know?" provides tips and techniques to help you work smarter, while a "See Also" leads you to other parts of the book containing related information about the task.

Real World Examples

This book uses real world examples to help convey "why" you would want to perform a task. The examples give you a context in which to use the task. You'll observe how *Home Sense, Inc.*, a fictional home improvement business, uses Word 2003 to get the job done.

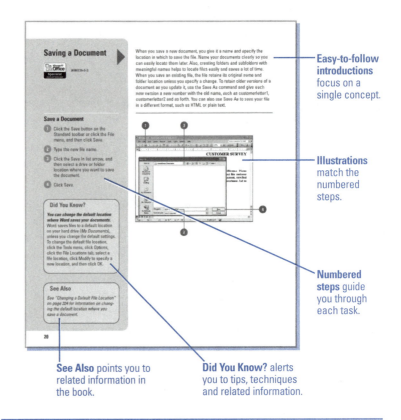

Easy-to-follow introductions focus on a single concept.

Illustrations match the numbered steps.

Numbered steps guide you through each task.

See Also points you to related information in the book.

Did You Know? alerts you to tips, techniques and related information.

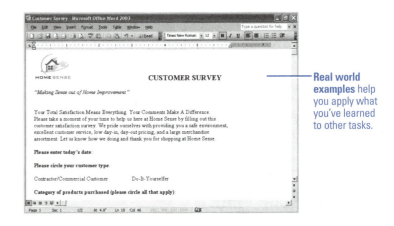

Real world examples help you apply what you've learned to other tasks.

Troubleshooting Guide

This book offers quick and easy ways to diagnose and solve common Word 2003 problems that you might encounter. The troubleshooting guide helps you determine and fix a problem using the task information you find. The problems are posed in question form and are grouped into categories that are presented alphabetically.

Troubleshooting points you to information in the book to help you fix your problems.

Show Me Live Software

In addition, this book offers companion software that shows you how to perform most tasks using the live program. The easy-to-use VCR-type controls allow you to start, pause, and stop the action. As you observe how to accomplish each task, Show Me Live highlights each step and talks you through the process. The Show Me Live software is available free at *www.perspection.com or www.quepublishing.com/showme*.

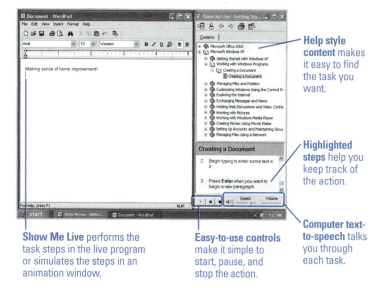

Help style content makes it easy to find the task you want.

Highlighted steps help you keep track of the action.

Computer text-to-speech talks you through each task.

Show Me Live performs the task steps in the live program or simulates the steps in an animation window.

Easy-to-use controls make it simple to start, pause, and stop the action.

Microsoft Office Specialist

This book prepares you fully for the Microsoft Office Specialist exam at the specialist and expert levels for Microsoft Office Word 2003. Each Microsoft Office Specialist certification level has a set of objectives, which are organized into broader skill sets. To prepare for the certification exam, you should review and perform each task identified with a Microsoft Office Specialist objective to confirm that you can meet the requirements for the exam. Throughout this book, content that pertains to an objective is identified with the Microsoft Office Specialist logo and objective number next to it.

Microsoft Office Specialist

About the Microsoft Office Specialist Program

The Microsoft Office Specialist certification is the globally recognized standard for validating expertise with the Microsoft Office suite of business productivity programs. Earning an Microsoft Office Specialist certificate acknowledges you have the expertise to work with Microsoft Office programs. To earn the Microsoft Office Specialist certification, you must pass one or more certification exams for the Microsoft Office desktop applications of Microsoft Office Word, Microsoft Office Excel, Microsoft Office PowerPoint, Microsoft Office Outlook, or Microsoft Office Access. The Microsoft Office Specialist program typically offers certification exams at the "specialist" and "expert" skill levels. (The availability of Microsoft Office Specialist certification exams varies by program, program version, and language. Visit *www.microsoft.com/officespecialist* for exam availability and more information about the program.) The Microsoft Office Specialist program is the only Microsoft-approved program in the world for certifying proficiency with Microsoft Office programs.

What Does This Logo Mean?

It means this book has been approved by the Microsoft Office Specialist program to be certified courseware for learning Microsoft Office Word 2003 and preparing for the certification exam. This book will prepare you fully for the Microsoft Office Specialist exam at the specialist and expert levels for Microsoft Office Word 2003. Each certification level has a set of objectives, which are organized into broader skill sets. Throughout this book, content that pertains to a Microsoft Office Specialist objective is identified with the Microsoft Office Specialist logo and objective number below the title of the topic:

 WD03S-1-1
WD03E-2-2

Logo indicates a task fulfills one or more Microsoft Office Specialist objectives.

353

Getting Started with Word

Introduction

Microsoft Office Word 2003 is a powerful word-processing program that enables you to easily compose and edit documents for print or online use. Word 2003 contains many new tools specifically designed to improve the way you interact with the program, and the way you collaborate with one another in preparing documents.

This chapter introduces you to the terminology and the basic Word skills you can use in the program. In Word, files are called **documents**. Each new document is similar to a blank page. As you type and add additional text and other objects, you document gets longer. Unlike looking at a piece of paper, Word provides many views, such as the Reading Layout view, that help you see the document in the best possible way for the task at hand.

You can navigate through various tasks with a click of the mouse, or by using shortcut keys on your keyboard. Word is set up with a variety of menus and dialog boxes that assist you in getting the job done right. Toolbars help you when you need to quickly perform a task, such as formatting text. When working with your documents, you can view more than one document, or resize the window to compare data. Moving around in your document is made easy by the browsing function in Word. With a click of a button, you are on your way to browsing your document in various ways—by footnote, graphic, or comments, to name a few.

The Office Assistant, along with Word's extensive on-line Help, can point you in the right direction. When you finish the design of your document you can save it in various formats, a Web page for example, to use in another office program. Microsoft also offers the Office Online Web site, a resource to check for updates and information on Word.

What You'll Do

Start Word

View the Word Window

Use Task Panes

Choose Menu Commands

Choose Dialog Box Options

Work with Toolbars

Move Around in a Document

Create a Document

Resize and Move a Window

Select, Copy, and Paste Text

Change Document Views

Read and Save a Document

Get Help While You Work

Get Help from the Office Assistant

Get Word Updates on the Web

Exit Word

Starting Word

Before you can begin using Word, you need to start the program. The easiest way to start Word is to use the Start menu, which you open by clicking the Start button on the taskbar. When Word starts, it displays a blank document so that you can begin working immediately.

Start Word

1. Click the Start button on the task bar.

2. Point to All Programs, and then point to Microsoft Office.

3. Click on Microsoft Office Word 2003. A blank document opens.

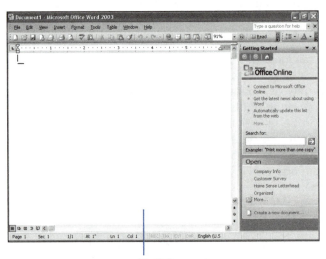

Blank document

Viewing the Word Window

Menu bar
The nine menus provide access to all Word options.

Title bar
The document name and Microsoft Word appear in the title bar. *Document1* is a temporary name Word uses until you assign a new one.

Close button

Insertion point
The blinking insertion point (also called a cursor) shows you where the next character will appear.

Standard and Formatting toolbars
These and other toolbars contain buttons that provide quick access to a variety of commands and features.

Document
You enter text and graphics here.

Document view buttons
Click to see your document in different ways.

Mouse pointer
In the document, the mouse pointer appears as an I-beam. The pointer changes shape depending on where you point in the window.

Status bar
The status bar provides information about current settings and commands.

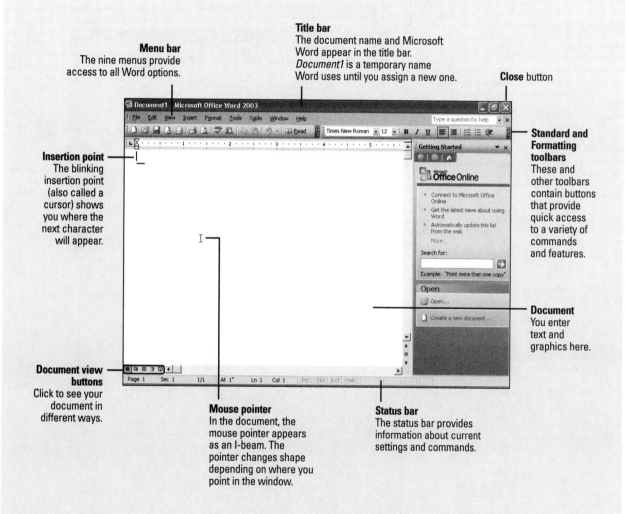

Using Task Panes

Use the Task Pane

1. When you start Word, the task pane appears on the right side of your screen.

2. Click an option on the task pane.

When you start Word, a task pane appears by default on the right side of the program window. The task pane displays various options that relate to the current task. There are several types of options available on the task pane. You can search for information, select options, and click links, like the ones on a Web page, to perform commands. You can also display different task panes, move back and forth between task panes, and close a task pane to provide a larger work area.

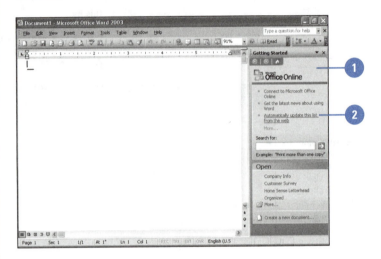

Open and Close Task Panes

1 Click the View menu, and then click Task Pane.

2 To open another task pane, click the list arrow on the task pane title bar, and then click the task pane you want.

3 To switch between task panes, click the Back and Forward task pane buttons.

4 Click the Close button on the task pane.

Did You Know?

You can jump to the Getting Started task pane. Click the Home button to jump back to the Getting Started task pane.

Home button

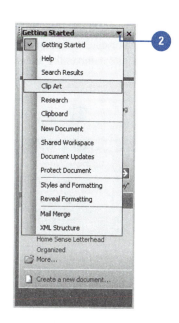

Choosing Menu Commands

A **menu** is a list of related commands or options, located at the top of the window. The menus are personalized as you work—when you click a menu name, you first see the commands you use most frequently. After a few moments, you see the entire list of commands. You can right-click a word or object to open a **shortcut menu**, which contains menu commands related to the specific item.

Choose a Command from a Menu

1. Click a menu name on the menu bar.

2. If necessary, click the double-headed arrow to expand the menu, or wait until the expanded list of commands appears.

3. Click the command you want. If the command is followed by an arrow, point to the command to see a list of related options, and then click the option you want.

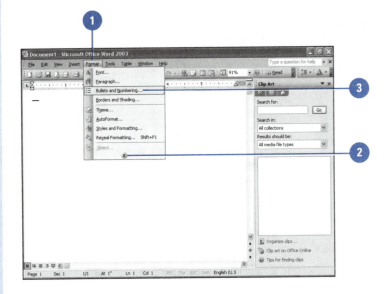

Choose a Command from a Shortcut Menu

1. Right-click an object (a text or graphic element).

2. Click a command on the shortcut menu. If the command is followed by an arrow, point to the command to see a list of related options, and then click the option you want.

   TIMESAVER *You can use a shortcut key to choose a command. Press and hold down the first key and then press the second key. For example, press and hold the Ctrl key and then press S to select the Save command.*

Choosing Dialog Box Options

A **dialog box** is a window that opens when you choose a menu command followed by an ellipsis (. . .). The ellipsis indicates that you must supply more information before the program can carry out the command you selected. After you enter information or make selections in a dialog box, click the OK button to complete the command. Click the Cancel button to close the dialog box without issuing the command. In many dialog boxes, you can also click an Apply button to apply your changes without closing the dialog box.

1

Choose Dialog Box Options

All dialog boxes contain the same types of options, including the following:

◆ **Tabs.** Click a tab to display its options. Each tab groups a related set of options.

◆ **Option buttons.** Click an option button to select it. You can usually select only one.

◆ **Up and down arrows.** Click the up or down arrow to increase or decrease the number, or type a number in the box.

◆ **Check box.** Click the box to turn on or off the option. A checked box means the option is selected; a cleared box means it's not.

◆ **List box.** Click the list arrow to display a list of options, and then click the option you want.

◆ **Text box.** Click in the box and type the requested information.

◆ **Button.** Click a button to perform a specific action or command. A button name followed by an ellipsis (...) opens another dialog box.

◆ **Preview box.** Many dialog boxes show an image that reflects the options you select.

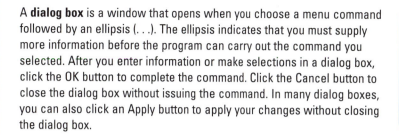

Buttons

Check box

List box

Option buttons

Text box

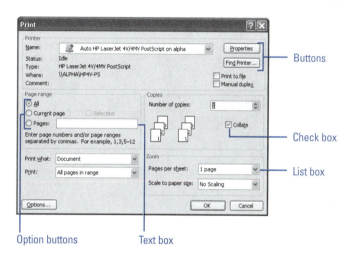

Tabs

Up and down arrows

Preview box

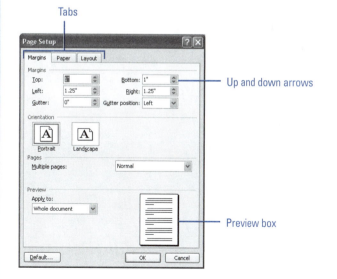

Working with Toolbars

A **toolbar** contains a collection of buttons you click to select frequently used menu commands. Most programs open with a Standard toolbar (with commands such as Save and Print) and a Formatting toolbar (with commands for selecting fonts and sizes) side by side. You can also display toolbars designed for specific tasks, such as drawing pictures, importing data, or creating charts. If you're not using a toolbar or want to position it in another place, you can hide or move it. When you move a toolbar, you can dock it to the edge of a window or allow it to float in a separate window. The toolbars are personalized as you work, showing only the buttons you use most often. Additional toolbar buttons are available by clicking the Toolbar Options list arrow at the end of the toolbar.

Choose a Command Using a Toolbar Button

1. If you are not sure what a toolbar button does, point to it to display a ScreenTip.

2. To choose a command, click the button. To see additional commands that might be available on the toolbar, click the toolbar list arrow.

Did You Know?

Toolbar buttons and keyboard shortcuts are faster than menu commands. You can learn the toolbar button equivalents of menu commands by looking at the toolbar button icon to the left of a menu command.

ScreenTip   Toolbar list arrow

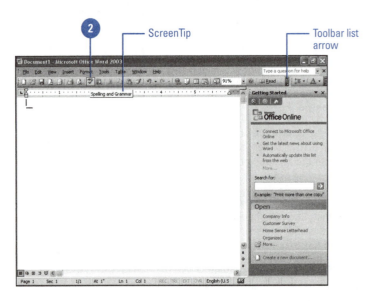

Display or Hide a Toolbar

1 Click the View menu, and then point to Toolbars.

2 Click the toolbar you want to display or hide.

A check mark next to the toolbar name indicates that it is currently displayed on the screen.

Did You Know?

You can choose a toolbar quickly. To quickly display the list of available toolbars, right-click a toolbar and then click the toolbar you want to use.

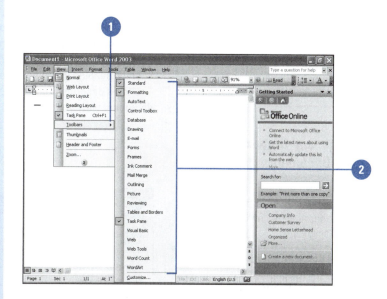

Move and Reshape a Toolbar

◆ To move a toolbar that is docked (attached to one edge of the window) or floating (unattached) over the window, click the gray dotted edge bar on the left edge of the toolbar, and then drag it to a new location.

◆ To move a toolbar that is floating (unattached) over the window, drag the title bar to a new location.

◆ To return a floating toolbar to its previously docked location, double-click its title bar.

◆ To change the shape of a floating toolbar, drag any border until the toolbar is the shape you want.

Drag any docked toolbar using the dotted gray bar.

Drag any floating toolbar using the Title bar.

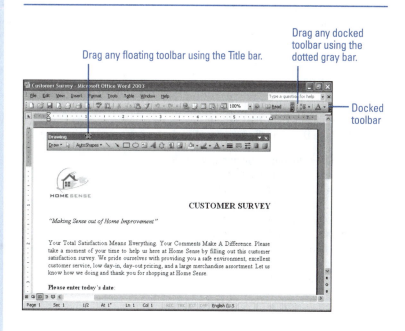

Docked toolbar

Moving Around in a Document

WW03S-1-3

Scroll, Page, and Browse Through a Document

◆ To scroll through a document one line at a time, click the up or down scroll arrow on the vertical scroll bar.

◆ To scroll quickly through a document, click and hold the up or down scroll arrow on the vertical scroll bar.

◆ To scroll to a specific page or heading in a document, drag the scroll box on the vertical scroll bar until the page number or heading you want appears in the yellow box.

◆ To page through the document one screen at a time, press Page Up or Page Down on the keyboard.

◆ To browse a document by page, edits, headings, or other items, click the Select Browse Object button, and then click that item. If a dialog box opens, enter the name or number of the item you want to find, and then click the Previous or Next button to move from one item to the next.

As your document gets longer, some of your work shifts out of sight. You can easily move any part of a document back into view. **Scrolling** moves the document line by line. **Paging** moves the document page by page. **Browsing** moves you through your document by the item you specify, such as to the next word, comment, picture, table, or heading. The tools described here move you around a document no matter which document view you are in.

The current page appears when you drag the vertical scroll box.

Up scroll arrow

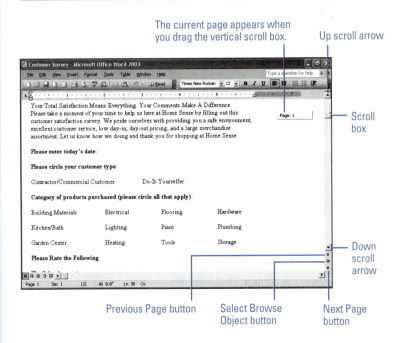

Scroll box

Down scroll arrow

Previous Page button

Select Browse Object button

Next Page button

Click to move from one comment to the next.

Select Browse Object button

Click to go to a specific item.

Click to move from one table to the next.

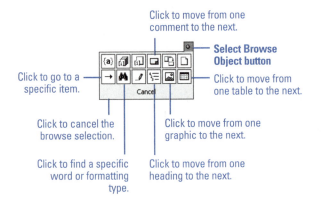

Click to cancel the browse selection.

Click to move from one graphic to the next.

Click to find a specific word or formatting type.

Click to move from one heading to the next.

Creating a Document

WW03S-1-1

When you open a new Word document, it's blank, ready for you to enter text. By default, this document is titled Document1. You can create new documents in several ways: using the New command on the File menu, the New Blank Document button on the Formatting toolbar, and by the New Document task pane. Word numbers new documents consecutively. You can open and work on as many new documents as you'd like. The insertion point (blinking cursor bar) appears in the document where text will appear when you type. As you type, text moves, or **wraps**, to a new line when the previous one is full. You can move the insertion point anywhere within the document so that you can insert new text and **edit** (or insert, revise, or delete) existing text.

Create a Document

1. Click the File menu, and then click New.

2. Click Blank Document.

3. Begin typing, and then press Enter when you want to begin a new paragraph or insert a blank line.

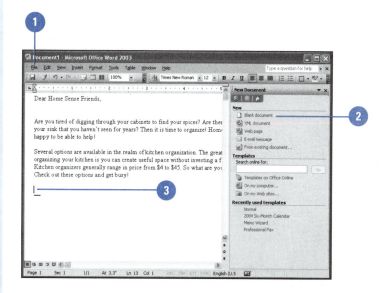

Edit Text in a Document

1. Click where you want to insert text, or select the text you want to edit.

2. Make the change you want:

   ◆ Type to insert new text.

   ◆ Press Enter to begin a new paragraph or insert a blank line.

   ◆ Press Backspace or Delete to erase text to the left or right of the insertion point.

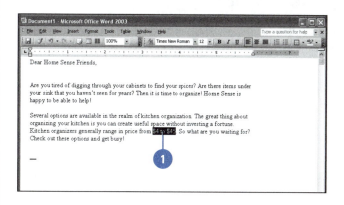

Resizing a Window

When you open a Word window, it appears in a preset size. You can change the size of the Word program window using the set of buttons, called resizing tools, in the upper-right corner of the Word window. The resizing tools appear in the blue title bar at the very top of the Word window. Resizing the window allows you to work with more than one document, or even more than one program, on your desktop at one time. When you resize a Word window, it only affects that particular document and window. It does not change the size of any other documents or windows you have open.

Resize a Window

◆ **Minimize a window.** To reduce a window to a button on the taskbar, click the Minimize button.

◆ **Maximize a window.** To maximize a window to fit the screen, click the Maximize button. Note that the button changes to Restore Down. This button toggles between these two settings.

◆ **Restore a window.** To revert from the full screen maximized view to a normal window, click the Restore Down button. Notice that the button changes to Maximize. This button toggles between these two settings.

◆ **Drag to resize a window.** To resize a window, position the mouse over any edge of the window and drag the sizing handle (double-ended arrow) to the size you want. If you drag a corner, the horizontal and vertical proportions of the window will be maintained as you resize it.

◆ **Close a window.** To close a window, click the Close button.

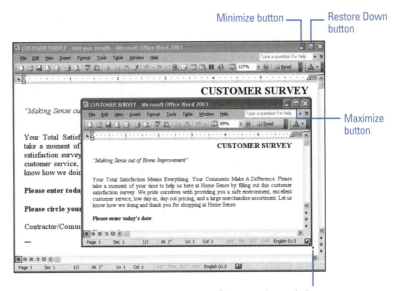

Minimize button — Restore Down button

Maximize button

Drag to resize a window

Moving a Window

When you open a Word window, it appears at a default location on your screen. You can change the location of a window to make it easier to work with multiple documents, or to move it out of the way without minimizing it so that you can work in another open window on the desktop.

Manually Move and Size Windows

◆ **Move a window.** To change a window's location on your screen, drag the title bar of the document window to a different location. By using a combination of resizing and moving, you can display documents side-by-side or in groupings onscreen.

Did You Know?

You can tell which window is active on your screen by looking at the title bar. When you display multiple documents or programs on the same screen, the title bar of the active window is a different color than the rest of the windows. If you have not changed any of the Windows color settings, the active window's title bar is blue, and all other windows are gray.

See Also

See "Working with Multiple Documents " on page 34 for information on using and arranging windows.

Drag to a new position

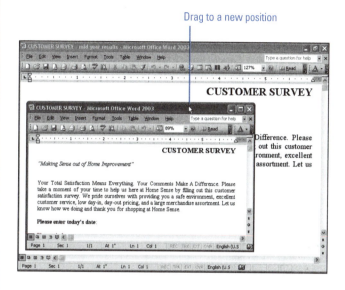

Selecting Text

The first step in working with text is to highlight, or **select**, the text you want. Once you've selected it, you can copy, move, format, and delete words, sentences, and paragraphs. When you finish with or decide not to use a selection, you can click anywhere in the document to **deselect** the text.

Select Text

1. Position the pointer in the word, paragraph, line, or part of the document you want to select.

2. Choose the method that accomplishes the task you want to complete in the easiest way.

   Refer to the table for methods to select text.

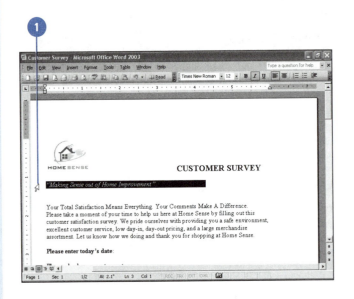

Did You Know?

You can have AutoComplete finish your words. As you enter common text, such as your name, months, today's date, and common salutations and closings, Word provides the rest of the text in a ScreenTip. Press Enter to have Word complete your words.

Selecting Text

To Select	Do This
A single word	Double-click the word.
A single paragraph	Triple-click a word within the paragraph.
A single line	Click in the left margin next to the line.
Any part of a document	Click at the beginning of the text you want to highlight, and then drag to the end of the section you want to highlight.
A large selection	Click at the beginning of the text you want to highlight, and then press and hold Shift while you click at the end of the text that you want to highlight.
The entire document	Triple-click in the left margin.
An outline heading or subheading in Outline view	Click the bullet, plus sign, or minus sign.

Copying and Pasting Text

You can copy or move items (including blocks of text) from one place to another within a document, or from one document to another. To do this, you **copy** the item (or block of text) you want to the Office Clipboard, and then **paste** it into the new location or document(s). Word stores each item copied on Office Clipboard. After you have placed two items on the Clipboard, the Clipboard opens so you can select which copied item you want to paste. After you paste an item, the Paste Options button appears next to the item in the document. You can click the Paste Options button to display a list of options on the shortcut menu. This button, known as a smart tag, allows you to immediately adjust how information is pasted or how automatic changes occur.

Copy and Paste Text in a Document

1. In the document you are copying from, select the item you want to copy.

2. Click the Copy button on the Standard toolbar.

   TIMESAVER *To copy a selected item, press Ctrl+C.*

3. Click the location where you want to insert the item to position the insertion point.

4. Click the Paste button on the Standard toolbar. Word pastes the text.

   TIMESAVER *To paste an item, press Ctrl+V.*

5. Click the Paste Options button, and then click an option to customize the way the text appears.

Did You Know?

You can perform Cut, Copy, and Paste operations using the Cut, Copy, and Paste commands on the Edit menu. The Cut and Copy commands are grayed out and unavailable until you select something in the document.

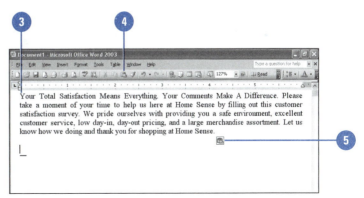

Changing Document Views

Word displays the contents of a document in different ways to help you work efficiently with your content. The available views include Normal, Web Layout, Print Layout, Outline, and Reading Layout. You can change the window view from the View menu, or you can click a Document view button at the bottom left corner of the Word window.

Normal view displays the document as a single, long piece of "paper," divided into pages by perforation marks. Word displays each new document in Normal view by default. This view is fine for composition but inadequate for editing or previewing your work prior to printing.

Web Layout view displays the document as it will appear on the Web. You can save documents as HTML code to make Web content creation easy.

Print Layout view displays a gray gap between each page to clearly delineate where each actual page break occurs. This view is best for previewing your work before printing, and it works well with the Zoom feature on the

Standard toolbar to increase and decrease the page view size and display multiple pages of the same document simultaneously onscreen.

Outline view displays the document as an outline with headings and subheadings. When you shift to Outline view, each heading has a clickable plus or minus sign next to it to expand or collapse the content under the heading. You can drag a plus, or minus sign to move the heading and all of its associated text.

Reading Layout view displays the screen size and removes distracting screen elements to provide a more comfortable view to read your documents. You can also display the Thumbnail pane or the Document Map to quickly jump to different parts of your document.

Full Screen view displays the document using the entire screen without a window and toolbars. When you're done, you can use the Close Full Screen button on the toolbar. This view is only available on the View menu.

Normal view

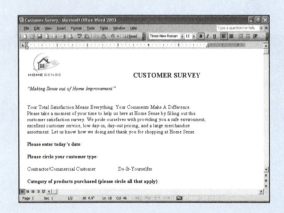

Web Layout view

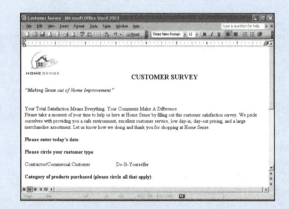

WW03S5-7

Print Layout view

Print Layout view (with Zoom view)

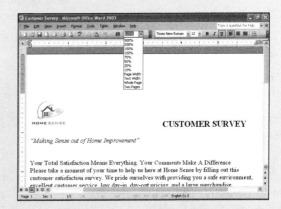

Outline view

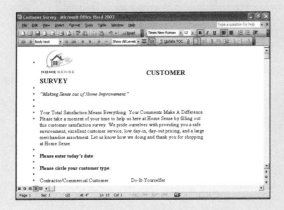

Reading Layout view

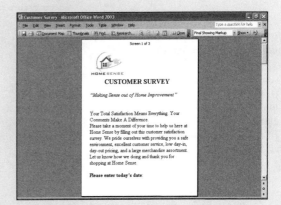

Reading a Document

WW03S-1-3, WW03S-5-7,
WW03E-2-5

You can avoid eye strain when you want to read a document with the Reading Layout view. The Reading Layout view is designed with tools optimized for reading a document. Word changes the screen size and removes distracting screen elements to provide a more comfortable view for reading your documents. In the Reading Layout view, you can display the Document Map or the Thumbnail pane to quickly jump to different parts of your document. If you have a Tablet PC, you can write comments and changes directly on the page using the tablet's stylus.

Read a Document

1. Click the Read button on the Standard toolbar.

   TIMESAVER *Press Alt+R to start reading.*

2. Click the Increase Text Size button or the Decrease Text Size button on the Reading Layout toolbar to display the text in a larger or smaller size.

3. Click the Allow Multiple Pages button or the Actual Page button on the Reading Layout toolbar to display two pages at once or a single page.

   TIMESAVER *Press Esc to deselect the document, type a number, and then press Enter to go to a page.*

4. When you're done, click the Close button on the Reading Layout toolbar.

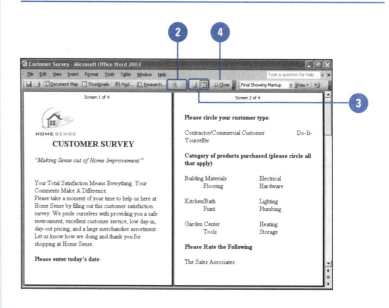

Did You Know?

You can highlight text and track changes in Reading Layout view. The Reviewing toolbar appears in Reading Layout view, where you can highlight text, track changes, insert comments, and use all the available commands.

Display Thumbnail View

① Click the Read button on the Standard toolbar.

② Click the Thumbnails button on the Reading Layout toolbar.

③ Click a thumbnail of a page to display the page.

④ Click the Thumbnails button on the Reading Layout toolbar again to turn it off.

⑤ When you're done, click the Close button on the Reading Layout toolbar.

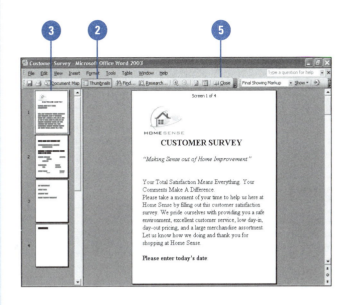

Display Document Map

① Click the Read button on the Standard toolbar.

② Click the Document Map button on the Reading Layout toolbar.

③ Click the part of the document you want to display.

④ Click the Document Map button on the Reading Layout toolbar again to turn it off.

⑤ When you're done, click the Close button on the Reading Layout toolbar.

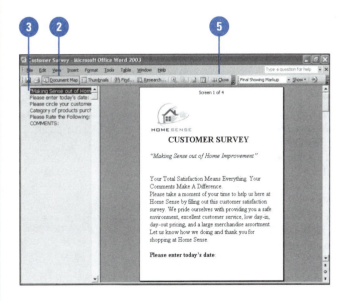

Saving a Document

WW03S-5-3

When you save a new document, you give it a name and specify the location in which to save the file. Name your documents clearly so you can easily locate them later. Also, creating folders and subfolders with meaningful names helps to locate files easily and saves a lot of time. When you save an existing file, the file retains its original name and folder location unless you specify a change. To retain older versions of a document as you update it, use the Save As command and give each new version a new number with the old name, such as customerletter1, customerletter2 and so forth. You can also use Save As to save your file in a different format, such as HTML or plain text.

Save a Document

1. Click the Save button on the Standard toolbar or click the File menu, and then click Save.

2. Type the new file name.

3. Click the Save In list arrow, and then select a drive or folder location where you want to save the document.

4. Click Save.

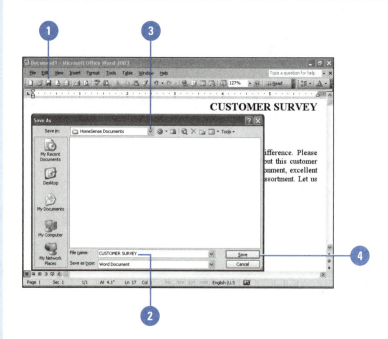

Did You Know?

You can change the default location where Word saves your documents. Word saves files to a default location on your hard drive (*My Documents*), unless you change the default settings. To change the default file location, click the Tools menu, click Options, click the File Locations tab, select a file location, click Modify to specify a new location, and then click OK.

See Also

See "Changing a Default File Location" on page 334 for information on changing the default location where you save a document.

Save a Document with a Different Name or Location

1. Click the File menu, and then click Save As.

2. Type the new file name.

3. Click the Save In list arrow, and then select a drive or folder location where you want to save the document.

4. Click the Create New Folder button.

5. Type the new folder name, and then click OK.

6. Click Save.

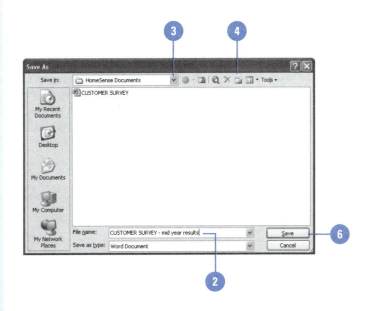

Save a Document in a Different Format

1. Click the File menu, and then click Save As.

2. Click the Save As Type list arrow, and then click the file type you want to use.

3. Click Save.

Did You Know?

You can rename a folder in the Save As and Open dialog boxes. Right-click the folder you want to rename, click Rename, type a new name, and then press Enter.

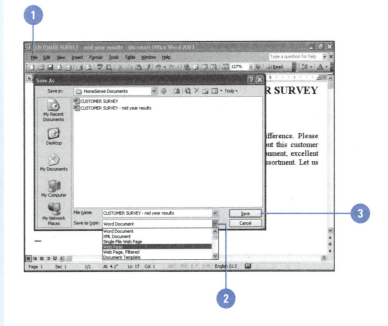

Getting Help While You Work

At some time, everyone has a question or two about the program they are using. The Office Online Help system provides the answers you need. You can search an extensive catalog of Help topics using a table of contents to locate specific information, or you can get context sensitive help in a dialog box. You can also ask your question in the Type A Question For Help box located on the right side of the menu bar. When you use any of these help options, a list of possible answers is shown to you in the Search Results task pane, with the most likely answer to your question at the top of the list.

Get Help Without the Office Assistant

 Click the Help button on the Standard toolbar.

 Locate the Help topic you want.

- ◆ Type one or more keywords in the Search For box, and then click the Start Searching button.

- ◆ Click Table Of Contents, and then click a topic.

  The topic you want appears in the right pane.

 Read the topic, and then click any hyperlinks to get information on related topics or definitions.

 When you're done, click the Close button.

 Click the Close button on the task pane.

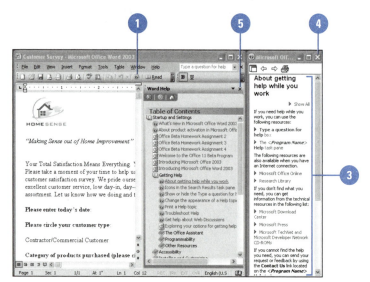

Get Help While You Work

1. Click the Type A Question For Help box.

2. Type your question, and then press Enter.

3. Click the topic that you want to read about.

4. When you're done, click the Close button on the task pane.

Get Help in a Dialog Box

1. Display the dialog box in which you want to get help.

2. Click the Help button.

3. Read the information in the Help window, and then click any links to display additional information.

4. When you're done, click the Close button.

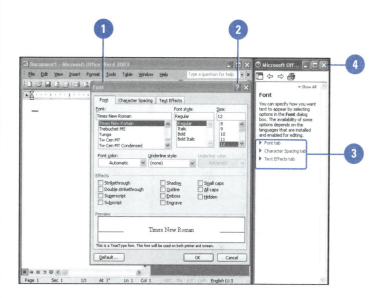

Getting Help from the Office Assistant

Often the easiest way to learn how to accomplish a task is to ask someone who knows. Now, with Office, that knowledgeable friend is always available in the form of the Office Assistant. The **Office Assistant** is an animated Help feature that you can use to access information that is directly related to the task you need help with. Using everyday language, just tell the Office Assistant what you want to do and it walks you through the process step by step. You can turn this feature on and off whenever you need to. If the personality of the default Office Assistant—Clippit—doesn't appeal to you, choose from a variety of other Office Assistants.

Ask the Office Assistant for Help

1. Click the Help menu, and then click Show Office Assistant.

2. If necessary, click the Office Assistant to display the help balloon.

3. Type your question about a task you want help with.

4. Click Search.

5. Click the topic you want help with, and then read the information.

6. After you're done, click the Close button.

7. To refine the search, click the Search list arrow, select a search area, and then click the Start Searching button.

8. When you're done, click the Close button on the task pane.

9. Click the Help menu, and then click Hide The Office Assistant.

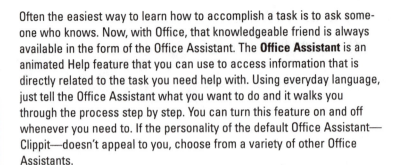

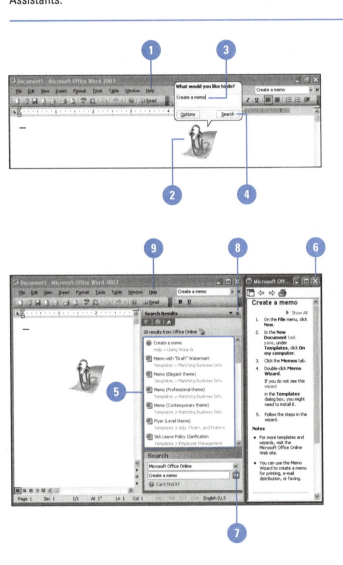

Hide the Office Assistant

1. Right-click the Office Assistant.

2. Click Hide.

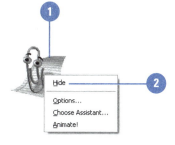

Turn Off the Office Assistant

1. Right-click the Office Assistant, and then click Options, or click the Options button in the Assistant window.

2. Click the Options tab.

3. Clear the Use The Office Assistant check box.

4. Click OK.

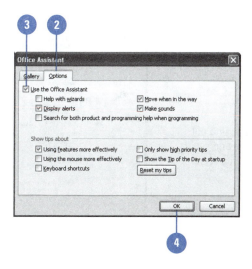

Did You Know?

You can change the Assistant character. Right-click the Assistant, and then click Choose Assistant. Click the Next and Back buttons to view the available Assistants, and then click OK. You might be asked to insert the original installation CD.

Getting Word Updates on the Web ▶

Word offers a quick and easy way to get updates of any new software downloads that improve the stability and security of the program. From the Help menu, simply select the Check For Updates command to connect to the Microsoft Office Online Web site, where you can have your computer scanned for necessary updates, and then choose which Office updates you want to download and install. You can use Microsoft Office Online Web site to check out other options that are available.Using the Office Online links on the Word Help task pane, you can check out Word-related news, obtain the most up-to-date help from Microsoft, and locate training and assistance with any aspect of Word.

Get Word Updates on the Web

1 Click the Help menu, and then click Check For Updates.

The Microsoft Office Online Web site opens, displaying the Downloads page.

2 Click Check For Updates to find out if you need Word updates, and then choose the updates you want to download and install.

3 When you're done, click the Close button.

Get the Latest Information on Word

1. Click the Help button on the toolbar.

2. Click one of the Office online links for information on a Word feature.

   ◆ Click Assistance to go to the Assistance Home Web page for information on ways to maximize the features you want to use in Word for greater efficiency.

   ◆ Click Training to go to the Training Home Web page to learn how to use the tools in Word more effectively.

   ◆ Click Communities to go the Microsoft Office Newsgroup Web page to communicate with other Word users.

   ◆ Click Downloads to go the Downloads Home Web page and get the very latest information on Word.

3. When you're done, click Close to go back to Word.

4. Click the Close button on the task pane.

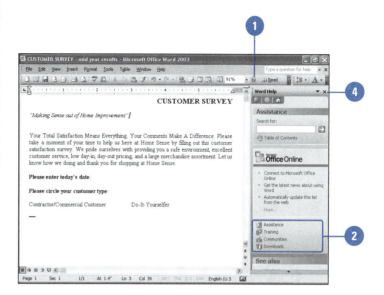

Exiting Word

When you finish working on a document, you can close it and open another document, or close it and quit Word. To protect your files, always quit Word before turning off your computer.

Close a Document and Exit Word

1. Click the File menu, and then click Close to close your document or click Exit to close your document and exit Word.

2. Click Yes to save any document changes; click No to close the document without saving any changes; or click Cancel to return to the document without closing it.

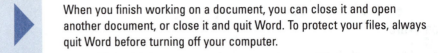

Click to close Word.

Click to close document.

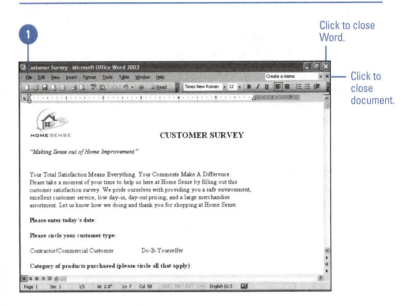

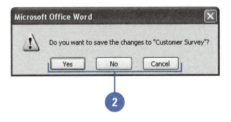

Working with Simple Documents

Introduction

You are now ready to get started with all the various features Word has to offer. Microsoft Office Word 2003 recognizes and can open files created in a variety of other programs including, but not limited to—Lotus 1-2-3, WordPerfect, Write, Excel, Outlook, Schedule, and Microsoft Works. If you are having a problem finding a certain document, Word can help you with the Search task pane.

Sometimes, you might need to be in two documents at the same time—copying information from one document to another, or refering to an older version of a report submitted in Word. You can arrange the documents in multiple windows so that you can view the information side-by-side.

With the AutoCorrect feature in Word, you can insert text automatically with AutoText, make changes with AutoCorrect, and you can also insert information the smart way with Smart Tags. The Redo and Undo functions help you to repeat an action or remove an action. This is helpful when you've accidentally deleted a word, or changed a formatting style unintentionally.

Using the Letter and Memo Wizards can be a fast way to create a document with some predefined elements. The wizards walk you through each step of the way in order to give you the document you want. You can also add an automatic date and time stamp to your documents that will update as you print each time.

Unfortunately, there will be an occurence of loss of power, a surge, or other system problems that will cause Word to shut down. If you are working inside a document, Word will try and recover the document to allow you to use it the next time you bring up Word. Should your system problems be more serious, Word can detect and repair problems through a diagnostic tool.

What You'll Do

Open an Existing Document

Open Files of Different Types

Find a File or Contents in a File

Work with Multiple Documents

Insert Text

Correct Text Automatically

Insert Information the Smart Way

Make Corrections

Insert the Date and Time

Create a Letter

Create a Memo

Recover a Document

Detect and Repair Problems

Recover an Office Program

Opening an Existing Document

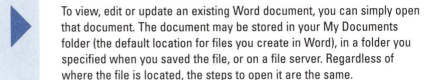

To view, edit or update an existing Word document, you can simply open that document. The document may be stored in your My Documents folder (the default location for files you create in Word), in a folder you specified when you saved the file, or on a file server. Regardless of where the file is located, the steps to open it are the same.

Open an Existing Document

1. Click the Open button on the Standard toolbar.

2. Click an icon on the Places bar to open a frequently used folder.

3. If necessary, click the Look In list arrow, and then click the drive where the file is located.

4. Double-click the folder in which the file is stored.

5. Click the file you want to open, and then click Open.

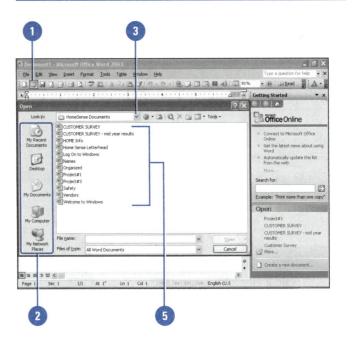

Opening Files of Different Types

Word recognizes and can open files created in a wide variety of other programs including, but not limited to: Lotus 1-2-3, WordPerfect, Windows Write, Excel, Outlook, Schedule, and Microsoft Works. When you open a document that was created in an older version of Word, Word opens it automatically into the current version.

Open a File in a Non-Word Format

1. Click the File menu, and then click Open.

2. Click the Files Of Type list arrow, and then select the type of file that you want to open.

3. Click the Look In list arrow, and then select the drive or Internet location, or click a button on the Places bar that contains the file you want to open.

4. Double click the file to open it.

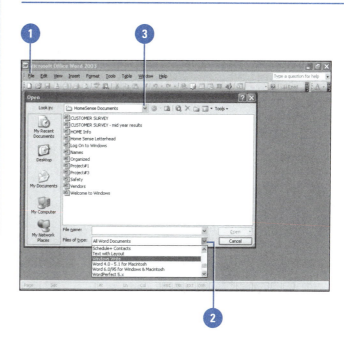

Finding a File or Contents in a File

The search feature available in the Open dialog box is also available using the Search task pane. You can use the Search task pane to find a file's name or location as well as search for specific text or property in a document. This becomes handy when you recall the content of a document, but not the name. When you perform a search, try to use specific or unique words to achieve the best results.

Find a File or Contents in a File

1. Click the File menu, and then click File Search.

2. Type the name of the file you are looking for or any distinctive words or phrases in the document.

3. Click the Search In list arrow, and then select or clear the check boxes to indicate where you want the program to search.

   Click the plus sign (+) to expand a list.

4. Click the Results Should Be list arrow, and then select or clear the check boxes to indicate the type of files you want to find.

5. Click Go.

6. To revise the find, click Modify.

7. When the search results appear, point to a file, click the list arrow, and then click the command you want.

8. When you're done, click the Close button on the task pane.

Did You Know?

You can use wildcards to search for file names. When you recall only part of the file name you want to open, type a question mark (?) for any one unknown character or an asterisk (*) for two or more unknown characters.

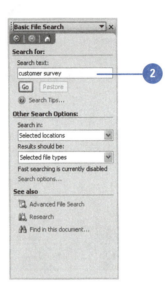

Find a Property in a File

1. Click the File menu, and then click File Search.

2. Click Advanced File Search.

3. Click the Property list arrow, and then select the property in which you want to search.

4. If necessary, click the Condition list arrow, and then select a criteria.

5. Type the value in which you want to search.

6. Click Add.

7. Click the Search In list arrow, and then select or clear the check boxes to indicate where you want the program to search.

   Click the plus sign (+) to expand a list.

8. Click the Results Should Be list arrow, and then select or clear the check boxes to indicate the type of files you want to find.

9. Click Go.

10. To revise the find, click Modify.

11. When the search results appear, point to a file, click the list arrow, and then click the command you want.

12. When you're done, click the Close button on the task pane.

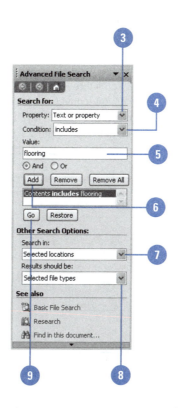

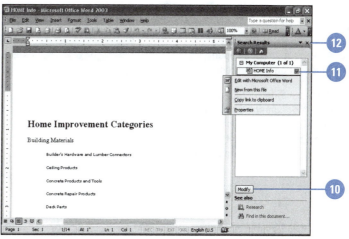

Working with Multiple Documents

WW03S-5-7

Multiple open documents are handy if you want to refer to an old report or copy parts of one letter into another. You can view each document in its own window or all open documents in horizontally tiled windows. If you need to compare two documents, you can view them side by side and scroll through them at the same time. To view different parts of a document (convenient for summarizing a long report), you can split it into two windows that you view simultaneously but edit and scroll through independently.

Switch Between Documents

◆ Click the Word Document button on the taskbar you want to display.

◆ Click the Window menu, and then click the document on which you want to work.

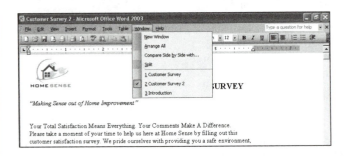

Arrange Multiple Document Windows

1 Click the Window menu.

2 Click a window command.

◆ Arrange All to fit all open windows on the screen.

◆ Compare Side By Side With ..., click a document, and then click OK to tile two windows and scroll through both documents at the same time.

Compare two documents side by side

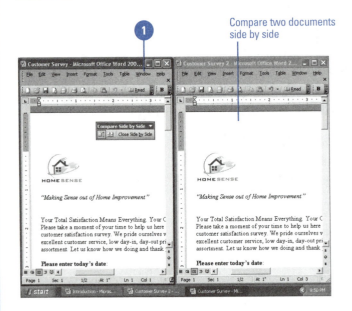

Did You Know?

You can move or copy text between documents. You can cut, copy, and paste text or drag text between two open windows or panes by having multiple windows open.

Work on Two Parts of the Same Document

1 Click the Window menu, and then click Split.

2 Drag the split bar until the two window panes are the sizes you want.

3 Click to set the split and display scroll bars and rulers for each pane.

4 Click to place the insertion point in each pane and scroll to the parts of the document you want to work on. Each pane scrolls independently. Edit the text as usual.

5 To return to a single pane, click the Window menu, and then click Remove Split.

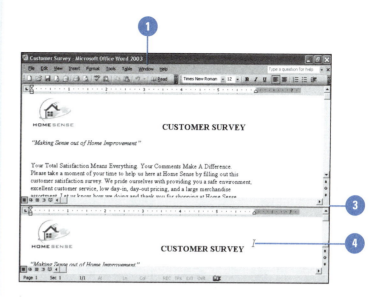

Did You Know?

You can resize window panes. As you work in two parts of the same document, you can resize the window panes to fit your task. Drag the split bar between the two panes to resize the windows.

You can switch between open Word documents using your keyboard. Hold down the Alt +Tab keys on the keyboard to move between open Word documents. This only works if you are using the default single document interface setting.

2

For Your Information

Working with Multiple Documents

When you create a new document, Word opens a separate instance of the document in a new window and displays an icon for that window on the taskbar. When Word creates new windows for each open document, it is a function of the single document interface. This feature was first introduced in Word 2000 so that users could easily navigate from Word to documents open in other programs. If you primarily work with several Word documents at the same time, you can turn off the single document interface and employ a multiple document interface. This enables you to shift between multiple documents in a single instance of Word using the Window menu. Each open document displays its own button on the Windows taskbar. You can switch to a multiple document interface, by clicking on the Tools menu, and then click Options. Click the View tab, and then clear the Windows In Taskbar check box.

Inserting Text

WW03S-1-2

In addition to cut and paste, you can use many other techniques for inserting text into your documents. You can insert automatic text to help make typing easier, and you can insert text boxes for areas of stylized text or additional notes to the side of your document. You can also add an entire Word file into a current document. When inserting text or files into Word, you can maximize your typing time by using the AutoText elements that Word has to offer.

Insert AutoText

1. Position the insertion point where you want the AutoText to be inserted.

2. Click the Insert menu, and then point to AutoText.

3. Point to a category, and then click an entry.

4. To see additional choices or add your own entries, click the Insert menu, point to AutoText, and then click AutoText.

5. To add an entry to the menu, type an entry in the Enter AutoText Entries Here box, and then click Add.

6. Scroll down the list to find the AutoText entry you want to make, and then click Insert.

Did You Know?

You can select AutoText options including greetings, closings, attention lines and other routinely used text. They are arranged in cascading sub-menus under AutoText on the Insert menu.

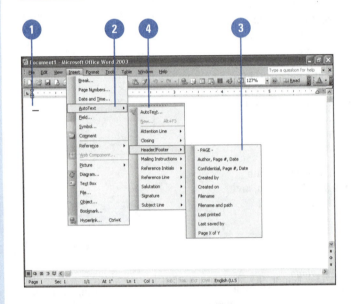

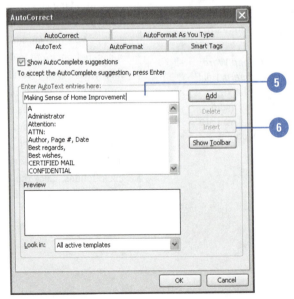

36

Insert a Text Box

1 Click the location in your document where you want to insert the text box.

2 Click the Insert menu, and then click Text Box.

3 Click anywhere inside the text box to edit its content.

4 When you have completed entering text into the box, click anywhere outside the border of the text box.

Did You Know?

You can resize a text box to fit your text. Drag the corner of the box to resize it just as you would any other window so that all of the text is displayed. A text box will not expand if you type text that extends beyond its visible borders.

Insert Files

1 Click the place in your document where you want to insert the file.

2 Click the Insert menu, and then click File.

3 Click the Look In list arrow to find the file to insert.

4 Select the file, and then click Insert.

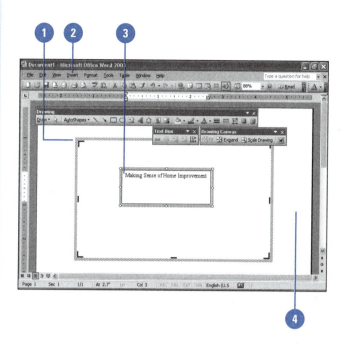

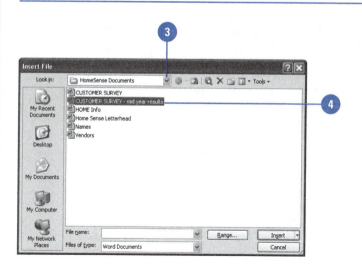

Correcting Text Automatically

 WW03S-1-2

Since the dawn of typing, people have consistently mistyped certain words or letter combinations. How many times do you misspell *and* or press and hold Shift too long? AutoCorrect fixes common misspellings and incorrect capitalization as you type. It also replaces typed characters, such as -- (two hyphens), with typographical symbols, such as — (an em dash). What's more, you can add your personal problem words to the AutoCorrect list. In most cases, AutoCorrect corrects errors after you press Enter or the Spacebar. When you point to a word that AutoCorrect changed, a small blue box appears under it. When you point to the small blue box, the AutoCorrect Options button appears, which gives you control over whether you want the text to be corrected. You can change it back to its original spelling, or you can stop AutoCorrect from automatically correcting text.

Replace Text as You Type

◆ To correct capitalization or spelling errors automatically, continue typing until AutoCorrect makes the required correction.

◆ To replace two hyphens with an em dash, turn ordinals into superscripts (for example, 1st to 1st), or stack a fraction (for example, 1/2), continue typing until AutoCorrect makes the appropriate change.

◆ To create a bulleted or numbered list, type **1.** or * (for a bullet), press Tab or Spacebar, type any text, and then press Enter. AutoCorrect inserts the next number or bullet. To end the list, press Backspace to erase the extra number or bullet.

Did You Know?

You can prevent automatic corrections. Click the Tools menu, click AutoCorrect Options, clear the Replace Text As You Type check box, and then click OK.

Examples of AutoCorrect Changes		
Type of Correction	**If You Type**	**AutoCorrect Inserts**
Capitalization	dOCUMENT	Document
Capitalization	TWo INitial CAps	Two Initial Caps
Capitalization	ann Marie	Ann Marie
Capitalization	microsoft	Microsoft
Capitalization	thursday	Thursday
Common typos	accomodate	accommodate
Common typos	can;t	can't
Common typos	windoes	windows
Superscript ordinals	2nd	2nd
Stacked fractions	1/2	½
Smart quotes	" "	" "
Em dashes	Madison--a small city in southern Wisconsin--is a nice place to live.	Madison—a small city in southern Wisconsin—is a nice place to live.
Symbols	(c)	©
Symbols	(r)	®
Hyperlinks	www.microsoft.com	www.microsoft.com

Change Correction as You Type

① Point to the small blue box under the corrected or changed word.

② Click the AutoCorrect Options button.

③ Click any of the following options:

◆ Change Back To

◆ Stop Automatically Correcting

◆ Control AutoCorrect Options to change the AutoCorrect settings

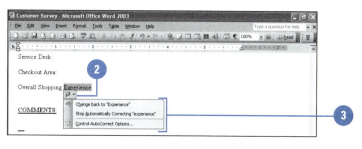

Add or Edit AutoCorrect Entries

① Click the Tools menu, and then click AutoCorrect Options.

② Click the AutoCorrect tab.

To edit an AutoCorrect entry, select the entry you want to change.

③ Type the incorrect text you want AutoCorrect to correct.

④ Type the text or symbols you want AutoCorrect to use as a replacement.

⑤ Click Add or Replace.

⑥ When you're done, click OK.

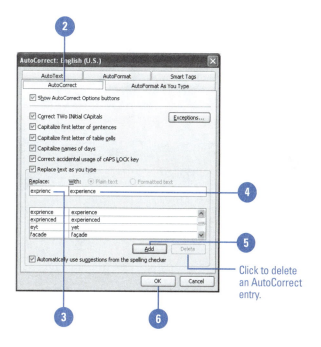

Click to delete an AutoCorrect entry.

Did You Know?

You can create exceptions to Auto-Correct. Specify terms that you don't want AutoCorrect to correct. Click Exceptions, and then add these items to the list of exceptions.

2

Inserting Information the Smart Way

When you type certain information, such as the date and time, personal names, places, telephone numbers, or recent e-mail recipients, a purple dotted line appears under the item, which indicates a Smart Tag is available. A Smart Tag provides options for commonly performed tasks associated with the information. For example, you can add a name and address that you just typed in a Word document to your Contacts list in Office Outlook. When you point to the purple dotted line, the Smart Tags Option button appears below it. When you click the button, a menu appears with a list of available options. The available options differ depending on the Smart Tag content.

Insert Information Using Smart Tags

1 Point to the purple dotted line under an item.

2 Click the Smart Tag Options button.

3 Click any of the available options:

◆ Remove This Smart Tag

◆ Smart Tag Options to change the smart tag settings

◆ Additional options appear depending on the Smart Tag content.

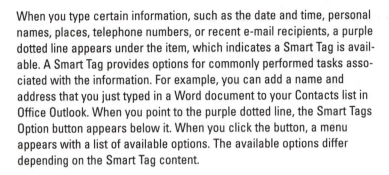

Did You Know?

You can turn off Smart Tags. Click the Tools menu, click AutoCorrect Options, click the Smart Tags tab, clear the Label Text With Smart Tags check box, and then click OK.

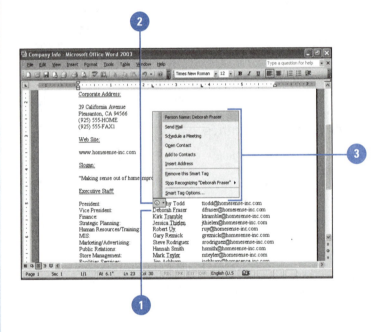

Change Smart Tag Options

① Click the Tools menu, and then click AutoCorrect Options.

② Click the Smart Tags tab.

③ Select the Label Text With Smart Tags check box.

④ Select the check boxes with the smart tags you want to use.

⑤ To check the active document for smart tags, click Check Document or click Recheck Document.

⑥ To download new Smart Tag types from the Web, click More Smart Tags.

⑦ When you're done, click OK.

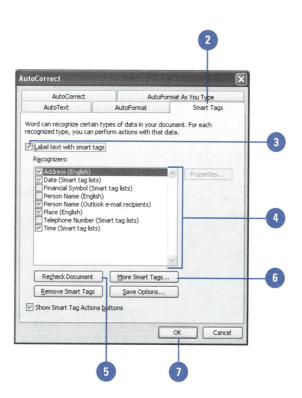

Did You Know?

You can embed the Smart Tags in your document. Click Save As to embed smart tags.

Making Corrections

Everyone makes mistakes and changes their mind at some point, especially when creating or revising a document. With Word you can instantly correct typing errors by pressing a key. You can also reverse more complicated actions, such as typing an entire word, formatting a paragraph, or creating a chart. With the Undo button, if you change your mind, you can just as easily click the Redo button to restore the action you reversed.

Undo or Redo an Action

◆ Click the Undo button to reverse your most recent action, such as typing a word, formatting a paragraph, or creating a chart.

   TIMESAVER *Press Ctrl+Z to undo.*

◆ Click the Redo button to restore the last action you reversed.

   TIMESAVER *Press Ctrl+Y to redo your undo.*

◆ Click the Undo button list arrow, and then select the consecutive actions you want to reverse.

◆ Click the Redo button list arrow, and then select the consecutive actions you want to restore.

Undo button ── ┌ ── Undo button list arrow

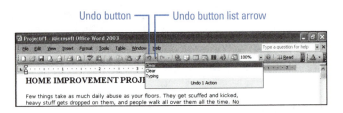

Redo button ── ┌ ── Redo button list arrow

Did You Know?

You can use Undo to reverse an AutoCorrect change. To reverse an AutoCorrect change, click the Undo button on the Standard toolbar as soon as AutoCorrect makes the change.

Correct Typing Errors Using the Keyboard

To Delete	Press
One character at a time to the left of the insertion point	Backspace
One word at a time to the left of the insertion point	Ctrl+Backspace
One character at a time to the right of the insertion point	Delete
One word at a time to the right of the insertion point	Ctrl+Delete
Selected text	Backspace or Delete

Inserting the Date and Time

WW03S-1-2

Insert the Date or Time

1 Click the Insert menu, and then click Date And Time.

2 Select the Update Automatically check box.

3 Double-click the date and time format you want.

Did You Know?

You can use the current date and time as the default setting. Click the Default button in the Date And Time Dialog box, and then click Yes.

Adding a Date and Time stamp to your documents allows you to print the information with the document each time it is revised or published. Various formats are offered to help you customize your document to the exact format you want. You can use just the date, just the time, or a combination of both. If you want the date and time to automatically update when you open the document, you can turn on the Update Automatically option. If you are working with mulitple languages, you can insert the date and time in another language.

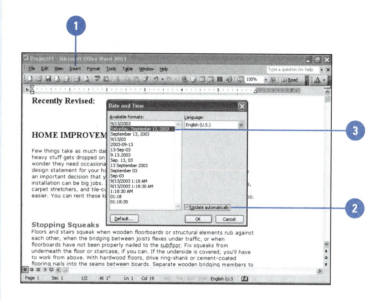

Creating a Letter

You can create a letter in Word as quickly as you can grab a pen and paper and start writing. With all of the text, formatting, spelling, and graphic features that Word has to offer, writing a letter is a very easy way to communicate with clients, friends, and family.

Create a Letter

1. Click the File menu, and then click New.

2. In the New Document task pane, click On My Computer under the Templates heading.

3. Click the Letters & Faxes tab.

4. Double-click the Letter Wizard icon.

5. Click the Send One Letter option.

6. On the Letter Format tab, choose a Page Design and any other options, and then click Next.

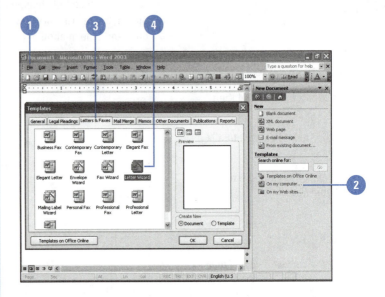

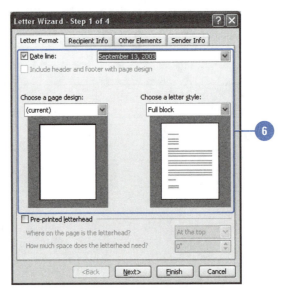

7. On the Recipient Info tab, enter the Recipients's Name, address, select a salutation, and then click Next.

8. On the Other Elements tab, enter the Reference Line and any other options, and then click Next.

9. On the Sender Info tab, enter the Sender's Name and any other options, and then click Finish.

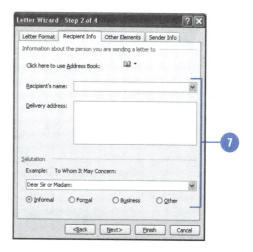

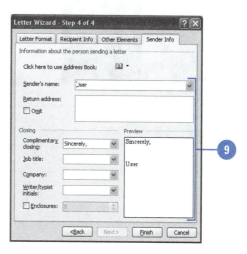

2

Creating a Memo

Memos are another commonly used document whose creation has been simplified via the use of Word templates. You can use the Memo Wizard to create and customize a memo form all your own. Add your company logo, change font attributes, adjust line spacing, and other important parts of your document and you have a customized memo.

Create a Memo

1. Click the File menu, and then click New.

2. In the New Document task pane, click On My Computer under the Templates heading.

3. Click the Memos tab.

4. Double-click the Memo Wizard icon.

5. Read the introduction, click Next, specify the Style you want to use, and then click Next.

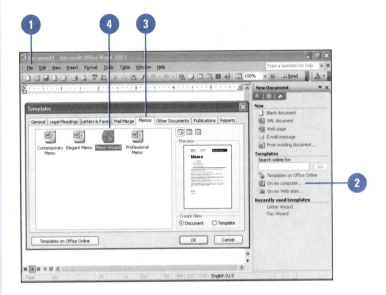

6 Specify the Title you want to use, and then click Next.

7 Specify the Heading Fields you want to use, and then click Next.

8 Specify the Recipients you want to use, and then click Next.

9 Specify the Closing Fields you want to use, and then click Next.

10 Specify the Header and Footer you want to use, click Next, and then click Finish.

Your interoffice memo appears.

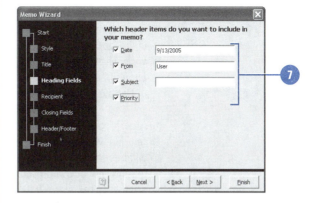

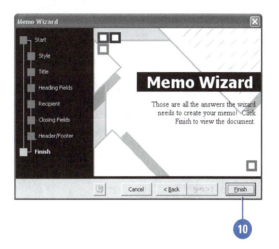

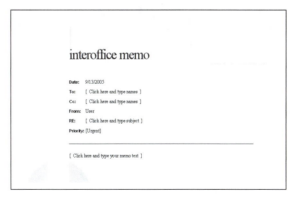

Recovering a Document

If Word encounters a problem and stops responding, the program tries to recover the file the next time you open Word. The recovered files appear in the Document Recovery task pane, which allows you to open the files, view what repairs were made, and compare the recovered versions. Each file appears in the task pane with a status indicator, either Original or Recovered, which shows what type of data recovery was performed. You can save one or all of the file versions. You can also use the AutoRecover feature to periodically save a temporary copy of your current file, which ensures proper recovery of the file. Occasionally, a file will become corrupt, either by transmission as an e-mail attachment over the Internet or through some other means. When this happens, you can attempt to recover the data from within the file by using Word's Open and Repair command in the Open dialog box.

Recover a Document

1. When the Document Recovery task pane appears, click the list arrow next to the name of each recovered file, and then perform one of the following:

   ◆ Click Open to view the file for review.

   ◆ Click Save As to save the file.

   ◆ Click Delete to close the file without saving.

   ◆ Click Show Repairs to find out how Word fixed the file.

2. When you're done, click the Close button.

Use AutoRecover

1. Click the Tools menu, and then click Options.

2. Click the Save tab.

3. Select the Save AutoRecover Info Every check box.

4. Enter the number of minutes, or click the up and down arrows to adjust the minutes.

5. Click OK.

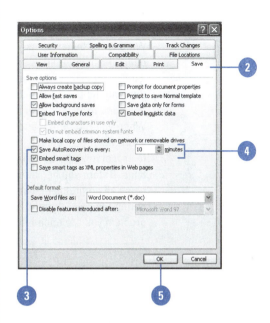

Recover the Text from a Damaged Document

1. Click the File menu, and then click Open.

2. Click the Look In list arrow, and then click the drive, folder, or Internet location holding the file you want to repair.

3. Click the Open button list arrow to display a list of options.

4. Click Open And Repair.

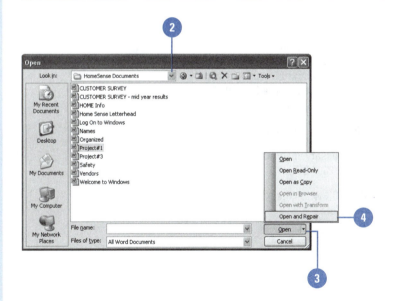

Did You Know?

You have to re-save a repaired file. Once your document is repaired, use the Save command to save the repaired file.

You can reinstall Word if repairs do no work. Use your Office CD to uninstall and reinstall Word.

Detecting and Repairing Problems

To help you keep your Office 2003 suite of programs running at its best, Office comes with its own diagnostic and repair tools. If you find that Word is not behaving as you think it should, its core files might have been damaged or inadvertently deleted. If Word encounters a problem itself, it prompts you to run its self-diagnostic tool, **Detect and Repair**. Running the Detect and Repair tool restores Word's default settings and finds and fixes problems that might diminish the performance of Word. When you run Detect and Repair, you can choose to preserve any of the shortcuts that you have created. You can also choose whether you want to preserve your customized settings or return Word to its default settings. Before you begin the Detect and Repair procedure, make sure you close all programs that are running (if not, you will be prompted to do so during the procedure). If the Detect and Repair procedure doesn't fix the problem you are encountering, try reinstalling Word.

Detect and Repair Problems

1 Click the Help menu, and then click Detect And Repair.

2 To save your shortcuts, select the Restore My Shortcuts While Repairing check box.

3 To save the settings you have specified for your Word features, clear the Discard My Customized Settings And Restore Default Settings check box.

4 Click Start to begin the process.

5 If necessary, insert the Microsoft Office 2003 CD.

6 Click OK when the procedure is complete.

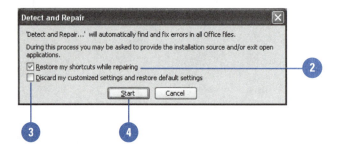

Perform Maintenance on Office Programs

① In Windows Explorer, double-click the Setup icon on the Office CD.

② Click one of the following maintenance buttons:

◆ Add Or Remove Features to determine which, and when, features are installed or removed

◆ Reinstall Or Repair to repair or reinstall Office

◆ Uninstall to uninstall Office

③ Click Next, and then follow the wizard instructions to complete the maintenance.

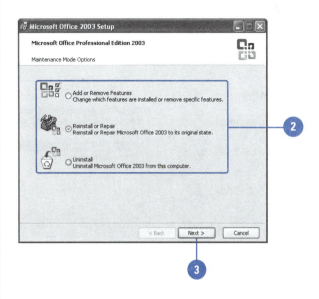

Did You Know?

You can set Detect and Repair to run automatically. In the Control Panel (Classic view), double-click Add Or Remove Programs, click Microsoft Office 2003, and then click Change/Remove. Click Repair Office, click Repair Errors In My Office Installation, and then click Finish.

2

Recovering an Office Program

If an Office program gets stuck exiting or stops responding during an operation, you can use the Microsoft Office Application Recovery program to exit the program, send an error report to Microsoft, and try to recover your unsaved work.

Recover an Office Program

1. Click the Start button on the taskbar, point to All Programs, and then point to Microsoft Office.

2. Point to Microsoft Office Tools, and then click Microsoft Office Application Recovery.

3. Click the Office program you want to recover.

4. Click Recover Application or End Application.

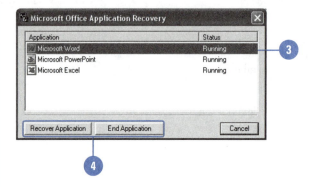

Formatting Documents

3

Introduction

Once you type a document and get the content how you want it, the finishing touches can sometimes be the most important. An eye catching document will draw the reader in, while a boring font without a lot of extra details will draw the reader away from all your hard work. To create that interest, Microsoft Office Word 2003 can help you change your document for a fresh look. One of the first elements you can change is your font attributes. Applying bold, underline, or italics when appropriate, can emphasize text. You might find that having different font sizes in your document to denote various topics will also enhance your document.

You can change the **kerning**—the amount of space between each individual character, for a special effect on a title or other parts of text. Other special effects can be applied to your document if you are using it in a presentation, such as animations. You can also apply a dropped capital letter to introduce a body of text, add a shading or border onto your document.

Word has various tools to help you format your document. You can search and replace formatting effects, display rulers, change a paragraph alignment, set paragraph tabs and indents, and change your line spacing.

There are times when typing a paragraph will not do your text justice. Creating a bulleted or numbered list might better show your information. Another way to organize items in a document is with a table. A **table** is an object that is inserted into the document that displays text in rows and columns. You can set up your table with existing text, or create the table, even draw it out, and enter in new text. Once created, you can adjust the cells (where the text is contained in the rows and columns). You can also adjust the table to insert or delete rows, columns or individual cells, change the alignment of text, sort the text, or even apply a border or shading to the table.

Formatting Text for Emphasis

WW03S-3-1

You'll often want to format, or change the style of, certain words or phrases to add emphasis to parts of a document. **Boldface**, *italics*, <u>underlines</u>, highlights, and other text effects are toggle switches, which you simply click to turn on and off. For special emphasis you can combine formats, such as bold and italics. Using one **font**—a collection of characters, numbers, and symbols in the same letter design—for headings and another for main text adds a professional look to your document. You can also apply font styles and effects to text, such as Strikethrough, Double Strikethrough, Superscript, Subscript, Shadow, Outline, Emboss, Engrave, Small Caps, All Caps, and Hidden.

Format Existing Text Quickly

1. Select the text you want to emphasize.

2. Click the Bold, Italic, Underline, or Highlight button on the Formatting toolbar.

   You can add more than one formatting option at a time. For example, *this text uses both boldface and italics.*

3. Click anywhere in the document to deselect the formatted text.

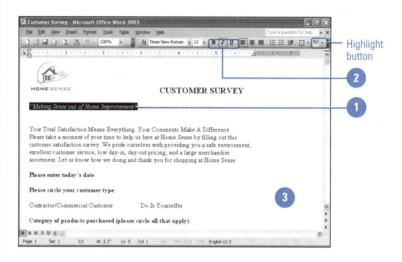

Change the Font or Size of Existing Text Quickly

1. Select the text you want to format.

2. Click the Font list arrow on the Formatting toolbar, and then click a new font.

3. Click the Font Size list arrow on the Formatting toolbar, and then click a new point size.

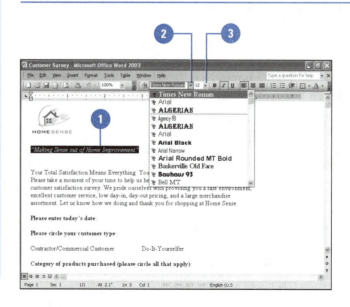

Apply Formatting Effects to Text

1 Select the text you want to format.

2 Click the Format menu, and then click Font.

3 Click the Font tab.

4 Click the formatting (Font, Font Style, Size, Font Color, Underline Style, and Underline Color) you want.

5 Click to select the effects (Strike-through, Double Strikethrough, Superscript, Subscript, Shadow, Outline, Emboss, Engrave, Small Caps, All Caps, and Hidden) you want.

6 Check the results in the Preview box.

7 To make the new formatting options the default for all new Word documents, click Default, and then click Yes.

8 Click OK.

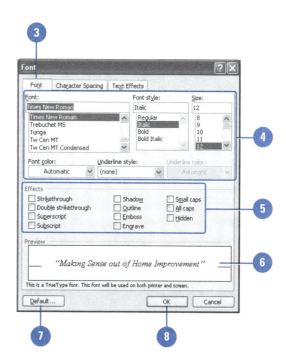

Did You Know?

You can format text as you type. You can add most formatting options to text as you type. First, select the formatting options you want, and then type the text. If necessary, turn off the format-ting options when you're done.

You can use Word to format your document. Click the Format menu, and then click AutoFormat. Select a docu-ment type (General Document, Letter, Email) and indicate if you want to review each change, and then click OK.

Changing Font Type and Size

Although it is usually not considered good style to use numerous fonts in a document, and certainly not within paragraphs, some designs incorporate multiple fonts. Also, you might want to globally change the font you are using after a document has been created. The most commonly used text sizes for regular text (not headers or other layout elements) are 10 and 12 point type. Again, nothing limits you from breaking with convention, and you will also want to manipulate point sizes to keep your headers from wrapping to two lines or make other aesthetic changes from time to time.

Change the Font Type

1 Select the text you want to change.

2 Use one of the following methods:

◆ Click the Format menu, and then click Font. Select the font you want, and then click OK.

◆ Click the Font button list arrow on the Formatting toolbar. Click the font you want, and it replaces the selected font in the original document.

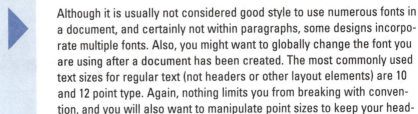

Change the Font Size

1 Select the text whose size you want to change.

2 Use one of the following methods:

◆ Click the Format menu, and then click Font. Select the font size you want, and then click OK.

◆ Click the Font Size button list arrow on the Formatting toolbar. Click the selected size and it resizes the selected text.

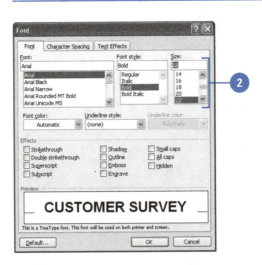

Changing Character Spacing

WW03S-3-1

Change Character Spacing

1. Select the text you want to format.

2. Click the Format menu, and then click Font.

3. Click the Character Spacing tab.

4. Click the Spacing list arrow, click an option, and then specify a point size to expand or condense spacing by the amount specified.

5. Click the Position list arrow, click an option, and then specify a point size to raise or lower the text in relation to the baseline (bottom of the text).

6. Select the Kerning For Fonts check box, and then specify a point size.

7. Check the results in the Preview box.

8. To make the new formatting options the default for all new Word documents, click Default, and then click Yes.

9. Click OK.

Kerning is the amount of space between each individual character that you type. Sometimes the space between two characters is larger than others, which makes the word look uneven. You can use the Font dialog box to change the kerning setting for selected characters. Kerning works only with TrueType or Adobe Type Manager fonts. You can expand or condense the character spacing to create a special effect for a title, or realign the position of characters to the bottom edge of the text—this is helpful for positioning the copyright or trademark symbols.

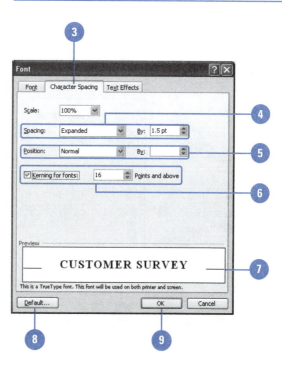

3

Formatting Text with Special Effects

WW03S-3-1

Apply Special Effects to Text

1 Select the text you want to format.

2 Click the Format menu, and then click Font.

3 Click the Text Effects tab.

4 Click an animation.

5 Check the results in the Preview box.

6 To make the new formatting options the default for all new Word documents, click Default, and then click Yes.

7 Click OK.

Did You Know?

You can view formatting marks.
Sometimes it's hard to see the number of spaces or tabs between words. You can change the view to display formatting marks, a period for space and an arrow for tabs. Click the Tools menu, click Options, click the View tab, select the formatting mark check boxes you want to view, and then click OK.

If you are using a document in an on-screen presentation, you can add animation effects to text. You can add animation effects, such as Las Vegas Lights, Marching Black Ants, and Sparkle Text to a title or heading. Animated effects appear only on the screen. When you select an animation, you can check the Preview box to make sure the animation is the one you want. When you are print document with an animation effect, the text prints, but the animation does not. You can only apply one animation effect at a time.

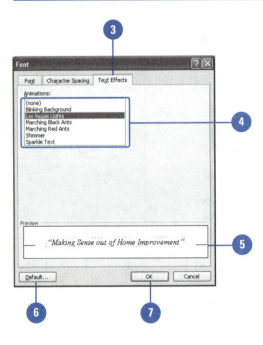

Revealing Formatting

WW03S-5-7

Word uses wavy blue underlines to indicate possible instances of inconsistent formatting. If you see a wavy blue underline while formatting a document, you can open the Reveal Formatting task pane to display the format of selected text, such as its font and font effects. The Reveal Formatting task pane allows you to display, change, or clear formatting for the selected text. You can also select text based on formatting so that you can compare the formatting used in the selected text with formatting used in other parts of the documents.

Select or Clear Text Formatting

1. Select the text whose formatting you want to select or clear away.

2. Click the Format menu, and then click Reveal Formatting.

3. Point to the Selected Text box, click the list arrow, and then click either Select All Text With Similar Formatting or Clear Formatting.

   To apply the formatting to your surrounding text, click Apply Formatting Of Surrounding Text.

4. When you're done, click the Close button on the task pane.

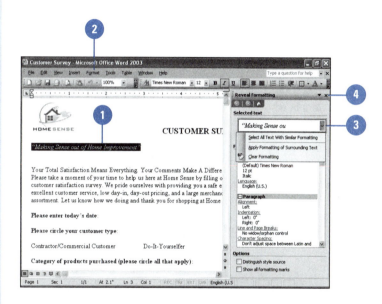

Compare Text Formatting

1. Select the first instance of formatting you want to compare.

2. Click the Format menu, and then click Reveal Formatting.

3. Select the Compare To Another Selection check box.

4. Select the second instance of formatting to compare.

5. When you're done, click the Close button on the task pane.

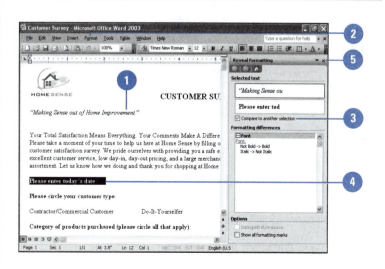

3

Finding and Replacing Formatting

 WW03S-3-1

Suddenly you realize all the bold text in your report would be easier to read in italics. Do you spend time making these changes one by one? No. The Find and Replace feature locates the formatting and instantly substitutes new formatting. If your search for a formatting change is an easy one, click Less in the Find And Replace dialog box to decrease the size of the dialog box. If your search is a more complex one, click More to display additional options. With the Match Case option, you can specify exact capitalization. The Go To tab quickly moves you to a place or item in your document.

Find Text or Formatting

1. Click the Edit menu, and then click Find.

2. If you want to locate formated text, type the word or words.

3. Click More, click Format, and then click the formatting you want to find. When you're done, click OK.

4. Click Find Next to select the next instance of the formatted text.

5. Click OK to confirm Word finished the search.

6. Click Cancel.

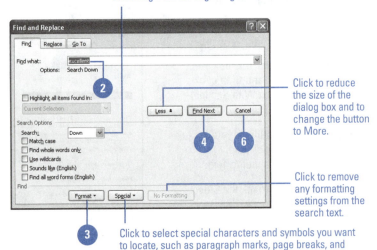

Unless you search All, you may be asked whether to continue searching from the beginning of the document.

Click to reduce the size of the dialog box and to change the button to More.

Click to remove any formatting settings from the search text.

Click to select special characters and symbols you want to locate, such as paragraph marks, page breaks, and em dashes.

Find an Item or Location

1. Click the Edit menu, and then click Go To.

2. Click an item in the Go To What box.

3. Enter the item number or name.

4. Click Next, Previous, or Go To to locate the item.

5. When you're done, click Close.

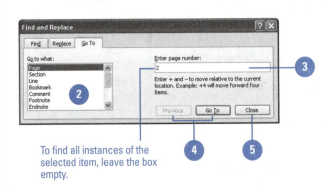

To find all instances of the selected item, leave the box empty.

Replace Text or Formatting

1. Click the Edit menu, and then click Replace.

2. If you want to locate formatted text, type the word or words.

3. Click the More button, click Format, and then click the formatting you want to find. When you're done, click OK.

4. Press Tab, and then type any text you want to substitute.

5. Click Format, and then click the formatting you want to substitute. When you're done, click OK.

6. To substitute every instance of the formatting, click Replace All.

   To substitute the formatting one instance at a time, click Find Next, and then click Replace.

   If you want to cancel the replace, click Cancel.

7. If necessary, click Yes to search from the beginning of the document.

8. Click OK to confirm Word finished searching.

9. Click the Close button.

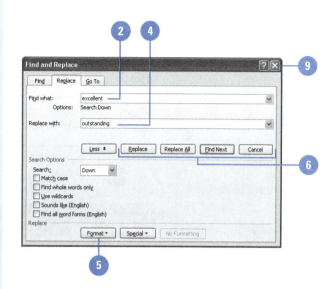

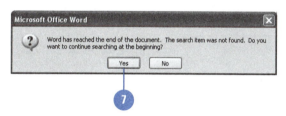

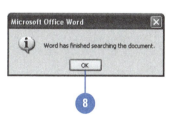

Did You Know?

You can find and replace special characters and document elements. In Word, you can search for and replace special characters (for example, an em dash) and document elements (for example, a tab character). Click More in the Find And Replace dialog box, click Special, and then click the item you want from the menu.

Displaying Rulers

Word rulers do more than measure. The **horizontal ruler** above the document shows the length of the typing line and lets you quickly adjust left and right margins and indents, set tabs, and change column widths. The **vertical ruler** along the left edge of the document lets you adjust top and bottom margins and change table row heights. You can hide the rulers to get more room for your document. As you work with long documents, use the document map to jump to any heading in your document. Headings are in the left pane and documents in the right.

Show and Hide the Rulers

1 Click the View menu, and then click Ruler.

- ◆ To view the horizontal ruler, click the Normal View button.

- ◆ To view the horizontal and vertical rulers, click the Print Layout View button.

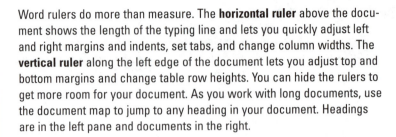

Horizontal ruler

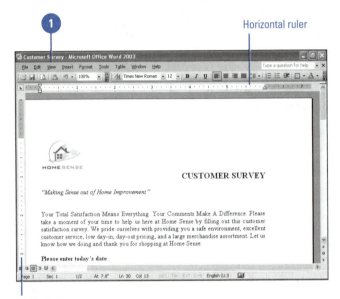

Vertical ruler

Did You Know?

You can change the ruler measurements. Change the ruler to show inches, centimeters, millimeters, points, or picas. Click the Tools menu, click Options, click the General tab, click the Measurement Units list arrow, and then select the measurement you want.

You can set your text to be hyphenated. Hyphenation prevents ugly gaps and short lines in text. Click the Tools menu, point to Language, click Hyphenation, select the Automatically Hyphenate Document check box, set the hyphenation zone and limit the number of consecutive hyphens (usually two), and then click OK.

Changing Paragraph Alignment

WW03S-3-2

Text starts out positioned evenly along the left margin, and uneven, or **ragged**, at the right margin. Left-aligned text works well for body paragraphs in most cases, but other alignments vary the look of a document and help lead the reader through the text. **Right-aligned text**, which is even along the right margin and ragged at the left margin, is good for adding a date to a letter. **Justified text** spreads text evenly between the margins, creating a clean, professional look, often used in newspapers and magazines. **Centered text** is best for titles and headings. You can use Click-And-Type to quickly center titles or set different text alignment on the same line, or you can use the alignment buttons on the Formatting toolbar to set alignment on one or more lines.

Align New Text with Click-And-Type

- Position the I-beam at the left, right, or center of the line where you want to insert new text.

  When the I-beam shows the appropriate alignment, double-click to place the insertion point, and then type your text.

Click-And-Type Text Pointers

Pointer	Purpose
	Left-aligns text
	Right-aligns text
	Centers text
	Creates a new line in the same paragraph
	Creates text around a picture

Align Existing Text

1. Position the I-beam, or select at least one line in each paragraph to align.

2. Click the appropriate button on the Formatting toolbar.

   - Align Left button
   - Center button
   - Align Right button
   - Justify button

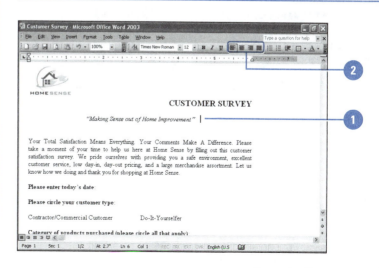

Setting Paragraph Tabs

WW03S-3-2

In your document, **tabs** set how text or numerical data aligns in relation to the document margins. A **tab stop** is a predefined stopping point along the document's typing line. Default tab stops are set every half-inch, but you can set multiple tabs per paragraph at any location. Choose from four text tab stops: left, right, center, and decimal (for numerical data). The bar tab inserts a vertical bar at the tab stop. You can use the Tab button on the horizontal ruler to switch between the available tabs.

Create and Clear a Tab Stop

1. Select one or more paragraphs in which you want to set a tab stop.

2. Click the Tab button on the horizontal ruler until it shows the type of tab stop you want.

3. Click the ruler where you want to set the tab stop.

4. If necessary, drag the tab stop to position it where you want.

   To display a numerical measurement in the ruler where the tab is placed, press and hold Alt as you drag.

5. To clear a tab stop, drag it off the ruler.

Did You Know?

You can display tab characters. If you don't see a tab character, that looks like an arrow when you press Tab, click the Show/Hide ¶ button on the Standard toolbar.

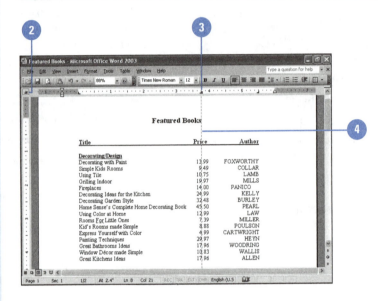

Tab Stops	
Tab Stop	**Purpose**
L	Aligns text to the left of the tab stop
⌐	Aligns text to the right of the tab stop
⊥	Centers text on the tab stop
⊥.	Aligns numbers on the decimal point
I	Inserts a vertical bar at the tab stop

Changing Line Spacing

WW03S-3-2

The lines in all Word documents are single-spaced by default, which is appropriate for letters and most documents. But you can easily change your document line spacing to double or 1.5 lines to allow extra space between every line. This is useful when you want to make notes on a printed document. Sometimes, you'll want to add space above and below certain paragraphs, for headlines, or indented quotations to help set off the text.

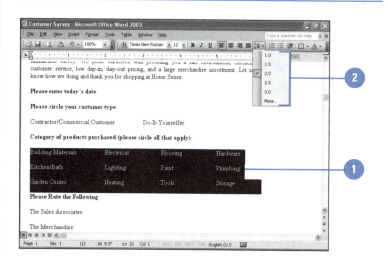

Change Line Spacing

1. Select the text you want to change.

2. On the Formatting toolbar, click the Line Spacing button list arrow, and then click a spacing option.

   ◆ To apply a new setting, click the number you want.

   TIMESAVER *Press Ctrl+1 for single-space, Ctrl+5 for 1.5 space, or Ctrl+2 for double-space.*

   ◆ Click More to enter precise parameters.

   ◆ To apply the setting you last used, click the Line Spacing button.

Change Paragraph Spacing

1. Choose the paragraph(s) whose spacing you want to change, and then select that text.

2. Click the Format menu, and then click Paragraph.

3. Click the Indents And Spacing tab.

4. Under the Spacing header, enter the custom spacing parameters you want both before and after the paragraph(s), and then click OK.

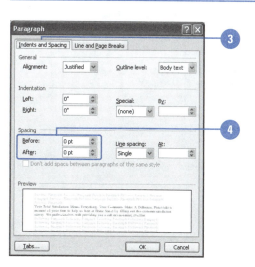

3

Setting Paragraph Indents

 WW03S-3-2

Indent Paragraph Lines Precisely

Click the paragraph or select multiple paragraphs to indent:

◆ To change the left indent of the first line, drag the First-line Indent marker.

◆ To change the indent of the second and subsequent lines, drag the Hanging Indent marker.

◆ To change the left indent for all lines, drag the Left Indent marker.

◆ To change the right indent for all lines, drag the Right Indent marker.

As you drag a marker, the dotted guideline helps you position the indent accurately. You can also press and hold Alt to see a measurement in the ruler.

Did You Know?

You can indent using the Tab key. You can indent the first line of a paragraph by clicking at the beginning of the paragraph, and then pressing Tab. You can indent the entire paragraph by selecting it, and then pressing Tab.

Quickly indent lines of text to precise locations from the left or right margin with the horizontal ruler. Indent the first line of a paragraph (called a **first-line indent**) as books do to distinguish paragraphs. Indent the second and subsequent lines of a paragraph from the left margin (called a **hanging indent**) to create a properly formatted bibliography. Indent the entire paragraph any amount from the left and right margins (called **left indents** and **right indents**) to separate quoted passages.

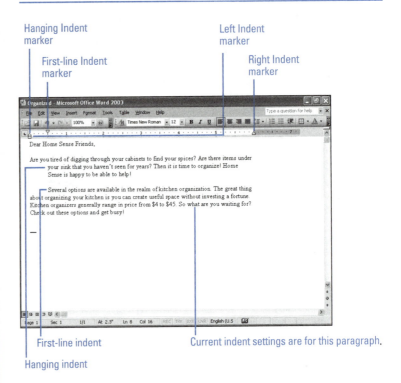

Hanging Indent marker

First-line Indent marker

Left Indent marker

Right Indent marker

First-line indent

Hanging indent

Current indent settings are for this paragraph.

Indent a Paragraph

1. Click the paragraph, or select multiple paragraphs to indent.

2. Click the Increase Indent button or Decrease Indent button on the Formatting toolbar to move the paragraph right or left one-half inch.

Set Indentation Using the Tab Key

1. Click the Tools menu, and then click AutoCorrect Options.

2. Click the AutoFormat As You Type tab.

3. Select the Set Left- And First-Indent With Tabs And Backspaces check box.

4. Click OK.

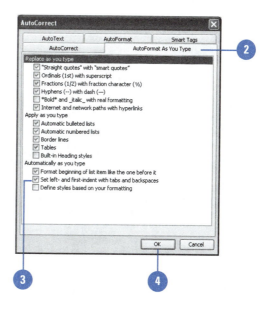

3

Adding Desktop Publishing Effects

WW03S-2-1, WW03S-3-2

A few simple elements—drop caps, borders, and shading—make your newsletters and brochures look like a professional produced them. A **drop cap** is the enlarged first letter of a paragraph. **Borders** are lines or graphics that appear around a page, paragraph, selected text, or table cells. For borders, you can change the line style, width, and colors, and you can add shadows and 3D effects. **Shading** is a color that fills the background of selected text, paragraphs, or table cells. For more attractive pages, add clips or columns.

Add a Dropped Capital Letter

1. Click the Print Layout View button.

2. Click the paragraph where you want the drop cap.

3. Click the Format menu, and then click Drop Cap.

4. Click a drop cap position.

5. Change the drop cap font.

6. Change the drop cap height.

7. Enter the distance between the drop cap and paragraph.

8. Click OK.

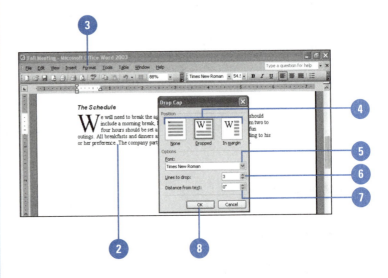

Add Shading

1. Select the text you want to shade.

2. Click the Format menu, and then click Borders And Shading.

3. Click the Shading tab.

4. Click a color.

5. Select a color style percentage.

6. Click OK.

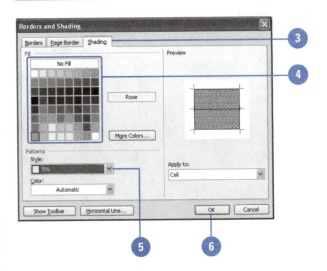

Add a Page Border

1. Click the Format menu, click Borders And Shading, and then click the Page Border tab.

2. Click a box setting.

3. Click a line style or click the Art list arrow, and then select a line or art style.

4. Enter a border width.

5. Select the pages you want to have borders.

6. Click OK.

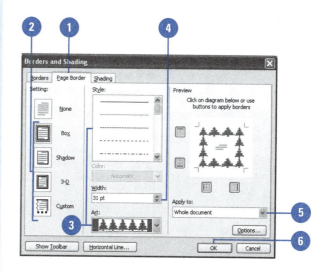

Add Borders

1. Select the text you want to have a border.

2. Click the Format menu, and then click Borders And Shading.

3. Click the Borders tab.

4. Click a setting.

5. Click a border style.

6. Select a border color and width.

7. Click OK.

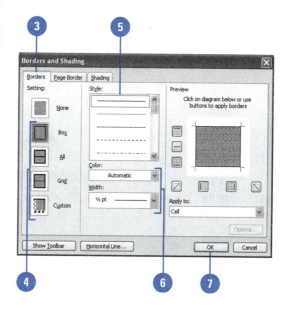

Did You Know?

You can add a border quickly. Click the Border button on the Formatting toolbar, and then select a common border.

You can use the Tables And Border toolbar to modify borders. Click the View menu, point to Toolbar, and then click Tables And Borders.

3

Creating Bulleted and Numbered Lists

WW03S-2-2

The best way to draw attention to a list is to format the items with bullets or numbers. You can even create multi-level lists. For different emphasis, change any bullet or number style to one of Word's many predefined formats. For example, switch round bullets to check boxes or Roman numerals to lowercase letters. You can also customize the list style or insert a picture as a bullet. If you move, insert, or delete items in a numbered list, Word sequentially renumbers the list for you.

Create a Bulleted List

1. Click where you want to create a bulleted list.

2. Click the Bullets button on the Formatting toolbar.

3. Type the first item in your list, and then press Enter.

4. Type the next item in your list, and then press Enter.

5. Click the Bullets button on the Formatting toolbar, or press Enter again to end the list.

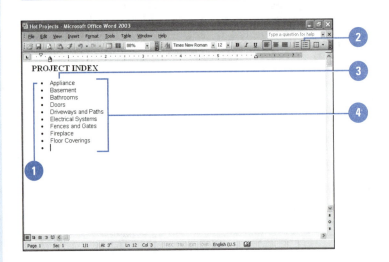

Create a Numbered List

1. Click where you want to create a numbered list.

2. Click the Numbering button on the Formatting toolbar.

3. Type the first item in your list, and then press Enter.

4. Type the next item in your list, and then press Enter.

5. Click the Numbering button on the Formatting toolbar, or press Enter again to end the list.

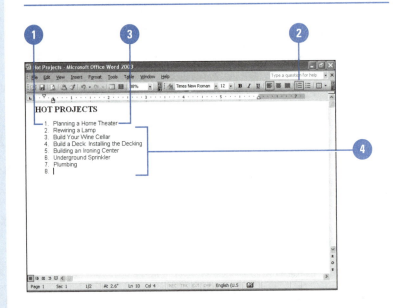

Change Bullet or Number Styles

1. Select the list, click the Format menu, and then click Bullets And Numbering.

2. Click the Bulleted tab or the Numbered tab.

3. Click a predefined format.

4. Click Customize to change the format style. You can change the Bullet (or Number) Position and Text Position options to specify where you want the bullet (or number) to appear and how much to indent the text.

5. To add a graphic bullet, click Picture, select the picture you want, and then click OK.

6. Click OK.

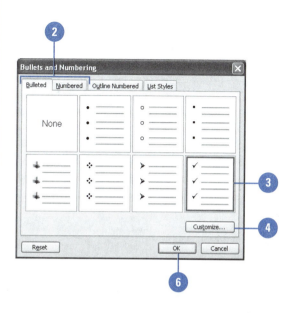

Create a Multi-Level Bulleted or Numbered List

1. Start the list as usual.

2. Press Tab to indent a line to the next level bullet or number, type the item, and then press Enter to insert the next bullet or number.

3. Press Shift+Tab to return to the previous level bullet or number.

4. End the list as usual.

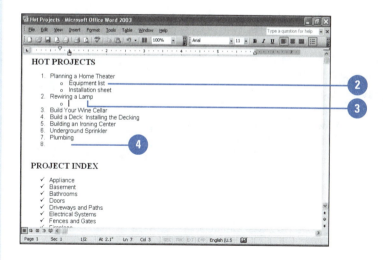

Did You Know?

You can quickly create a numbered list. Click to place the insertion point at the beginning of a line, type **1.**, press the Spacebar, type the first item, and then press Enter. Press Enter or Backspace to end the list.

Creating a Table

WW03S-2-1

A Word table organizes your information into rows and columns. The intersection of a row and column is called a **cell**. You can create a table from existing text separated by paragraphs, tabs, or commas, or you can draw a custom table with various sized cells and then enter text. Once you create your table you enter text into cells just as you would in a paragraph, except pressing Tab moves you from cell to cell. The first row in the table is good for column headings, whereas the leftmost column is good for row labels. To enter text in cells, you must move around the table. Knowing how to select the rows and columns of a table is also essential to working with the table itself. If you decide not to use a table, you can convert it to text.

Create a Table

1. Position the insertion point where you want to create a table.

2. Click the Table menu, point to Insert, and then click Table.

3. Enter the number of columns (vertical) and rows (horizontal) you want.

4. Click the option to adjust the table size.

5. Click OK.

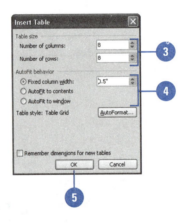

Create a Table from Existing Text

1. Select the text for the table.

2. Click the Table menu, point to Convert, and then click Text To Table.

3. Enter the number of columns.

4. Click the option to adjust the table size.

5. Click a symbol to separate text into cells.

6. Click OK.

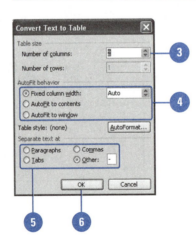

Draw a Custom Table

1. Click the View menu, point to Toolbars, and then click Tables And Borders.

2. Click the Draw Table button on the Tables And Borders toolbar.

3. Draw the table.

   ◆ A rectangle creates individual cells or the table boundaries.

   ◆ Horizontal lines create rows.

   ◆ Vertical lines create columns.

   ◆ Diagonal lines split cells.

4. If necessary, press and hold Shift, and then click one or more lines to erase them.

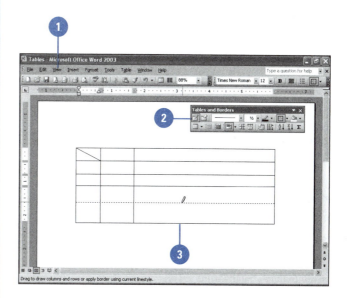

Entering Text in a Table

Once you create your table, you enter text into cells just as you would in a paragraph, except pressing Tab moves you from cell to cell. As you type in a cell, text wraps to the next line, and the height of a row expands as you enter text that extends beyond the column width. The first row in the table is good for column headings, whereas the left-most column is good for row labels. Before you can modify a table, you need to know how to select the rows and columns of a table.

Enter Text and Move Around a Table

1 The insertion point shows where text that you type will appear in a table. After you type text in a cell:

◆ Press Enter to start a new paragraph within that cell.

◆ Press Tab to move the insertion point to the next cell to the right (or to the first cell in the next row).

◆ Press the arrow keys or click in a cell to move the insertion point to a new location.

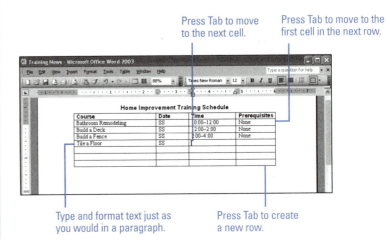

Press Tab to move to the next cell.

Press Tab to move to the first cell in the next row.

Type and format text just as you would in a paragraph.

Press Tab to create a new row.

Select Table Elements

Refer to this table for methods of selecting table elements, including:

◆ The entire table

◆ One or more rows and columns

◆ One or more cells

Selecting Table Elements

To Select	Do This
The entire table	Click ⊞ next to the table, or click anywhere in the table, click the Table menu, point to Select, and then click Table.
One or more rows	Click in the left margin next to the first row you want to select, and then drag to select the rows you want.
One or more columns	Click just above the first column you want to select, and then drag with ↓ to select the columns you want.
The column or row with the insertion point	Click the Table menu, point to Select, and then click Column or Row.
A single cell	Drag a cell or click the cell with ➶.
More than one cell	Drag with ➶ to select a group of cells.

Sorting Table Contents or Lists

 WW03E-2-1

After you enter contents in a table or create a bulleted or numbered list, you can reorganize the information by sorting the information. For example, you might want to sort information in a client list alphabetically by last name or numerically by their last invoice date. **Ascending order** lists information from A to Z, earliest to latest, or lowest to highest. **Descending order** lists information from Z to A, latest to earliest, or highest to lowest. You can sort a table columns based on one or more adjacent columns. A sort, for example, might be the telephone directory numerically by area code and then alphabetically by last name.

Sort Table Contents or Lists

1. Select the table column, adjacent columns, or list you want to sort.

2. Click the Table menu, and then click Sort.

3. If necessary, click the Sort By list arrow, and then select a column name.

4. Click the Type list arrow, and then click table cell content type.

5. Click the Ascending or Descending option.

6. If necessary, click the second Sort By list arrow, select another column name, and then select the related sorting options you want.

7. Click the Header Row or No Header Row option as it applies to the table.

8. Click OK.

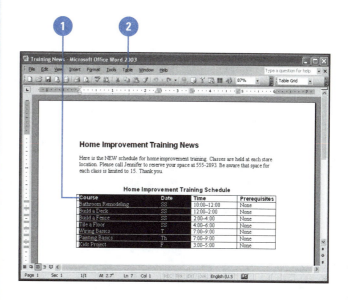

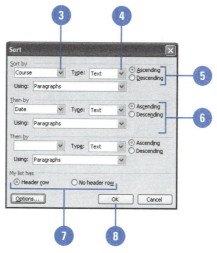

Adjusting Table Cells

WW03S-2-1, WW03E-2-3

Merge and Split Table Cells and Tables

◆ To merge two or more cells into a single cell, select the cells you want to merge, click the Table menu, and then click Merge Cells.

◆ To split a cell into multiple cells, click the cell you want to split, click the Table menu, and then click Split Cells. Enter the number of rows or columns (or both) you want to split the selected cell into, clear the Merge Cells Before Split check box, and then click OK.

◆ To split a table into two tables separated by a paragraph, click in the row that you want as the top row in the second table, click the Table menu, and then click Split Table.

◆ To merge two tables into one, delete the paragraph between them.

Did You Know?

You can quickly adjust columns and rows. Position the pointer over the boundary of the column or row you want to adjust until it becomes a resize pointer. Drag the boundary to a new location.

Often there is more to modifying a table than adding or deleting rows or columns; you need to make cells just the right size to accommodate the text you are entering in the table. For example, a title in the first row of a table might be longer than the first cell in that row. To spread the title across the top of the table, you can merge (combine) the cells to form one long cell. Sometimes, to indicate a division in a topic, you need to split (or divide) a cell into two. You can also split one table into two at any row. Moreover, you can modify the width of any column and height of any row to better present your data.

The four cells in this row will be combined into one.

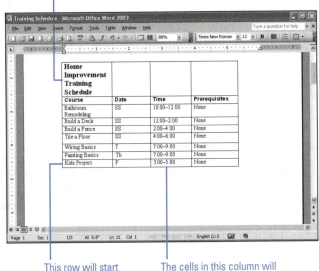

This row will start a new table.

The cells in this column will be divided into two.

Merged cells

Split cells

Home Improvement Training Schedule			
Course	Date	Time	Prerequisites
Bathroom Remodeling	SS	10:00–12:00	None
Build a Deck	SS	12:00–2:00	None
Build a Fence	SS	2:00–4:00	None
Tile a Floor	SS	4:00–6:00	None
Wiring Basics	T	7:00–9:00	None
Painting Basics	Th	7:00–9:00	None
Kids Project	F	3:00–5:00	None

Split tables

Adjust Column Widths and Row Heights

① Select the columns or rows you want to change.

② Click the Table menu, and then click Table Properties.

③ Click the Column tab.

④ To specify an exact width, click the Measure In list arrow, and then click Inches.

⑤ Type an inch measurement.

⑥ Click the Row tab.

⑦ Click the Row Height Is list arrow, and then click Exactly or At Least.

⑧ Type an inch measurement.

⑨ Click OK.

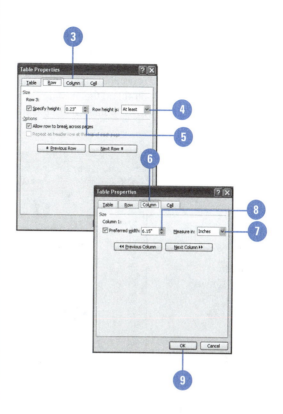

Change Table Properties

① Select the rows to change.

② Click the Table menu, and then click Table Properties.

③ Click an alignment option, and then specify an indent from the left (when you select the Left alignment option).

④ Click a text wrapping option.

⑤ Click OK.

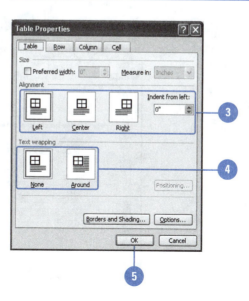

Modifying a Table

 WW03S-2-1, WW03E-2-3

As you begin to work on a table, you might need to modify its structure by adding more rows, columns, or cells to accommodate new text, graphics, or other tables. The table realigns as needed to accommodate the new structure. When you insert rows, columns, or cells, the existing rows shift down, the existing columns shift right, and you choose what direction the existing cells shift. Similarly, when you delete unneeded rows, columns, or cells from a table, the table realigns itself.

Insert Additional Rows

1. Select the row above or below which you want the new rows to appear.

2. Drag to select the number of rows you want to insert.

3. Click the Table menu, point to Insert, and then click Rows Above or Rows Below.

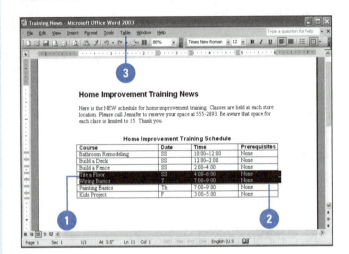

Insert Additional Columns

1. Select the column to the left of which you want the new columns to appear.

2. Drag to select the number of columns you want to insert.

3. Click the Insert Columns button on the Standard toolbar.

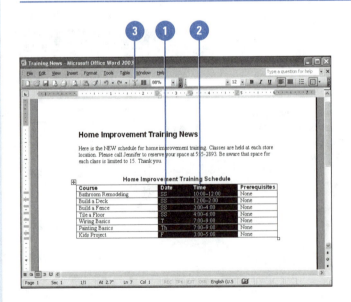

Insert Additional Cells

1 Select the cells where you want the new cells to appear.

2 Click the Insert Cells button on the Standard toolbar.

3 Select the direction in which you want the existing cells to shift.

4 Click OK.

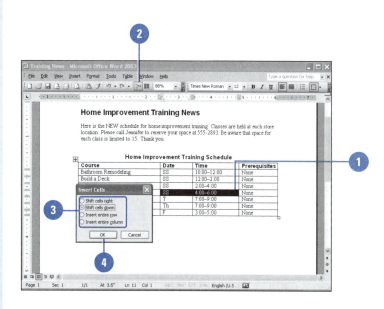

Delete Rows, Columns, or Cells

1 Select the rows, columns, or cells you want to delete.

2 Click the Table menu, point to Delete, and then click Columns, Rows, or Cells.

3 If necessary, select the direction in which you want the remaining cells to shift to fill the space, and then click OK.

Did You Know?

You can set column widths to fit text. Word can set the column widths to fit the cell contents or to fill the space between the document margins. Click in the table, click the Insert Table button list arrow on the Tables And Borders toolbar, and then click AutoFit To Contents or AutoFit To Window.

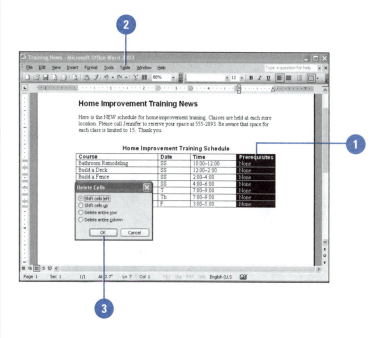

3

Formatting a Table

WW03S-2-1, WW03E-2-3

Tables distinguish text from paragraphs. In turn, formatting, alignment, and text direction distinguish text in table cells. Start by applying one of Word's predesigned table formats using AutoFormat. Then customize your table by realigning the cell contents both horizontally and vertically in the cells, changing the direction of text within selected cells, such as the column headings, and resizing the entire table. You can modify borders and shading using the Tables And Borders toolbar to make printed tables easier to read and more attractive.

Format a Table Automatically

1. Select the table you want to format.

2. Click the Table menu, and then click Table AutoFormat.

3. Click a format.

4. Preview the results.

5. When you find a format you like, click Apply.

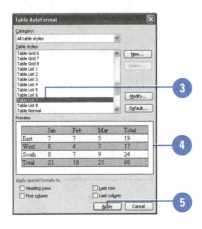

Align Text Within Cells

1. Click the View menu, point to Toolbars, and then click Tables And Borders.

2. Select the cells, rows, or columns you want to align.

3. Click the Cell Alignment button list arrow on the Tables And Borders Toolbar.

4. Click one of the alignment buttons.

Did You Know?

You can create nested tables. Select the table or cells, click the Edit menu, click Cut or Copy, right-click the table cell, and then click Paste As Nested Table.

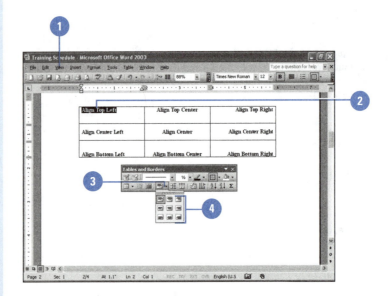

Change Text Direction Within Cells

1. Click the View menu, point to Toolbars, and then click Tables And Borders.

2. Select the cells you want to change.

3. Click the Change Text Direction button on the Tables And Borders toolbar until the text is the direction you want.

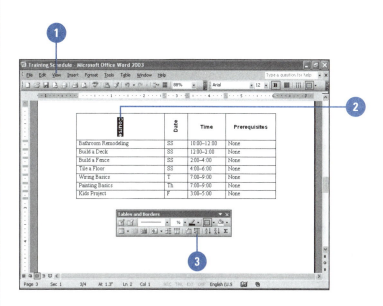

Resize the Entire Table Proportionally

1. Click to place the insertion point in the table.

2. Position the pointer over the table resize handle in the lower-right corner of the table.

3. Drag the resize handle until the table is the size you want.

Did You Know?

You can sort entries in a table column. Display the Tables And Borders toolbar, select the cells in the column you want to sort, and then click the Sort Ascending or Sort Descending button.

You can calculate the sum of a table column. Display the Tables And Borders toolbar, click in the blank cell in the bottom of the column you want to total, and then click the AutoSum button.

Drag the table from here to move it to a new location.

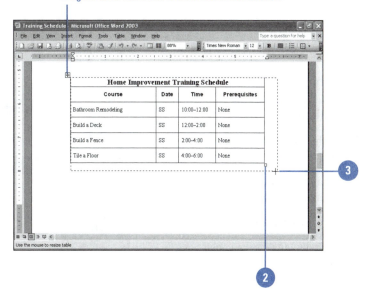

3

Applying Borders and Shading

 WW03S-2-1

To enhance the appearance of the text in a table, you can format it using the buttons on the Formatting toolbar, just as you would when formatting any text in a Word document. You can also format the structure of the table by adding borders and shading. Borders and Shading can help the table in your document come alive for your readers. You can quickly add a border using the one of the built-in layouts and adding your line style, color, and width preferences.

Apply a Border

1. Select the table you want to format.

2. Click the Format menu, and then click Borders And Shading.

3. Click the Borders tab.

4. Click to select the type of Setting you want for your border.

5. Click to select the type of Style.

6. Apply any other options you want.

7. Look in the preview box to see the new border.

8. Click OK.

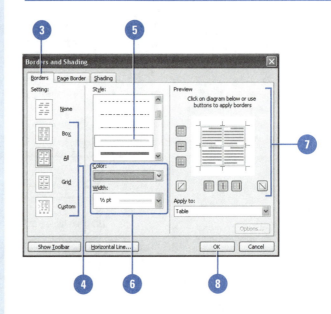

Apply Shading

1. Select the table you want to format.

2. Click the Format menu, and then click Borders And Shading.

3. Click the Shading tab.

4. Click to select the shading color you want to apply to your table.

5. Apply any other options you want.

6. Look in the preview box to see the new shading color.

7. Click OK.

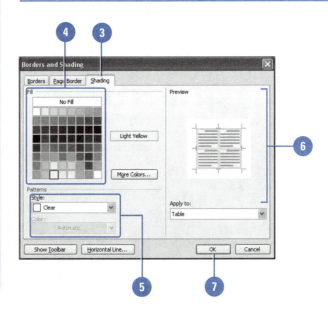

Using Templates and Applying Styles

Introduction

To help with formatting and saving time, Microsoft Office Word 2003 provides a number of **templates**—documents with pre-defined formatting, styles, macros, and other tools which define how text and graphics appear. Imagine, having templates available to browse through and select the best one, without having to do all of the work.

Word has a set of templates for creating letters, faxes, memos, reports, and other commonly used document types. Additionally, there are multiple templates for some of these document types, so you can choose a style that suits your needs.

If you don't want to use one of the pre-defined templates for your document, you can create your own template using the Template Wizard. With the click of a mouse, you can be brought through a series of steps and screens to create your document. You can take a pre-defined template, change it, and save it as a new template. You can also copy elements from one template to another and create a new template.

Styles are a way to make your documents appear consistent. Whether it's a similar font, a certain paragraph alignment, or the color of your text, you can select all of these options and save it as a style. You can then apply that style to any document that you have now or will create in the future. And just like fashion, as styles change, you can modify them to have a different look. Styles can be applied using the Format Painter Pointer or through the use of the Styles and Formatting toolbar.

Creating a Document from a Template

WW03S-5-1

Create a Document from a Template Manually

1. Click the File menu, and then click New.

2. Click On My Computer, under the Templates heading.

3. Click the Publications tab, and then select the template you want.

4. Click the Document option. This creates a new document based on the template you choose.

5. Click OK.

A **template** is a document with pre-defined formatting and styles. Each of its sections contains placeholder text which displays the exact formatting for that particular type of text. You can create a new document based on a template, so you can use the formatting provided in that template. You can do this manually, or, with some templates, you can use a wizard to help you populate the document. (A **wizard** is a series of dialog boxes which help you prepare a more complex document, such as a report or manual.)

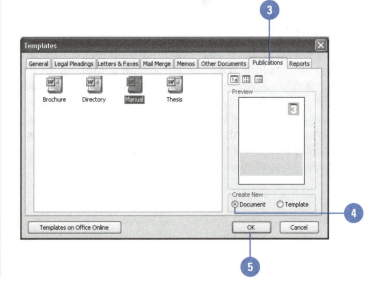

Create a Document Using a Wizard

1. Click the File menu, and then click New.

2. Click On My Computer, under the Templates heading.

3. Click a tab, select the type of template wizard you want, and then click OK.

4. Click Next, and then follow the wizard to create your document.

   Depending on the type of wizard you select, your steps will vary.

5. When you're done, click Finish.

See Also

See "Creating a Letter" on page 44 or "Creating a Memo" on page 46 for more examples of using a wizard to create documents.

Did You Know?

The Recently Used Template list in the New Document Task Pane automatically updates itself. The task pane changes over time, updating itself to reflect the types of documents you most frequently create.

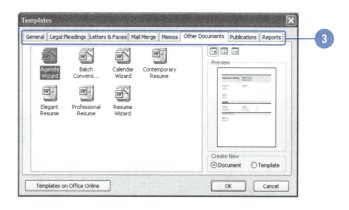

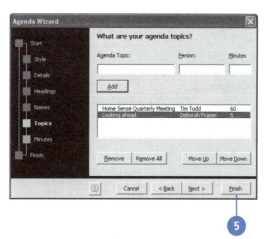

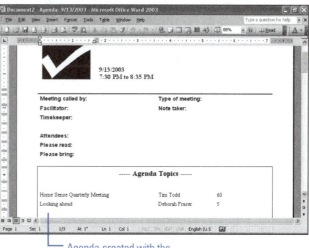

Agenda created with the Agenda Wizard.

4

Creating Your Own Template

You can create your own template for a new presentation of a common document type, or to present an entirely new type of document. You can create a template from any existing document or template. This means you only have to create your own formats once, then save the document as a template and use it over and over again.

Create a Template Based on an Existing Template

1. Click the File menu, and then click New.

2. Under the Templates heading, click On My Computer.

3. Select a template, and then click the Template option.

4. Click OK.

5. Click the File menu, and then click Save As.

6. Click the Save As Type list arrow, and then click Document Template.

7. Type a name for the new template.

8. Click Save.

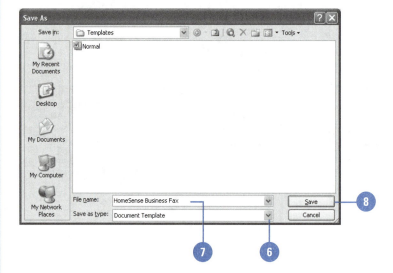

9 Add the text and graphics you want in all future documents that use this template, and then delete the unwanted elements. Make any additional changes in formatting and page layout.

10 Click the Save button.

Did You Know?

You can save a template so it appears in the Templates dialog box. When you save your template in the Templates folder, it appears on the General tab of the Templates dialog box. The Templates folder is typically located in Documents And Settings/*username*/Application Data/Microsoft/Templates.

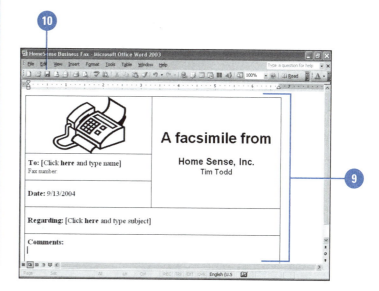

Customizing a Template

If you find that you are consistently modifying the same template (for example, modifying the Contemporary Letter template to function as letterhead for your company), you can save time by making your modifications once and overwriting the existing template with those changes. The next time you open the template, your changes will already be present instead of the placeholder text.

Customize an Existing Template

1. Click the File menu, and then click New.

2. Click On My Computer.

3. Click a document type tab, and then click an existing template.

4. Select the Template option.

5. Click OK.

6. Customize the placeholder text that you want to modify by typing those entries that will be consistent from one document to the next.

7. Click the File menu, and then click Save As.

8. Click the Save As Type list arrow, and then click Document Template.

9. Browse to the folder containing the template you have customized, and then double-click the existing template file. A Warning dialog box opens asking if you want to overwrite the existing template with the customized template.

10. Click Save.

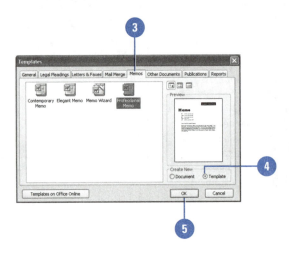

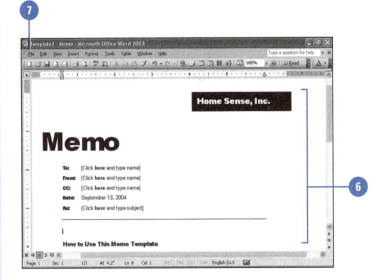

Copying Between Templates

To save time, Word allows you to copy features from one template to another. Once you create a style, macro, or Toolbar button you never have to create it again. You can simply copy it to another template to use it with a whole new set of documents. You can also replace all the styles in a document with those from a different template by attaching the new template to that document.

Copy Functionality Between Templates

1. With one template open, click the Tools menu, and then click Templates And Add-Ins.

2. Click Organizer on the Templates tab.

3. Click a tab on the Organizer dialog box with the part of the template that you want to copy.

4. To copy items either to or from a different template, click Close File.

5. Click Open File, and then open the template (or file) you want.

6. Click the items you want to copy in either list, and then click Copy.

7. Select any additional tabs to apply that part of the template.

8. Click Close.

Did You Know?

Templates can be password protected from unwanted changes. If the Copy button is unavailable in the Organizer dialog box, check to see if the template has been password protected against tracked changes, comments, or forms. If so, these settings must be changed before the elements can be copied to the template.

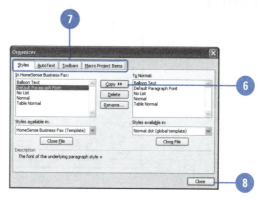

Working with Templates

WW03S-5-1

When you start Word, a blank document opens based on a default template. The default template defines the page margins, default font, and other settings. Instead of using the default template, you can create your own template. A custom template can store text, styles, formatting, macros, and page information for use in other documents. Start with a predefined Word template, or use one you created. Quickly try a new look by attaching a different template to your current document. The attached template's styles replace the styles in your document.

Save a Document as a Template

1 Open a new or existing document.

2 Add any text, graphics, and formatting you want to appear in all documents based on this template. Adjust margin settings and page size, and create new styles as necessary.

3 Click the File menu, and then click Save As.

4 Click the Save As Type list arrow, and then click Document Template.

5 Make sure the Templates folder or one of its subfolders appears in the Save In box.

6 Type a name for the new template.

7 Click Save.

You can open and modify the template just as you would in any other document.

See Also

See "Creating a Document from a Template" on page 84 for information on creating a new document using a template.

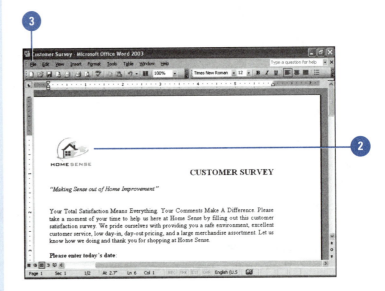

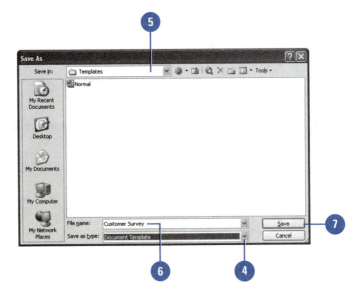

Attach a Template to an Existing Document

1. Open the document to which you want to apply a new template.

2. Click the Format menu, click Theme, and then click Style Gallery.

3. Click a template name to preview it.

4. Click OK to add the template styles to the document.

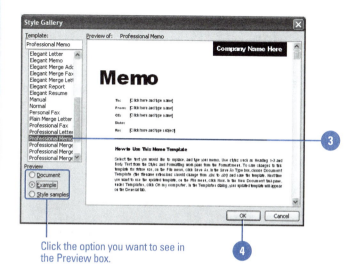

Click the option you want to see in the Preview box.

Load an Add-In

1. Click the Tools menu, and then click Templates And Add-Ins.

2. Click the add-in you want to load.

3. To add one to the list, click Add, navigate to the folder that contains the add-in, click the Files Of Type list arrow, select Word Add-Ins, click the add-in, and then click OK.

4. Click OK.

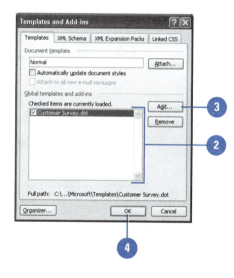

Did You Know?

You are probably using the Normal template. By default, all Word documents use the Normal template, which formats text in 12-point Times New Roman and offers three different heading styles.

Creating and Modifying Styles

 Microsoft® Office Specialist Approved Courseware

WW03S-3-1, WW03E-1-1

Word provides a variety of styles to choose from, but sometimes you need to create a new style or modify an existing one to get the exact look you want. When you create a new style, specify if it applies to paragraphs or characters, and give the style a short, descriptive name that describes its purpose so you and others recall when to use that style. A **paragraph style** is a group of format settings that can be applied only to all of the text within a paragraph (even if it is a one-line paragraph), while a **character style** is a group of format settings that is applied to any block of text at the user's discretion. To modify a style, adjust the formatting settings of an existing style.

Create a New Style

1. Select the text whose formatting you want to save as a style.

2. Click the Format menu, click Styles And Formatting, and then click the New Style button.

3. Type a short, descriptive name.

4. Click the Style Type list arrow, and then click Paragraph to include the selected text's line spacing and margins in the style, or click Character to include only formatting, such as font, size, and bold, in the style.

5. Click the Style For Following Paragraph list arrow, and then click the name of a style you want to be applied after a paragraph with the new style.

6. To add the style to the document template, select the Add To Template check box.

7. Click OK.

8. When you're done, click the Close button on the task pane.

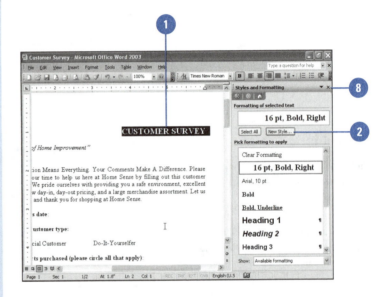

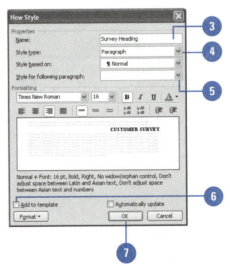

Modify a Style

1 Click the Format menu, and then click Styles And Formatting.

2 Click the style list arrow you want to modify.

3 Click Modify.

4 Click Format, and then click the type of formatting you want to modify:

♦ To change character formatting, such as font type and boldface, click Font.

♦ To change line spacing and indents, click Paragraph.

5 Select the formatting options you want.

6 Check the Preview box, and then review the style description. Make any formatting changes necessary.

7 Click OK.

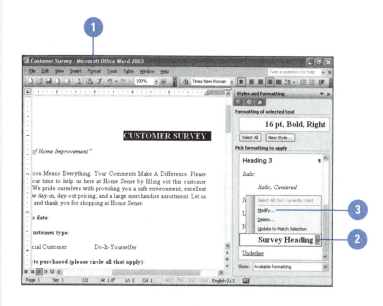

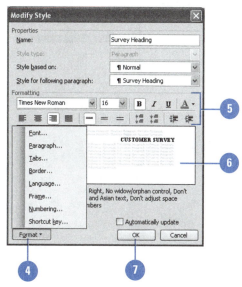

Did You Know?

You can save time by using the Styles feature. Once you format a document with styles, you can try different looks quickly. Modify each style, and then watch all text tagged with that style change automatically.

You can view different style lists. When looking at the list of styles in the Styles And Formatting task pane, you can select what types of styles to view from the Show list arrow: Available Formatting, Formatting In Use, Available Styles, and All Styles.

4

Applying a Style

WW03S-3-1, WW03E-1-1

Apply a Style with the Format Painter

1 Select the text with the formatting you want to copy.

2 Click the Format Painter button on the Standard toolbar.

3 Select the text you want to format with the Format Painter pointer.

The **Format Painter** copies and pastes formatting from one batch of selected text to another without copying the text. When you want to apply multiple groupings of formatting, save each as a style. A **style** is a collection of formatting settings saved with a name in a document or template that you can apply to text at any time. If you modify a style, you make the change once, but all text tagged with that style changes to reflect the new format.

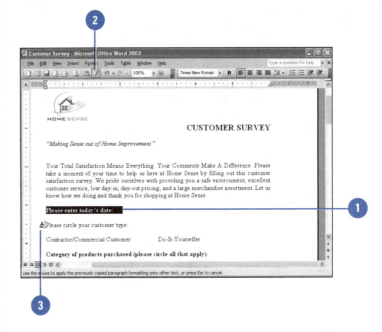

Apply a Style

1. Select the text to which you want to apply a style.

2. Click the Styles And Formatting button on the Formatting toolbar.

3. Click the style you want to apply.

Did You Know?

Additional styles are available within a document. Open the Styles And Formatting task pane, click the Show list arrow, and then click All Styles.

You can also request a style by name. Click or type a style name in the Style box on the Formatting toolbar.

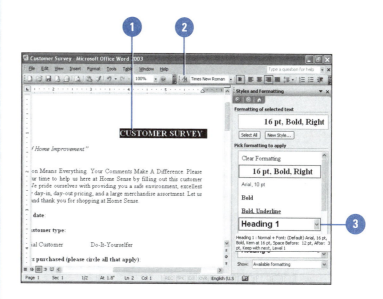

Adding Graphics and Multimedia to Documents

5

Introduction

Now that your text is entered into your document, adding graphical and multimedia elements will bring your document to a whole new level. In Microsoft Office Word 2003, you can insert many objects that give your document a finished look. When viewing graphic and multimedia objects, they are typically classified into 4 general types—clip art, pictures, sound, and video.

Microsoft offers a wide array of copyright-free clip art that you can add into your Office programs. As you use clip art, you might want to organize it in the Clip Organizer for easy access in the future. Clip art isn't just pictures, you can also add video or sound clips, or even create your own, and store them in the Organizer. You can import your own clips into the Clip Organizer. For example, if you have a company logo that you plan to include in more than one document, add it to the Clip Organizer.

If you find that you've gone through and search all that Word has to offer, you can go online and access the additional clips that Microsoft provides on it's Office Online Web site. Search for additional clip art, pictures, movie, and sound clips. You can also insert your own digital photos or a photo from a scanner. If you need to adjust the pictures or other clips, you can do that through the Picture toolbar. Add brightness or contrast, crop a picture, change colors or set a transparent background.

WordArt is another feature that adds detail to your document. If you want to draw attention to a title or section header, you can apply some WordArt, adjust color or shadowing, and you've got a custom look. Unlike WordArt, a background or a watermark are graphical objects that sit "behind" the text. For instance, if you want to have a stamp across your document pages labeled CONFIDENTIAL, you would add a watermark.

What You'll Do

Insert Multimedia Clips

Insert Clip Art

Add and Remove Clips

Organize Clips into Categories

Access Clip Art on the Web

Insert a Picture

Insert a Picture from a Scanner or Camera

Recolor and Modify a Picture

Crop and Resize a Picture

Add WordArt

Modify WordArt Text

Apply WordArt Text Effects

Create a Background

Add a Watermark

Add a Video and a Sound Clip

Record a Sound File

Inserting Multimedia Clips

Word provides access to hundreds of professionally designed pieces of clip art. These clips include clip art, pictures, photographs, sounds, and videos. All Office 2003 programs include **Microsoft Clip Organizer**, which organizes these objects into categories and gives you tools to help locate the clips you need quickly. You can extend the usefulness of the Clip Organizer by importing your own objects. The Insert Clip Art task pane helps you search for clip art and access the clip art available in the Clip Organizer.

Clip Art

Clip art objects (pictures and animated pictures) are images made up of geometric shapes, such as lines, curves, circles, squares, and so on. These images, known as vector images, are mathematically defined, which makes them easy to resize and manipulate. A picture in the Microsoft Windows Metafile (.WMF) file format is an example of a vector image.

Pictures

Pictures, on the other hand, are not mathematically defined. They are **bitmaps**, images that are made up of dots. Bitmaps do not lend themselves as easily to resizing because the dots can't expand and contract when you enlarge or shrink your picture. You can create a picture using a bitmap graphics program such as Adobe Photoshop, Microsoft Paint, or Paint Shop Pro by drawing or scanning an image or by taking a digital photograph.

Sounds

A **sound** is a file that makes a sound. Some sounds play on your computer's internal speakers (such as the beep you hear when your operating system alerts you to an error), but others require a sound card and speakers. You can use the Windows accessory called **Windows Media Player** to listen to sound clips.

Videos

A **video** can be animated pictures, such as cartoons, or it can be digital video prepared with digitized video equipment. Although you can play a video clip on most monitors, if it has sound, you need a sound card and speakers to hear the clip.

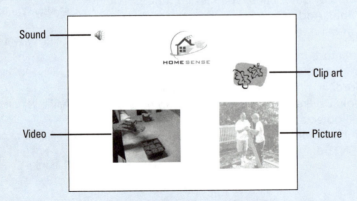

Inserting Clip Art

 WW03S-1-4

Insert a Clip

1. Click where you want to insert clip art.

2. Click the Insert menu, point to Picture, and then click Clip Art.

3. Type the word or phrase that describes the clip art you want to find.

4. Click the Search In list arrow, and then select the check boxes with the collection in which you want to search.

   Use the plus (+) and minus (-) signs to navigate the list.

5. Click the Results Should Be list arrow, and then select the check boxes with the type of media you want to search.

6. Click the Go button.

7. Click the clip art image you want to insert.

8. When you're done, click the Close button on the task pane.

Did You Know?

You can find more clip art on the Web. Click the Clip Art On Office Online button to open your Web browser and connect to a clip art Web site to download files.

You can insert clips from Microsoft's Clip Gallery or your own files. **Clips**—copyright-free images or pictures, sounds, and motion clips—enhance any document. A motion clip is an animated picture—also known as an animated GIF—frequently used in Web pages or videos. You can also insert personal files you scanned or created in a drawing program, and you can organize clip art in various collections using the Microsoft Clip Organizer.

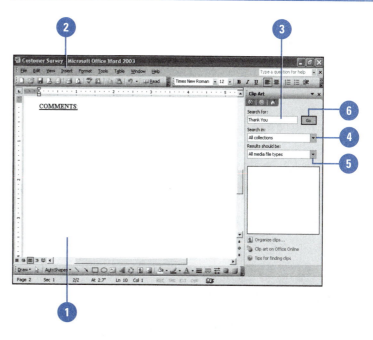

Adding and Removing Clips

You might want to add pictures and categories to the Clip Organizer for easy access in the future. You can import your own clips (pictures, photographs, sounds, and videos) into the Clip Organizer. For example, if you have a company logo that you plan to include in more than one document, add it to the Clip Organizer. You can also add groups of clips to the Clip Organizer. If you no longer need a picture in the Clip Organizer, you can remove it, which also saves space on your computer.

Add a Clip

1. Click the Insert Clip Art button on the Drawing toolbar, and then click Organize Clips on the Clip Art task pane.

2. Click the File menu, click Add Clips To Organizer, and then click On My Own.

3. Click the Look In list arrow, and then select the drive and folder that contain the clip you want to import.

4. Click the Files Of Type list arrow, and then select the file type.

5. Click the clip you want to import.

6. Click Add.

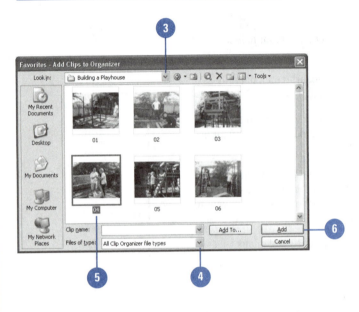

Remove a Clip

1. Click the Insert Clip Art button on the Drawing toolbar, and then click Organize Clips on the Clip Art task pane.

2. Point to the clip you want to remove, and then click the list arrow.

3. To delete the clip from all Clip Organizer categories, click Delete From Clip Organizer.

   To remove the clip from just one category, click Delete From the listed category.

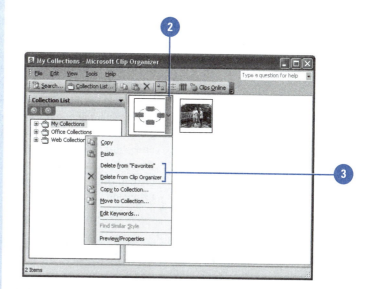

5

Organizing Clips into Categories

The clips that come with Microsoft Office Word 2003 are already organized, but if you've added clips without organizing them, it's probably hard to find what you need in a hurry. The Microsoft Clip Organizer sorts clip art images, pictures, sounds, and motion clips into categories. The Clip Organizer allows you to organize and select clips from Microsoft Office, from the Web, and from your personal collection of clips. To help you locate a clip quickly, you can place it in one or more categories. You can also assign one or more keywords to a clip and modify the description of a clip. When you add media files, Clip Organizer automatically creates new sub-collections under My Collections. These files are named after the corresponding folders on your hard disk. To help you find clips later on, Clip Organizer also creates search keywords based on the file's extension and folder name.

Categorize a Clip

1. Click the Insert Clip Art button on the Drawing toolbar, and then click Organize Clips on the Clip Art task pane.

2. Click the File menu, point to Add Clips To Organizer, and then click On My Own.

3. Locate the folder that contains the clip you want to add, and then select the clip.

4. Click the Add To button, and then click the collection to which you want to add the clip, or click New to create a new folder. Click OK.

5. Click Add.

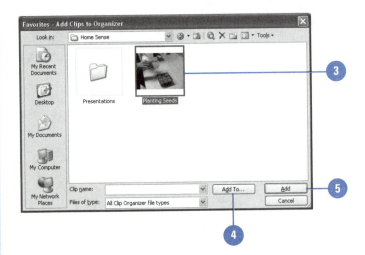

Did You Know?

You can create a new collection. In the Clip Organizer, click the File menu, click New Collection, type a new collection name, and then click OK.

Change Clip Properties

1. Click the Insert Clip Art button on the Drawing toolbar.

2. In the Clip Art task pane, click Organize Clips.

3. Find and point to the clip you want to categorize or change the properties of, click the list arrow, and then click one of the following:

   ◆ Click Copy To Collection to place a copy of the clip in another category.

   ◆ Click Move To Collection to move the clip to another category.

   ◆ Click Edit Keywords to edit the caption of the clip and to edit keywords used to find the clip.

4. Click Close to close the Clip Organizer dialog box.

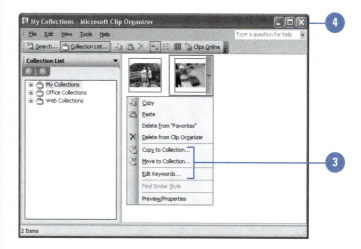

Accessing Clip Art on the Web

If you can't find the image that you want in the Clip Organizer, you can search for additional images in Clip Art On Office Online, a clip gallery that Microsoft maintains on its Web site. To access Clip Art On Office Online, you can click the link at the bottom of the Clip Art task pane or click the Clips Online button on the Clip Organizer toolbar. This launches your Web browser and navigates you directly to the Office Online Web site, where you can access thousands of free clip art images.

Open Clips Online

1. Click the Insert menu, point to Picture, and then click Clip Art.

2. Click Clip Art On Office Online.

3. If necessary, establish a connection to the Internet.

   Your Web browser displays the Microsoft Office Online Clip Art and Media Home Web page.

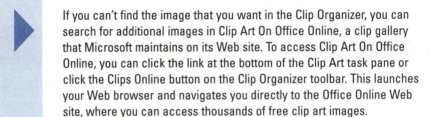

View Clips in a Category

1. If necessary, click the Accept button on the Clips Online Web page.

2. Scroll down to the Browse Clip Art And Media section, and then click the name of the category you want.

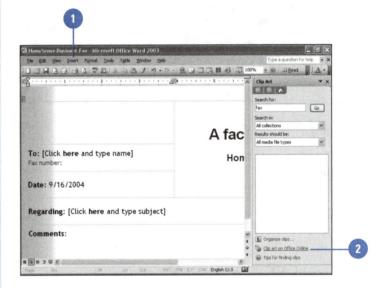

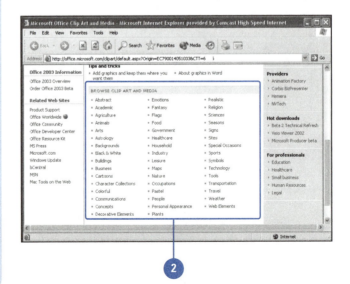

Search for a Clip

1. Click the Search list arrow on the Office Online Web page, and then select the media type you want: Clip Art, Photos, Animations, or Sounds.

2. Click the Search For box.

3. Type a keyword.

4. Click the green Click To Search arrow.

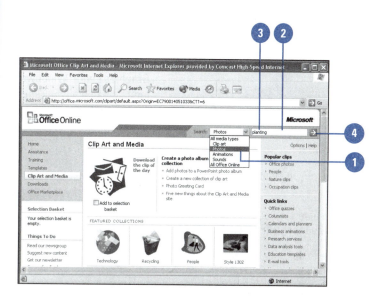

Download a Clip

1. Once you have displayed a list of clips on the Office Online Web page, select the check box below a clip to add it to your selection basket.

   You can select as many as you want. Clear the check box to deselect a clip.

2. Click Download 1 Item (will vary depending on the number of items you are downloading), review the Terms of Use, and then click Accept.

3. If a security virus warning dialog box appears, click Yes, and then click Continue.

4. Click Download Now, and then click Open.

5. The clip is stored on your hard disk and shown in your Clip Organizer where you can categorize it.

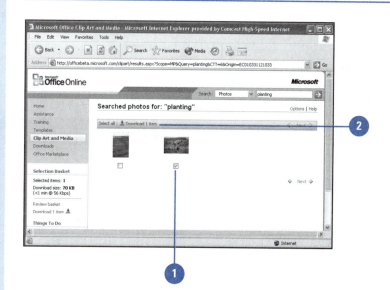

5

Inserting a Picture

WW03S-1-4

You can add pictures, such as your company logo, into an Office document that you created in a drawing program. You can insert popular graphic formats, such as Windows Enhanced Metafile (.wmf), Windows Metafile (.emf), JPEG File Interchange format (.jpg), Portable Network Graphics (.png), Windows Bitmap, and Graphics Interchange Format (.gif), to name a few. When you insert a picture, the Picture toolbar appears, which you can use to modify the appearance of the picture.

Insert a Picture

1. Click where you want to insert a picture.

2. Click the Insert menu, point to Picture, and then click From File.

3. Open the folder with the picture you want to insert.

4. Click the picture you want to use.

5. Click Insert.

Did You Know?

You can display the Picture toolbar. If the Picture toolbar doesn't appear when you select a clip or picture, right-click any toolbar, and then click Picture.

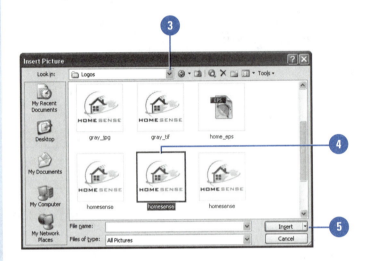

Inserted picture.

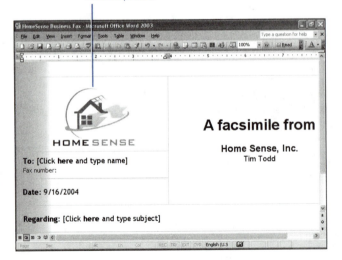

Inserting a Picture from a Scanner or Camera

If you have a scanner or digital camera connected to your computer, you can scan or download a picture into a document and you have the choice of storing it in the Clip Art Organizer. You can also use a digital still or video camera, or a live Web camera. For a video or Web camera, you can capture an image and use it in a document. When you scan an image, you can use the default or custom settings to scan and insert the image.

Insert a Picture from a Scanner or Camera

1. Click the Insert menu, point to Picture, and then click From Scanner Or Camera.

2. Click the Device list arrow, and then select the device connected to your computer.

3. Select the resolution (the visual quality of the image).

4. Select or clear the Add Pictures To Clip Organizer check box.

5. To use default settings, click Insert.

6. To specify your own settings to scan a picture or capture and select a camera image, click Custom Insert, and then follow the device instructions.

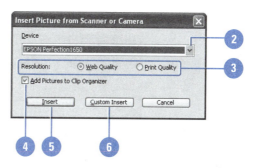

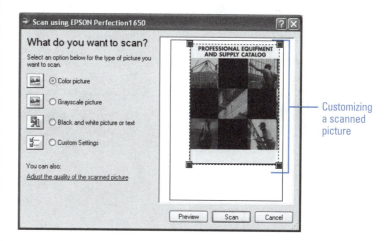

Customizing a scanned picture

5

Recoloring a Picture

You can recolor clip art and other objects to match the color scheme of your document. For example, if you use a flower clip art as your business logo, you can change shades of pink in the spring to shades of orange in the autumn. You can also use a transparent background in your clip art to avoid conflict between its background color and your document's background. With a transparent background, the clip art takes on the same background as your document.

Choose a Color Type

1. Click the picture whose color you want to change.

2. Click the Color button on the Picture toolbar.

3. Click one of the Color options.

   ◆ Automatic gives the image the default coloring.

   ◆ Grayscale converts the default coloring into whites, blacks, and grays scaled between white and black.

   ◆ Black & White converts the default coloring into only white and black. You may lose detail in your object when you choose this option.

   ◆ Washout converts the default coloring into whites and very light colors. This option makes a nice background.

Did You Know?

You can't modify some pictures in Word. If the picture is a bitmap (.BMP, .JPG, .GIF, or .PNG), you need to edit its colors in an image editing program, such as Adobe Photoshop, Microsoft Paint, or Paint Shop Pro.

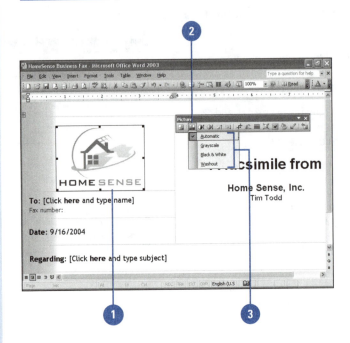

Recolor a Picture

1. Click the picture you want to recolor.

2. Click the Recolor Picture button on the Picture toolbar.

3. Click the check box next to the original color you want to change.

4. Click the corresponding New list arrow, and then select a new color.

5. Repeat steps 3 and 4 for as many colors as you want.

6. Click OK.

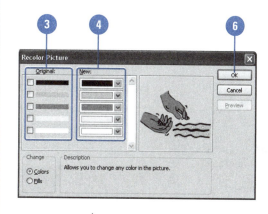

Set a Transparent Background

1. Click the picture you want to change.

2. Click the Set Transparent Color button on the Picture toolbar.

3. Move the pointer over to the object color you want to set as transparent.

4. When you're done, click outside the image.

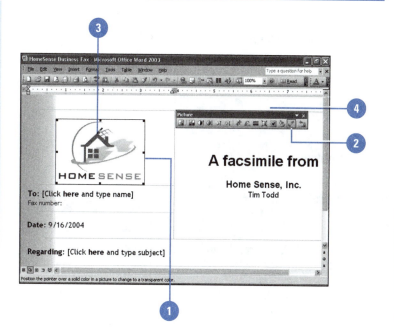

Modifying a Picture

WW03E-1-3

You can also control the image's colors, brightness, and contrast using the Picture toolbar. Maybe you've got the perfect picture, but the colors are off, and don't work with your document style. Or, you have a great picture, but the shadows are making it too dark. With Word's modifying tools, you can make adjustments to your pictures. You can also enhance the picture by adding a border around it so it looks more finished.

Change Brightness

1 Click the picture whose brightness you want to increase or decrease.

2 Choose the image brightness you want.

◆ Click the More Brightness button on the Picture toolbar to lighten the object colors by adding more white.

◆ Click the Less Brightness button on the Picture toolbar to darken the object colors by adding more black.

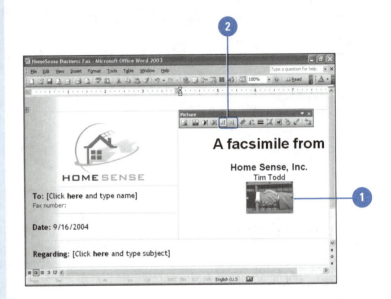

Change Contrast

1 Click the picture whose contrast you want to increase or decrease.

2 Choose the contrast you want.

◆ Click the More Contrast button on the Picture toolbar to increase color intensity, resulting in less gray.

◆ Click the Less Contrast button on the Picture toolbar to decrease color intensity, resulting in more gray.

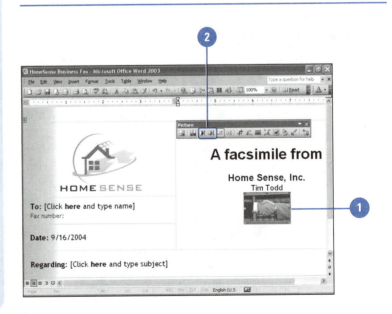

Add a Border Around a Picture

1. Click the picture or clip art image.

2. Click the Line Style button on the Picture toolbar.

3. Click the line style you want as a border around the picture.

Did You Know?

You can reset a picture to original settings. Select the image, and then click the Reset Picture button on the Picture toolbar.

You can set an image color to transparent. Select the image, and then click the Set Transparent Color button on the Picture toolbar.

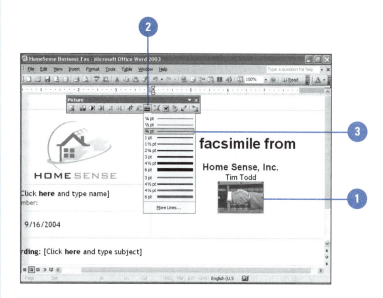

Cropping and Resizing a Picture

WW03E-1-3

You can crop clip art to isolate just one portion of the picture. Because clip art uses vector image technology, you can crop, or cut out, even the smallest part of it and then enlarge it, and the clip art will still be recognizable. You can also crop bitmapped pictures, but if you enlarge the area you cropped, you lose picture detail. You can crop an image by hand using the Crop button on the Picture toolbar. You can also crop or scale a picture using the Format Picture dialog box, which gives you precise control over the dimensions of the area you want to modify.

Crop a Picture Quickly

1. Click the picture you want to crop.

2. Click the Crop button on the Picture toolbar.

3. Drag the sizing handles until the borders surround the area you want to crop.

4. Click outside the image when you are finished.

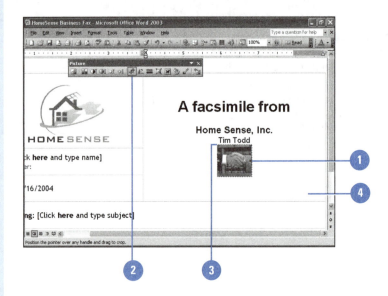

Redisplay a Cropped Picture

1. Click the picture you want to restore.

2. Click the Crop button on the Picture toolbar.

3. Drag the sizing handles to reveal the areas that were originally cropped.

4. Click outside the image when you are finished.

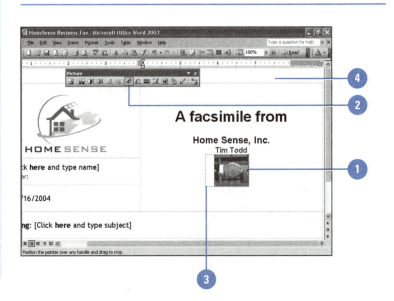

Crop a Picture Precisely

1. Right-click the picture you want to crop, and then click Format Picture.

2. Click the Picture tab.

3. Adjust the values in the Left, Right, Top, and Bottom boxes to crop the image to the exact dimensions you want.

4. Click OK.

See Also

See "Rotating and Flipping an Object" on page 234 for information on rotating and flipping a picture.

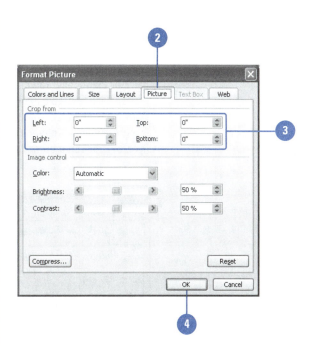

Scale a Picture

1. Right-click the picture you want to scale, and then click Format Picture.

2. Click the Size tab.

3. Adjust the values in the Height and Width boxes to scale the image to the dimensions you want.

4. To keep the proportions equal, select the Lock Aspect Ratio and Relative To Original Picture Size check boxes.

5. Click OK.

Did You Know?

You can use the mouse and Shift key to scale a picture. Press and hold Shift, and then drag a resize handle.

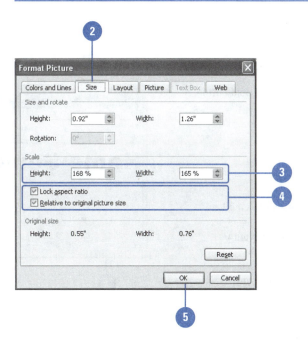

Adding WordArt

To add life to your documents, you can add a WordArt object to your document. **WordArt** is an Office component that allows you to add visual enhancements to your text that go beyond changing a font or font size. You can select a WordArt style that stretches your text horizontally, vertically, or diagonally. You can also change the character spacing and reshape the text. Like many enhancements you can add to a document, WordArt is an object that you can move, resize, and even rotate. WordArt is a great way to enhance a newsletter or resume, jazz up an invitation or flyer, or produce a creative report cover or eye-catching envelope.

Create WordArt

1. Right-click any toolbar, and then click Drawing to display the Drawing toolbar.

2. Click the Insert WordArt button on the Drawing toolbar.

3. Double-click the style of WordArt you want to insert.

4. Type the text you want in the Edit WordArt Text dialog box.

5. Click the Font list arrow, and then select the font you want.

6. Click the Size list arrow, and then select the font size you want.

7. If necessary, click the Bold button, the Italic button, or both.

8. Click OK.

Did You Know?

You can display the WordArt toolbar. When you click a WordArt object, its selection handles and the WordArt toolbar reappear. If the toolbar doesn't appear, click the View menu, point to Toolbars, and then click WordArt.

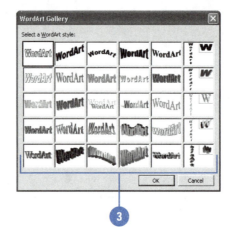

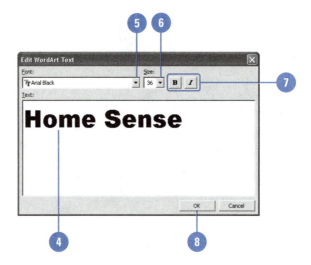

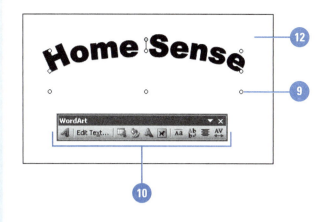

9 With the WordArt object selected, drag any handle to reshape the object until the text is the size you want.

10 Use the WordArt toolbar buttons to format or edit the WordArt.

11 Drag the WordArt object to the location you want.

12 Click outside the WordArt text to deselect the object and close the toolbar.

Did You Know?

You can change the WordArt fill color to match the background. Click the WordArt object, click the Format WordArt button, click the Colors And Lines tab, click the Fill Color button list arrow, click Fill Effects, click the Patterns tab, click the Background list arrow, choose a background color, click OK, and then Click OK again.

You can add a fill effect to WordArt. To fill a WordArt object with a pattern or special effect, click the Fill Color button list arrow on the Drawing toolbar, click Fill Effects, and then click the fill effect you want.

Using WordArt Toolbar Buttons

Icon	Button Name	Purpose
	Insert WordArt	Create new WordArt
Edit Text...	Edit Text	Edit the existing text in a WordArt object
	WordArt Gallery	Choose a new style for existing WordArt
	Format WordArt	Change the attributes of existing WordArt
	WordArt Shape	Modify the shape of an existing WordArt object
	Text Wrapping	Wrap text around an object.
	WordArt Same Letter Heights	Make uppercase and lowercase letters the same height
	WordArt Vertical	Change horizontal letters into a vertical formation
	WordArt Alignment	Modify the alignment of an existing object
	WordArt Character Spacing	Change the spacing between characters

5

Modifying WordArt Text

With WordArt, in addition to applying one of the preformatted styles, you can also create your own style by shaping your text into a variety of shapes, curves, styles, and color patterns. The WordArt toolbar gives you tools for coloring, rotating, and shaping your text. You can also format your WordArt using tools on the Drawing toolbar. The Drawing toolbar makes it easy to see your format changes.

Edit WordArt Text

1 Click the WordArt object you want to edit.

2 Click the Edit Text button on the WordArt toolbar.

3 Edit the text.

4 Click OK.

Did You Know?

You can format the WordArt text. Click the Edit Text button on the WordArt toolbar, make your changes, or click the Bold or Italic button, and then click OK.

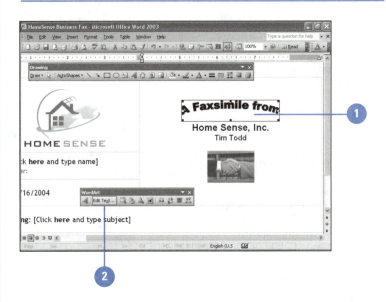

Change the Shape of WordArt

1 Click the WordArt object.

2 Click the WordArt Shape button on the WordArt toolbar.

3 Click the shape you want to apply to the text.

4 Click outside the object to deselect it.

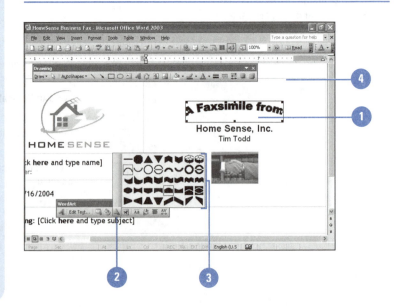

Color WordArt

1. Click the WordArt object.

2. Click the Fill Color button list arrow on the Drawing toolbar, and then click the fill color you want, or click Fill Effects to apply a special effect, such as a pattern or gradient.

3. Click the Line Color button list arrow on the Drawing toolbar, and then click the line color you want.

4. Click outside the object to deselect it.

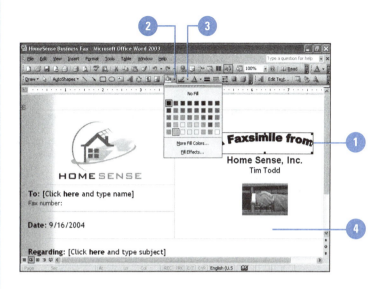

Did You Know?

You can change the WordArt fill color to match the background. Click the WordArt object, click the Format WordArt button on the WordArt toolbar, click the Colors And Lines tab, click the Fill Color button list arrow, click No Fill, and then click OK.

Align WordArt

1. Click the WordArt object.

2. Click the WordArt Alignment button on the WordArt toolbar.

3. Click the alignment you want.

4. Click outside the object to deselect it.

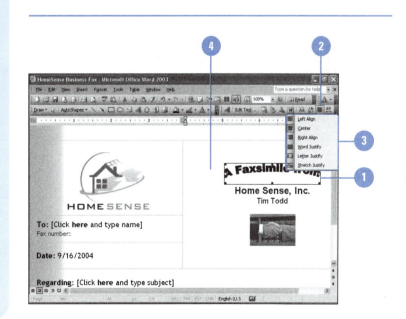

5

Applying WordArt Text Effects

You can apply a number of text effects to your WordArt objects that determine letter height, justification, and spacing. The effects of some of the adjustments you make are more pronounced for certain WordArt styles than others. Some of these effects make the text unreadable for certain styles, so apply these effects carefully.

Make Letters the Same Height

1. Click the WordArt object.

2. Click the WordArt Same Letter Heights button on the WordArt toolbar.

3. Click outside the object to deselect it.

Format Text Vertically

1. Click the WordArt object.

2. Click the WordArt Vertical button on the WordArt toolbar.

3. Click outside the object to deselect it.

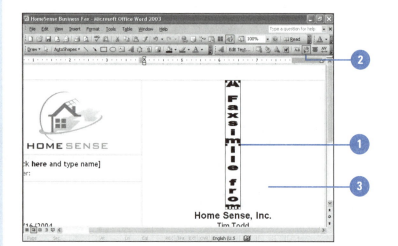

Adjust WordArt Character Spacing

1. Click the WordArt object.

2. Click the WordArt Character Spacing button on the WordArt toolbar.

3. Click a spacing setting— Very Tight, Tight, Normal, Loose, or Very Loose— to determine the amount of space between characters.

4. If you want, select or clear the Kern Character Pairs option to adjust the space between characters.

5. Click outside the object to deselect it.

Did You Know?

You can change the WordArt size or position. Click the WordArt object, click the Format WordArt button on the WordArt toolbar, click the Size or Position tab, change the size or positioning settings, and then click OK.

You can change WordArt character spacing. Although the default spacing for the WordArt Gallery objects is usually optimal, if you change the font you might want to experiment with character spacing.

You can change WordArt text to semi-transparent. Click the WordArt object, click the Format WordArt button on the WordArt toolbar, click the Colors And Lines tab, drag the Transparency slider to make the object more or less transparent, and then click OK.

5

Creating a Background

WW03E-3-2

By default, all Word documents are created on a standard white page. This is adequate for the vast majority of documents, but occasionally you might want to jazz things up a bit. Backgrounds and watermarks are excellent effects that can enhance the look of your Internet and hard copy documents. Backgrounds are intended for display exclusively in Web Layout view, whereas watermarks are designed for printed documents. In Word, you can add a background color or texture to a Web page, online document, or e-mail message.

Add a Background Color or Texture

1 Click the Format menu, and then click Background.

2 Click one of the following options:

◆ Click a color choice to apply a uniform color. The background color is applied.

◆ Click More Colors to view additional colors. Click a color, and then click OK.

3 Click Fill Effects to add the following effects:

◆ Click the Gradient tab, select one or two colors and a shading style, and then click OK.

◆ Click the Texture tab, click a background texture, and then click OK.

◆ Click the Pattern tab, select a pattern, foreground and background colors in which to display the pattern, and then click OK.

◆ Click the Picture tab, click Select Picture, locate and double-click the picture you want, and then click OK.

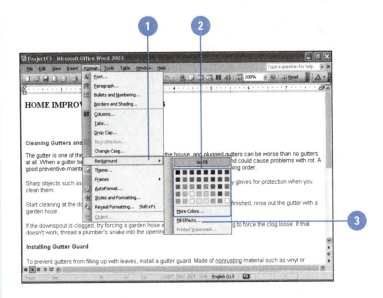

Adding a Watermark

 WW03E-3-2

Create a Watermark from a Picture

1. Click the Format menu, point to Background, and then click Printed Watermark.

2. Click the Picture Watermark option.

3. Click the Select Picture button.

4. Navigate to the picture you want to select and insert, and then click Insert.

5. Select any Scale or Washout options, and then click Apply.

6. Click Close.

Create a Watermark from Text

1. Click the Format menu, point to Background, and then click Printed Watermark.

2. Click the Text Watermark option.

3. Select the Text options you wish to apply.

4. Click Apply.

5. Click Close.

A watermark is a background effect—some text or a graphic, that prints in a light shade behind your text on your document. You can use a washed out version of your company logo, or you can add text such as SAMPLE, DRAFT, PROPOSAL, or CONFIDENTIAL. Watermarks are useful for making your documents look more professional. If you decide to change your watermark, it's as easy as typing in some new text.

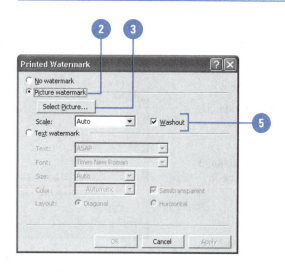

Click to clear watermark.

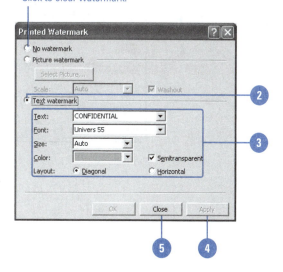

5

Adding a Video Clip

If you have a video clip that you want to associate with your document, you can insert it as an object. Word supports all standard video playback modes including Windows Media files and G2 Real Player files. Now, developing a document doesn't have to be a bland file. With the addition of clip art, sounds, and video, your document will be a complete package.

Insert a Video Clip

1 Click the Insert menu, and then click Object.

2 Click the Create From File tab.

3 Click Browse. Locate the video file you want to insert, and then double-click it.

4 To insert the selected video file as a linked object, click the Link To File check box to select it.

5 Click OK to insert the file.

6 To test the video file, double-click the video clip link.

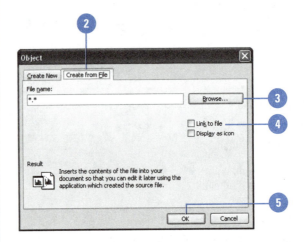

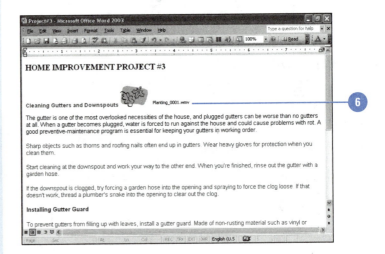

Adding a Sound Clip

Audio files can add snap as well as amplifying information in your Word documents, whether they are intended for Web publication or not. The Microsoft Clip Organizer comes with sound clips you can insert into your documents.

Insert a Sound Clip

1. Position the insertion point where you want the sound file located.

2. Click the Insert menu, and then click Object.

3. Click the Create From File tab.

4. Click Browse. Locate the sound file you want to insert, and then double-click it.

5. To insert the selected sound file as a linked object, click the Link To File check box to select it.

6. Click OK.

7. To test the sound file, double-click its button.

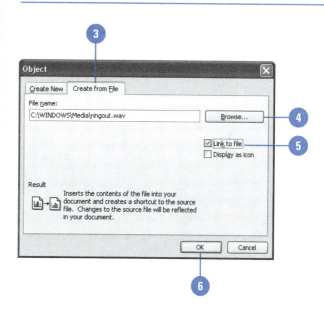

Insert a Sound from the Clip Organizer

1. Click the Insert menu, point to Picture, and then click Clip Art.

2. Type sounds in the Search For box, and then click the Go button.

3. Click the sound you want to insert.

4. When you're done, click the Close button on the task pane.

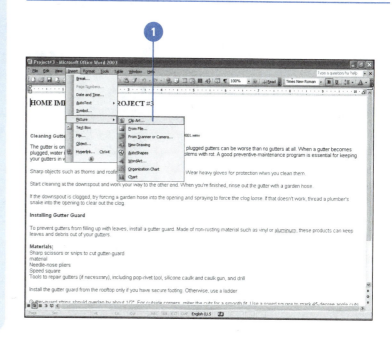

5

Recording a Sound File

You can create a new sound file and insert the file directly into your Word document. Having a customized sound can be your voice introducing the document, or a sound theme that you want to have your reader play at a certain point in the document. Either way, with the right sound equipment, you can add an extra personalized touch to your document.

Record a Sound File

1. Click the Insert menu, and then click Object.

2. Click the Create New tab.

3. Select the type that best suits your audio requirements. To use Sound Recorder, click Wave Sound.

4. Click OK.

5. Record the sound using your sound program.

6. When you're done, stop the recording and then, if necessary, save it in accordance with the instructions for that program.

7. Close your sound program.

8. To play the sound, double-click the sound icon.

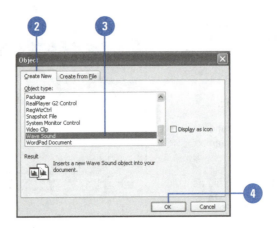

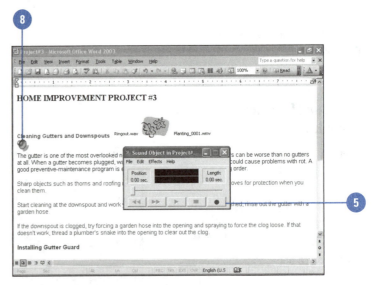

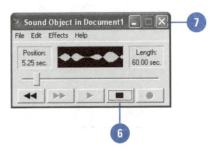

Working with Technical Documents

Introduction

Microsoft Office Word 2003 has many additional features that help you develop a more technical document. Research papers, business proposals and the like, all require more than just a document with some graphics or special text formatting.

You can find research material and incorporate it into your work quickly and easily. You can access informational services and insert the material right into your document without leaving Word. Material such as dictionaries, thesauruses, research sites, language translations, stock quotes, and company information are all at your finger tips.

With all of this research, it might be necessary to create footnotes or endnotes to reference your sources. You can format the notes to be similar in text to your document, or have an entirely different look. When working with a lot of text, you can create a bookmark to help you jump to various topics in your document.

Creating captions for your graphics is easy with Word. Once you've created captions, you can create a Table of Figures—similar to a Table of Contents, but this item keeps track of your graphics. You can format text in your document to have number lines. This is helpful if you need to locate a specific section of text—such as a legal briefing—in a long document. You can also create an outline in Word to help organize your document.

Some more technical features such as summing up the values in your tables and calculating values, are done with the help of Word's Formula feature. You can also document an equation for that scientific or mathematical paper. The ability to copy data from Excel, create a graph or organization chart, and create a diagram are all features that help make Word a useful tool when creating more technical documents.

What You'll Do

Insert Symbols and AutoText

Insert Research Material

Create Footnotes or Endnotes

Modify Footnotes or Endnotes

Format Footnotes or Endnotes

Create a Bookmark

Create Captions

Create a Table of Figures

Number Heading Styles

Number Lines

Create an Outline

Sum Table Rows and Columns

Calculate a Value in a Table

Create an Equation

Copy Data from Excel

Create a Graph Chart

Create an Organization Chart

Create a Diagram

Inserting Symbols and AutoText

 WW03S-1-1, WW03S-1-2

Word comes with a host of symbols and special characters for every need. Insert just the right one to keep from compromising a document's professional appearance with a hand-drawn arrow («) or missing mathematical symbol (å). **AutoText** stores text and graphics you want to reuse, such as a company logo, boilerplate text, or formatted table. For example, you can use AutoText to quickly insert the text *To Whom It May Concern* or a graphic of your signature. You can use the AutoText entries that come with Word, or create your own.

Insert Symbols and Special Characters

1. Click the document where you want to insert a symbol or character.

2. Click the Insert menu, and then click Symbol.

3. Click the Symbols tab or the Special Characters tab.

4. To see other symbols, click the Font list arrow, and then click a new font.

5. Click a symbol or character.

6. Click Insert.

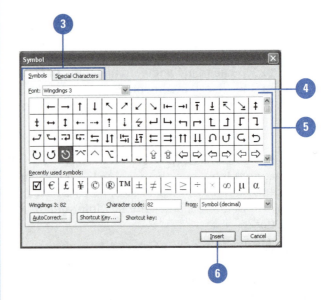

Did You Know?

You can assign a shortcut key to insert a symbol within the document. Click the Insert menu, click Symbol, click a symbol, click Shortcut Key, enter the shortcut key information requested, and then click Close.

Insert AutoText

1. Click where you want to insert AutoText.

2. Click the Insert menu, and then point to AutoText.

3. Point to an AutoText category.

4. Click the AutoText entry you want.

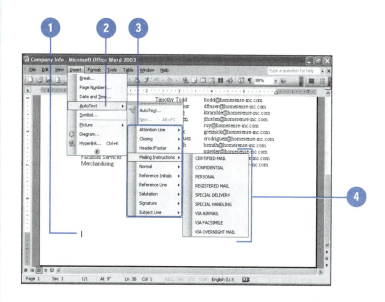

Create AutoText

1. Select the text or graphic in which you want to create an AutoText entry.

2. Click the Insert menu, point to AutoText, and then click New.

3. Type an AutoText name, or use the suggested one.

4. Click OK.

Did You Know?

You can delete an AutoText entry. Click the Insert menu, point to AutoText, click AutoText, select the AutoText entry you want to delete, click Delete, and then click OK.

You can use the AutoText toolbar for quick access. Click the View menu, point to Toolbars, and then click AutoText.

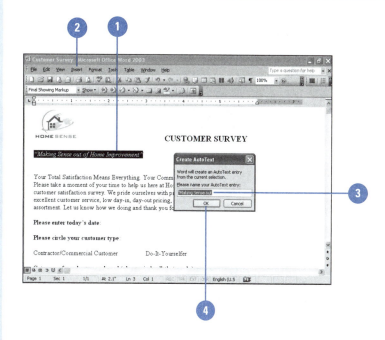

6

Inserting Research Material

 WW03S-1-6

Locate and Insert Research Material

1 Click the Tools menu, and then click Research.

2 Type the topic you want to research.

3 Click the Reference list arrow, and then select a reference source, or select All Reference Books.

4 Click the Start Searching button.

5 Copy and paste the material into your Office document.

6 When you're done, click the Close button on the task pane.

With the Research task pane, you can find research material and incorporate it into your work quickly and easily. The Research task pane allows you to access informational services and insert the material right into your document without leaving Word. The Research task pane can help you access dictionaries, thesauruses, research sites, language translations, stock quotes, and company information. You can also add and remove the services from the Research task pane.

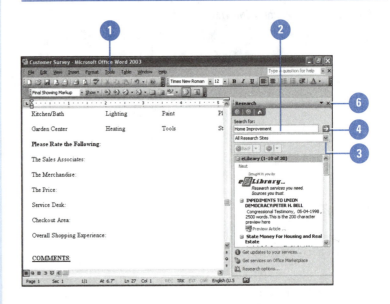

Change Research Options

① Click the Tools menu, and then click Research.

② Click Research Options.

③ Do one or more of the following:

◆ To activate or remove research services, select or clear the check boxes you want.

◆ To add research services, click Add Services, select or type the Internet address for a service you want, and then click Add.

◆ To remove a service provider, click Update/Remove, select a provider, click Remove, and then click Close.

◆ To turn on parental control, click Parental Control, select the options you want, and then click OK.

④ Click OK.

⑤ When you're done, click the Close button on the task pane.

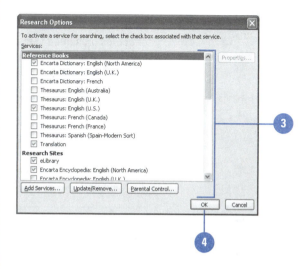

6

Creating Footnotes or Endnotes

  WW03E-3-4

Footnotes are used to provide additional information that is inappropriate for the body of the text, and to document your references for information or quotes presented in the body of the document. Footnotes are appropriate for academic, scientific, and, occasionally, business purposes. Footnotes appear at the bottom of the page on which the information is cited, and Word automatically inserts a reference mark at the insertion point to associate the information presented with the note at the bottom of the page. Creating and manipulating endnotes is identical to performing the same functions for footnotes. Endnotes differ from footnotes in that they appear at the end of the document or section (in the case of longer documents), not the bottom of the page on which the reference mark appears.

Create a Footnote or Endnote

1 Position the insertion point where you want to insert a footnote.

2 Click the Insert menu, point to Reference, and then click Footnote.

3 Click the Footnotes option or the Endnotes option.

4 Click the list arrow next to the Footnotes or Endnotes option, and then select the location where you want to place the footnote or endnote.

5 Verify that the Number Format option of 1,2,3… is selected.

6 Click Insert to insert a reference mark in the text. Word moves the insertion point to the bottom of the page corresponding to the number of the reference mark.

7 Type the text of your footnote or endnote.

8 Click inside the body of the document to reposition the insertion point at the desired location to continue with your work.

9 Click Close.

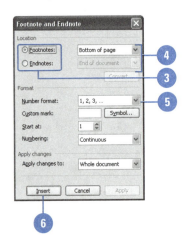

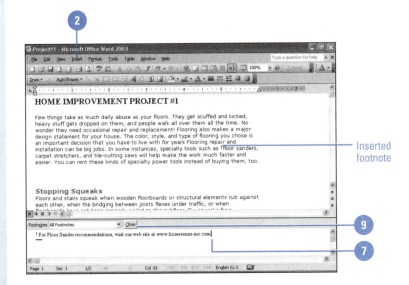

Inserted footnote

Modifying Footnotes or Endnotes

Microsoft® Office Specialist Approved Courseware

WW03E-3-4

Change a Footnote or an Endnote Format

1. Click the Insert menu, point to Reference, and then click Footnote.

2. Click the Number Format list arrow, and then click a,b,c... or another format.

3. If necessary, Click the Apply Changes To list arrow, and then click Whole Document.

4. Click Apply.

Did You Know?

You can modify a Reference mark. To move, copy, or delete a note, you work with the note reference mark in the document window, not the text in the Notes pane. You move, copy, or delete a note in the same way you would text in a document.

You can quickly view your footnotes or endnotes. Although footnotes and endnotes do not appear in Normal and Outline views, you can double-click a reference mark to open the Notes. You can also view footnotes and endnotes by pointing to a reference mark to display the footnote or endnote in a ScreenTip.

Footnote or endnote reference marks appear as 1,2,3... by default. Word provides you with various options in order to customize the reference marks the way you wish. If you'd like to change your footnotes or endnotes to be a,b,c or Roman numerals i, ii, iii, you can do that through the Insert menu. You can format the location of the footnote or endnote to be at the bottom of the text, or at the bottom of the page. You can also have Word renumber your footnotes or endnotes after each section of your document.

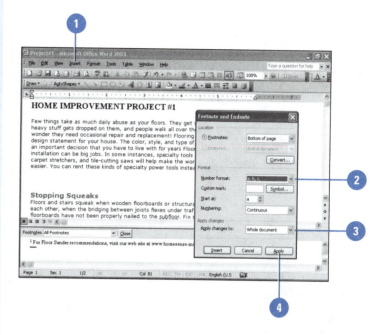

6

Formatting Footnotes or Endnotes

WW03E-3-4

Format All Footnotes or Endnotes in a Document

1 In the body text (not the footnote or endnote section), select the footnote or endnote reference mark.

2 Click the Format menu, and then click Styles and Formatting.

3 Click Select All. Under the Formatting Of Selected Text heading, the Footnote Reference style appears.

4 Under the Pick Formatting To Apply heading, click a formatting style, or use formatting buttons on the Formatting toolbar to format the reference marks the way you want.

5 When you're done, click the Close button on the task pane.

After you insert a footnote or endnote, you can change the font and other formatting. You format a footnote or endnote in the same way you format any other text in a document. To experiment with these font settings, select a reference mark of a footnote that you have created, and then, under the Format menu, change the font attributes as necessary. Once you get a look that goes well with your document, you can change all the footnotes or endnotes to be the new font style.

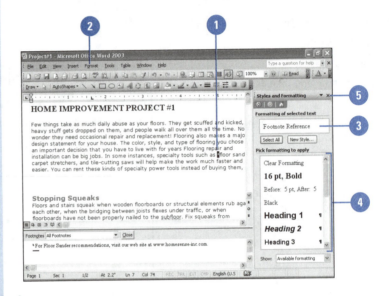

Format a Footnote or Endnote

1. In the body text (not the footnote or endnote section), select the footnote or endnote reference mark.

2. Right-click the selected reference mark, and then click Font.

3. Click the Font tab.

4. Select the Formatting options you want.

5. Click OK.

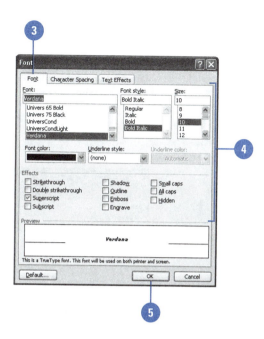

For Your Information

Editing Footnotes and Endnotes

Editing the actual text of a footnote is just like editing any text, except that you must first access the footnote because it is not visible in all the views used by Word. If necessary, click the Print Layout View button. Scroll down the page until you find the footnote in question, click to position your insertion point, and then edit.

But what if you are editing the rest of the document, not the footnotes themselves, and your edits would change the page on which the footnote would appear, for example? Adding or deleting text can change the position of your notes. As you change the body text, Word repositions your notes. When your edits affect footnoted sentences, or when you move, copy, or delete notes in your document, Word renumbers the other notes for you. When you move, copy, or delete a note, you work with the note reference mark in the document window, not the text in the Notes pane. You can move, copy, or delete a note in the same way you would text in a document.

6

Creating a Bookmark

WW03E-2-5

Instead of scrolling through a long document to find a specific word, phrase or section you can use bookmarks. **Bookmarks** are used to mark text so that you, or your reader, can return to it quickly. Using bookmarks as a destination lets you navigate through a long document quickly. You can also navigate documents with bookmarks by selecting a bookmark as a destination in the Go To dialog box.

Create a Bookmark

1. Click in your document where you want to insert a Bookmark.

2. Click the Insert menu, and then click Bookmark.

3. Type a one word descriptive name for your Bookmark.

4. Click Add.

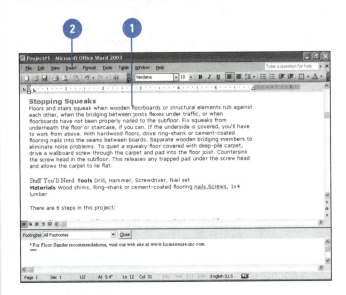

Go to a Bookmark Location

1. Click the Edit menu, and then click Go To.

2. On the Go To tab, click Bookmark.

3. Click the Enter Bookmark Name list arrow, and then select the bookmark you want to move to.

4. Click Go To.

5. If you want, choose another bookmark.

6. Click Close.

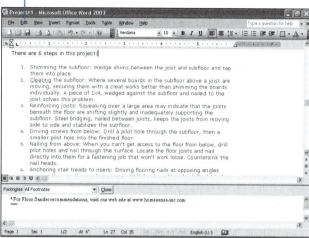

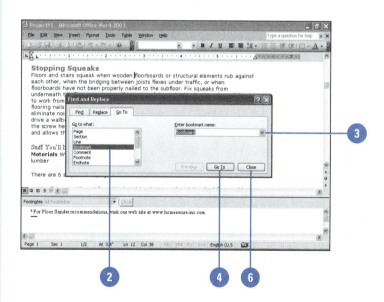

6

Creating Captions

WW03E-3-4

Captions are helpful not only to associate images with the text that refers to them, but also to provide the reader with amplifying information about the figure, table, chart, or other illustration displayed. You can use preset captions provided, such as Figure, or you can create your own custom caption for your document.

Insert a Caption

1. Select the image that you want to caption.

2. Click the Insert menu, point to reference, and then click Caption.

3. If you want to use a Label other than the default setting of Figure, which is appropriate for most art, click the Label list arrow, and then click Equation or Table.

4. If you want to use a numbering sequence other than the default setting of 1,2,3…, click Numbering, make your selections, and then click OK.

5. Click OK.

Did You Know?

You can have Word automatically add a caption field. Whenever you insert a particular type of file, such as a bitmapped image, click AutoCaption. In the Add Caption When Inserting list, click the check boxes to select the instances where you want the feature to apply, select the Label, Positioning and Numbering options you want, and then click OK.

You can add custom labels for captions. Click New Label, type the name of the New Label, and then click OK.

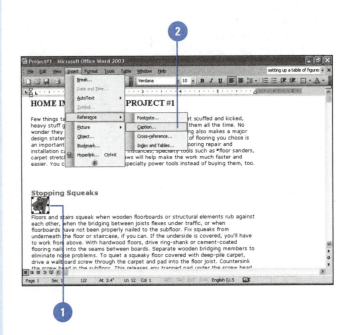

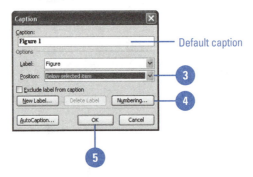

Default caption

Creating a Table of Figures

WW03E-3-3

If you are creating a document in which there are many illustrations (art, photographs, charts, diagrams etc.), it is often helpful to the reader of your document to provide a Table of Figures. A **Table of Figures** is like a Table of Contents except that it deals only with the graphic content of a document, not the written content. To create the Table of Figures, Word looks for text with the Style code that you specify (Figure, Table, etc.). You can also add a **tab leader** to make the table easier to read.

Create a Table of Figures

1. Put your cursor where you want the Table of Figures to appear.

2. Click the Insert menu, point to Reference, and then click Index And Tables.

3. Click the Table Of Figures tab.

4. Click the Tab Leader list arrow, and then select the tab leader you want to use.

5. Click the Formats list arrow, and then select the format you want to use for the Table of Figures.

6. If you want to create a Table of Figures from something other than the default Figure style, or the Table style, click Options.

7. Click the Style list arrow, select the text formatting that you want Word to search for when building the Table of Figures, and then click Close. All figure callouts of the selected style are tagged for inclusion in the Table of Figures.

8. Click OK.

9. Click OK.

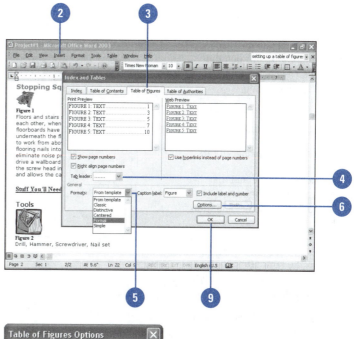

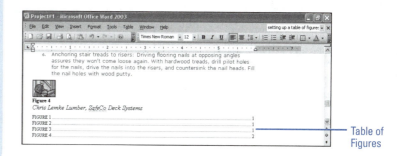

Table of Figures

6

Numbering Heading Styles

If you use the pre-defined heading styles provided by Word, such as those that appear in the Normal.dot template (Heading 1, Heading 2, Heading 3), you can also optionally number headings with a format of your choosing. Some examples of the proper times to use numbered headings include legal documents, scientific or other academic papers, and so forth. Consult the Formatting and Styles guide of the institution you are preparing the document for to determine whether this formatting is preferred.

Create a Numbered Heading Using Styles

1. In your document, position the cursor where you want to place the numbered heading.

2. Click the Format menu, and then click Bullets And Numbering.

3. Click the Outline Numbered tab.

4. Click a numbering format that contains the text "Heading 1", "Heading 2", and so on, and then click OK.

5. Click the Styles and Formatting button on the Formatting toolbar, and then select the heading style that you want.

6. Type the text of the heading, and then press Enter.

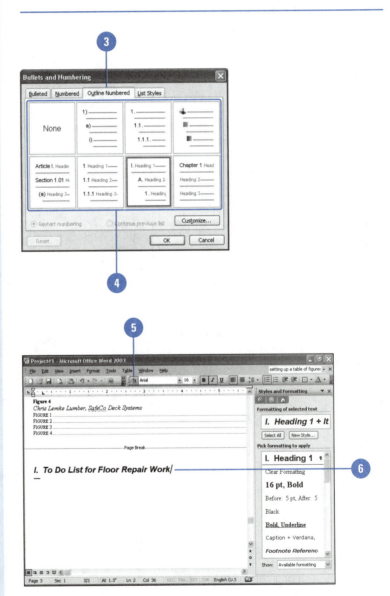

Did You Know?

You can edit your headings in a list.
After a heading has been entered, you can edit the numbering level by selecting the heading, and then on the Formatting toolbar, clicking the Increase Indent button to demote the heading to a lower level (changing a level 2 Head to a level 3 Head), or the Decrease Indent button to promote the heading (changing a level 2 Head to a level 1 Head).

Apply Numbering to Custom Heading Styles

1. Select the text in which you want to apply a style.

2. Click the Format menu, and then click Bullets And Numbering.

3. Click the Outline Numbered tab.

4. Click a numbering format that contains the text "Heading 1", "Heading 2", and so on, and then click Customize.

5. Click More to expand the Customize Outline Numbered List dialog box.

6. Click the heading level you want to number.

7. Click the Font button, format the selected heading level number, and then click OK.

8. Click the Link Level To Style list arrow, and then select the name of the custom style of text that you want to use for the level of numbering that you selected in Step 6.

9. Repeat Steps 6-8 for each custom heading style that you want to number, and then click OK.

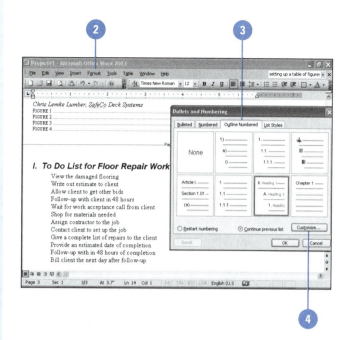

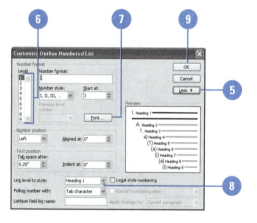

Numbering Lines

Many legal documents use the formatting convention of numbering every line of text to make it easier for multiple parties to refer to very specific text in a longer document in the context of their discussions. Other types of documents that sometimes use this convention are movie and television scripts. You can have Word automatically number each line of text within a document.

Number Each Line in a Document

1 Click the View menu, and then click Print Layout.

2 Click the Edit menu, and then click Select All.

3 Click the File menu, and then click Page Setup.

4 Click the Layout tab.

5 If you're adding line numbers to part of a document, click the Apply To list arrow, and then click Selections.

6 Click Line Numbers.

7 Click the Add Line Numbering check box to select it, and then select the options you want.

8 Click OK.

9 Click OK.

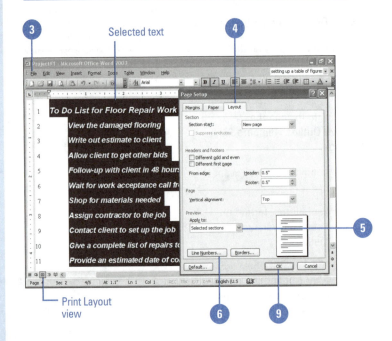

Selected text

Print Layout view

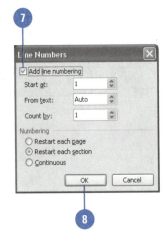

Creating an Outline

WW03S-2-2

Create an Outline from Scratch

1. In a new document, click the Outline View button.

2. Type each heading, and then press Enter.

3. To assign a heading to a different level and apply the corresponding heading style, place the insertion point in the heading, and then click the Promote or Demote button on the Outlining toolbar until the heading is at the level you want.

4. To move a heading to a different location, place the insertion point in the heading, and then click the Move Up or Move Down button on the Outlining toolbar until the heading is moved where you want it to go.

5. When you're done, click the Normal view button.

Did You Know?

You can create an outline in Normal view while you type. Click at the beginning of a line, type **1.**, press the Tab key, type a main heading, and then press Enter. You can type another main heading or press the Tab key to add a subheading under the main heading.

Outlines are useful for organizing information, such as topics in an essay. An outline typically consists of main headings and subheadings. You can create an outline from scratch in Outline view or change a bulleted or numbered list into an outline using the Bullets And Numbering command on the Format menu. In Outline view, you can use buttons on the Outlining toolbar or drag the mouse pointer to move headings and subheadings to different locations or levels.

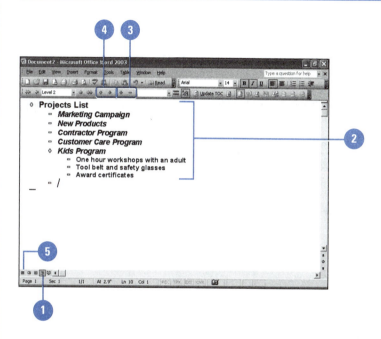

6

Summing Table Rows and Columns

Microsoft®
Office
Specialist
Approved Courseware

WW03E-2-2

The fastest way to total the rows or columns of a table is by clicking the AutoSum button on the Tables and Borders toolbar. The disadvantage of using this method is that if you subsequently edit the values in the rows and columns of the table, the sums will not automatically update. You would need to remember to click AutoSum again for each row and column that was updated. To ensure sum totals are automatically calculated anytime the data in a table changes, use the equation functions of Word.

Add the Contents of Rows and Columns

1. Click the cell in which you want the sum to appear.

2. Click the Table menu, and then click Formula.

   ◆ If the cell you selected is at the bottom of a column of numbers, Microsoft Word proposes the formula =SUM(ABOVE).

   ◆ If the cell you selected is at the right end of a row of numbers, Word proposes the formula =SUM(LEFT).

3. Click OK.

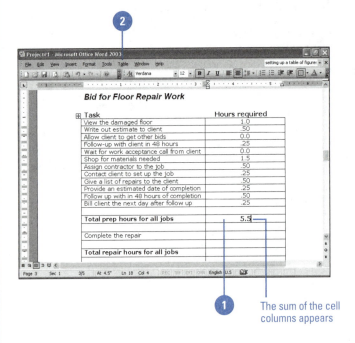

The sum of the cell columns appears

Word provides a formula

Calculating a Value in a Table

 Microsoft® Office Specialist Approved Courseware

WW03E-2-2

Calculate a Value

1. Click the cell in which you want the result to appear.

2. Click the Table menu, and then click Formula. If Word proposes a formula that you do not want to use, delete it from the Formula box.

3. Click the Paste Function list arrow, and then select a function.

4. To reference the contents of a table cell, type the cell references in the parentheses in the formula. For instance, to average the values in cells a1 through a4, the formula would read =Average(a1,a4). If you are doing the average of a row in the last column of the row, simplify this to =Average(left).

5. In the Number Format box, enter a format for the numbers. For example, to display the numbers as a decimal percentage, click 0.00%. For now, enter 0 to display the average as the nearest whole number. To display a true average, enter 0.00 in the Number Format box.

6. Click OK.

Sometimes the simple equations proposed by Word do not adequately cover what you are trying to calculate in the table. When that is the case, you need to create a custom equation to do the work. The Formula dialog box give you a choice of 18 paste functions to help you create your formula. Should you need help, you can activate Help to see examples of how to use each paste function, or for more complex formulas, try Microsoft's Online Community to look for advice from other users.

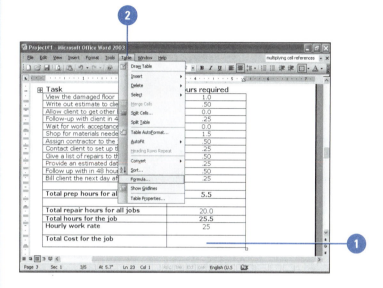

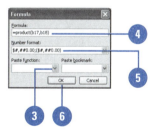

The value is calculated and displayed.

6

Creating an Equation

If you are creating a scientific or academic paper that involves complex equations, you may need to display them in the text without actually using them in conjunction with a table. The standard keyboard does not have all of the mathematical symbols you might need to create the equation, so you must use the Equation Editor.

Create an Equation

1 Click the Insert menu, and then click Object.

2 In the Object type box, click Microsoft Equation 3.0, and then click OK.

3 Build the equation by selecting symbols from the Equation toolbar, and then by typing variables and numbers.

4 Press Enter to show the equation and return to your document.

Did You Know?

You can get help using the Equation Editor. If you need help, click Equation Editor Help Topics on the Help menu.

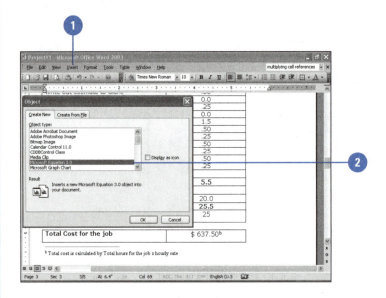

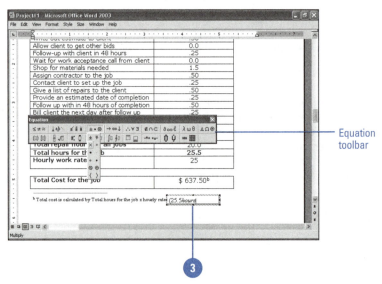

Equation toolbar

Copying Data from Excel

If you want to copy small sections of data from an Excel document, you can use the Cut and Paste or Copy and Paste routines that you have learned previously. If you want to import an entire Excel chart, the process is a little more involved.

Copy Data from Excel

1 Open both the Word document and the Excel worksheet that contain the data you want to create a linked object or embedded object from.

2 Switch to Excel, and then click and drag to select the entire worksheet, a range of cells, or the chart you want.

3 Click the Edit menu, and then click Copy.

4 Switch to the Word document, and then click where you want the information to appear.

5 Click the Edit menu, and then click Paste Special.

6 Click Microsoft Office Excel Worksheet Object.

7 Click OK.

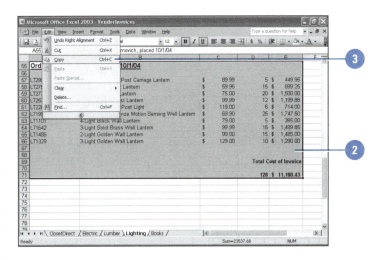

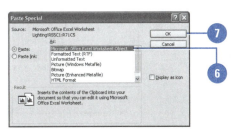

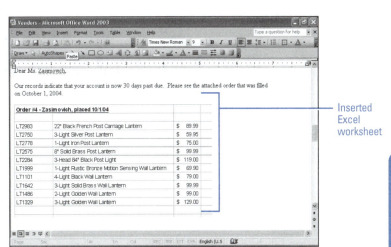

Inserted Excel worksheet

> **Did You Know?**
>
> *You can change your linked Excel object.* To make any format changes to the Excel data, (such as column width) double-click the Excel object, and then make your changes.

6

Creating a Graph Chart

WW03S-1-5

A chart often makes numerical data more visual and easier to grasp. With Microsoft Graph, you can create a chart in a document. Just enter your numbers and labels in the **datasheet**, a spreadsheet-like grid of rows and columns that holds your data in cells (intersections of rows and columns), and watch Graph create the **chart**, a graphical representation of the data. The chart has an X-axis (horizontal axis) and a Y-axis (vertical axis), which serve as reference lines for the plotted data. (In a 3-D chart, the vertical axis is the Z-axis.) Each **data series**, all the data from a row or column, has a unique color or pattern on the chart. The chart is made up of different elements that help display the data from the datasheet. You can format **chart objects**, individual elements that make up the chart, such as an axis, legend, or data series, to suit your needs.

Create a New Graph Chart

1. Click the Insert menu, point to Picture, and then click Chart.

2. Click the datasheet's upper-left button to select all the cells, and then press Delete to erase the sample data.

3. Enter new data in each cell, or click the Import Data button on the Standard toolbar to insert data from another source, such as Excel.

4. Edit and format the data in the datasheet as you like.

5. Click anywhere outside of the chart to return to the document.

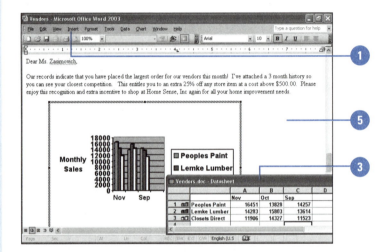

For Your Information

Using a Datasheet

To perform most tasks on the datasheet, you must first select a specific cell or range of cells. A selected cell, called the **active cell**, has a heavy border around it. To enter data into the datasheet, you can perform one or more of the following: type your own data into the datasheet, import information directly from another program, such as Microsoft Excel, or copy and paste a specified range of data or a complete worksheet into Graph. Once the data is entered into the datasheet, you can easily modify and format the associated chart.

Format a Chart Object

1. Click the chart in the document you want to format.

2. Double-click the chart object you want to format, such as an axis, legend, or data series.

3. Click the tab (Patterns, Scale, Font, Number, or Alignment) that corresponds to the options you want to change.

4. Select the options you want to apply.

5. Click OK.

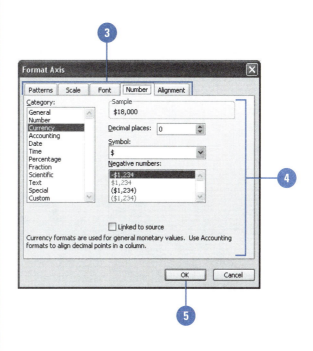

Customize a Chart

1. Double-click the chart in the document you want to customize.

2. Click the Chart menu, and then click Chart Options.

3. Click the tab (Titles, Axes, Gridlines, Legend, Data Labels, or Data Table) that corresponds to the chart object you want to customize.

4. Make your changes.

5. Click OK.

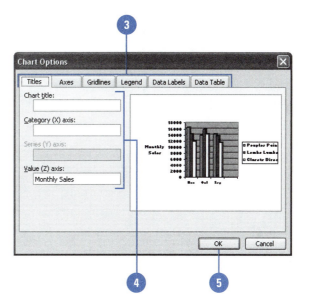

6

Creating an Organization Chart

WW03S-1-5

An **organization chart** shows the personnel structure in a company or organization. You can create an organization chart, also known as an **org chart**, in any Office document. When you insert an org chart, **chart boxes** appear into which you enter the names and titles of company personnel. Each box is identified by its position in the chart. For example, Managers are at the top, Subordinates are below, Coworkers are side to side, and so on.

Create a New Org Chart

1 Click the Insert menu, point to Picture, and then click Organization Chart.

2 Click a chart box, and then type a name.

3 Click the chart box to which you want to attach the new chart box.

4 Click the Insert Shape button list arrow on the Organization Chart toolbar, and then click a shape option.

5 When you're done, click anywhere outside the org chart to return to Word.

Did You Know?

You can edit an org chart. Double-click the organization chart, and then click the chart title or chart box you want to edit.

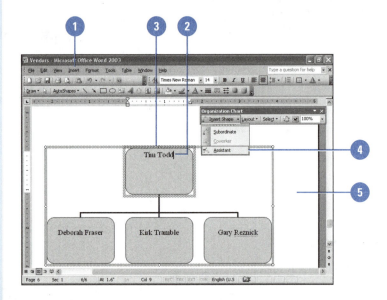

Open and Format an Org Chart

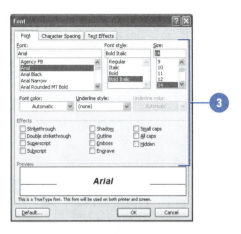

① Click the org chart in the document.

② Click the Format menu, and then click Font.

③ Click the Font, Character Spacing or Text Effects tabs, make the necessary changes, and then click OK.

④ Click the Format menu, and then click Organization Chart.

⑤ Click the Colors and Lines, Size, Layout or Web tabs, and then make the necessary changes.

⑥ Click OK.

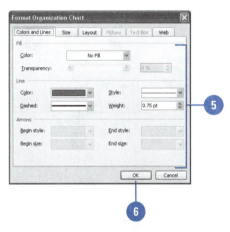

Did You Know?

You can change your shapes on an org chart. After selecting your org chart, click the AutoFormat button on the Organization Chart toolbar, select a new style, and then click OK.

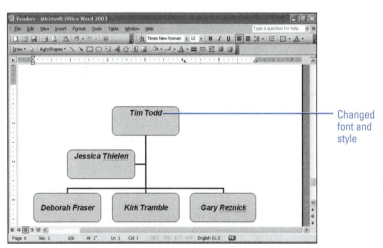

Changed font and style

Creating a Diagram

 WW03S-1-5

A **diagram** illustrates conceptual material that is easier to see visually than having to read textually. When looking at a workflow for example, it's easier to understand the components when you see them. Word offers a variety of built-in diagrams from which to choose, including pyramid, cycle, radial, and Venn diagrams as well as organization charts. Using built-in diagrams makes it easy to create and modify charts without having to create them from scratch.

Create a New Diagram

1. Click the Insert menu, and then click Diagram.

2. Select a diagram.

3. Click OK.

4. Click each text box to add your text.

5. Select diagram elements, and then use the Diagram toolbar to format the diagram with preset styles, add color and patterns, change line styles, add elements, and move them forward or backward.

6. Click anywhere outside of the diagram to return to the document.

Did You Know?

You can change a diagram. To edit a diagram, click the diagram, and then click the element you want to edit.

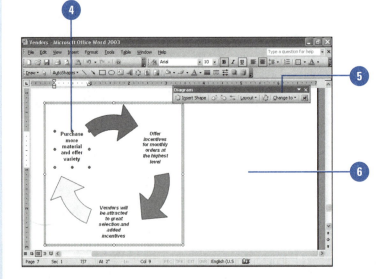

Working with Long Documents

Introduction

When working with long documents, the ability to split up the tasks can be crucial to meeting a deadline. Microsoft Office Word 2003 can do just that. By creating a master document in an Outline format, you can simply select the sections of the master that will be sectioned off as a subdocument. Word creates a number of subdocuments off the master, based on how you decide to group them. Once the subdocuments are created, they become separate files that others can open, develop, save and re-insert into the master.

Using master documents and subdocuments by many individuals could be a formatting nightmare. Word has an automatic formatting tool to help you create an overall format for your long document. In order to help your readers process your document, headers and footers, along with a cross reference, are a great way to keep them focused on the material at hand.

Once your long document is created and will be bound in some fashion, it's important to make sure that you have enough white space around the margins so that text won't get cut off during the binding process. And, as you navigate through the document, be sure to check for any special items that might require your attention. You can use the Go To function to quickly move from object to object, section to section, or page to page, to name a few. The Select Browse Object button is also a way to navigate through your long document. Browse by comments, graphics, tables or footnotes. The availability for Word to seek out these objects and for you to review them is crucial to your long document being a success.

Other documents items, such as a Table of Contents, an Index, or a Document Summary can all be done very easily in Word. When you need to know that final word count, you can find it quickly through the Tools menu.

Creating a Multiple-Author Document

WW03E-3-5

When several people are going to collaborate on a document by dividing the workload by section or heading, you can create a master document so that everyone can work concurrent with one another instead of passing one file around. The process of creating a master document begins with an outline. When the outline is complete, individual headings or sections can have subdocuments assigned to them. These subdocuments can be distributed to the collaborators and completed separately. When ready, they can then be combined back into the master document so that all the information is contained in a single file. After you have created a master document, those sections that you have designated as subdocuments can be created and saved as separate files. These files can then be reinserted into the master document as they are completed.

Create a Master Document

1 Click the New Blank Document button on the Standard toolbar.

2 Click the View menu, and then click Outline.

3 Enter headings to outline the presentation of topics in the master document, pressing Enter after each entry.

4 Select a heading, and then click one of the buttons on the Outlining toolbar to assign a heading style (Heading 1 through Heading 9).

◆ Click the Promote or Demote button on the Outlining toolbar to increase or decrease the heading level of the headlines and body text.

5 Select the heading that you want to make into a subdocument.

6 Click the Create Subdocument button on the Outlining toolbar.

7 Click the File menu, and then click Save As.

8 Select the location, type a name, and then click Save.

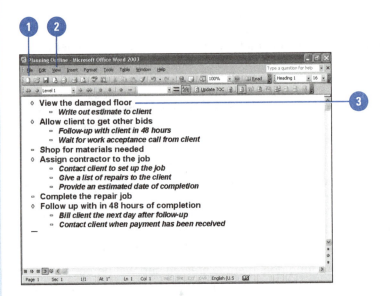

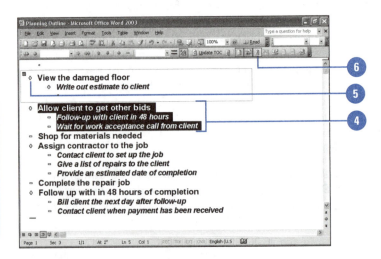

Insert a Subdocument

1. Open the Master document in which you want to add a subdocument.

2. If the subdocuments are collapsed such that just the headings are visible, click the Expand Subdocument button on the Outlining toolbar.

3. Position the insertion point where you want the subdocument inserted.

4. Click the Insert Subdocument button on the Outlining toolbar.

5. Locate and select the subdocument file you want to insert, and then click Open.

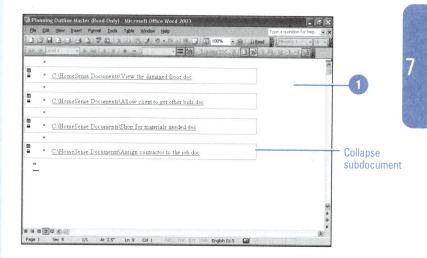

Collapse subdocument

Did You Know?

You can collapse, or hide, all of your subdocuments. To hide (collapse) the subdocuments in a master document, click the Collapse Subdocuments button on the Outlining toolbar. All subdocuments are collapsed in Outline view. To show (expand) the subdocuments, click the Expand Subdocuments button on the Outlining toolbar.

You can select a heading by clicking its outline marker. When you click an outline marker for a heading, all the subheadings below the heading are selected.

You can unlock a master document. Click the Expand Subdocuments button on the Outlining toolbar to remove the lock on the files.

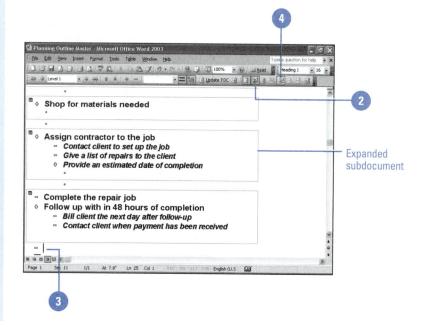

Expanded subdocument

Creating Documents Using Automatic Formatting

Word can automatically perform some formatting functions for you as you type a document. For example, you can change straight quotation marks to smart (curly) quotes, hyphens to en-dashes or em-dashes, an asterisk before and after text to bold text, or an underscore before and after text to italic text. You can also type a number and text or a bullet and text to start a numbered or bulleted list. If you had AutoFormat disabled when you created the document, you still have the option of using the feature to find and correct errors in formatting.

Set Up Automatic Formatting

1 Click the Tools menu, and then click AutoCorrect Options.

2 Click the AutoFormat As You Type tab.

3 Select or clear the AutoFormat check boxes you want to use.

4 Click OK.

Your choices take effect, but they only apply to text you will be entering subsequently. In this case, AutoFormat does not correct errors retroactively.

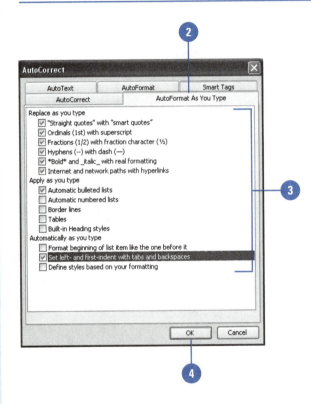

Revise Documents with AutoFormat

1. Click the Format menu, and then click AutoFormat.

2. Click Options.

3. Click the AutoFormat tab to select the formatting options you want.

4. Click the other tabs to make any additional changes to your document.

5. Click OK.

6. Click the AutoFormat Now option to have Word automatically format the document, or click the AutoFormat And Review Each Change option to review, and then accept or reject each change.

7. Click OK.

8. Click Review Changes to look at changes individually.

9. Click Style Gallery if you want to preview your document, and then click OK.

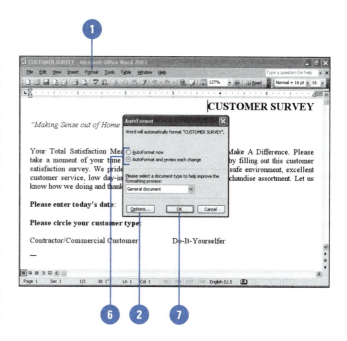

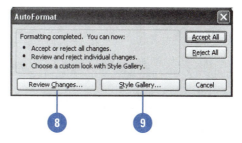

Creating Headers and Footers

WW03S-3-4

Create and Edit Headers and Footers

1 Click the View menu, and then click Header And Footer.

2 If necessary, click the Switch Between Header And Footer button on the Header And Footer toolbar to display the footer text area.

3 Click the header or footer box, and then type the text you want.

4 To insert common phrases, click the Insert AutoText button on the Header And Footer toolbar, and then click the text you want.

5 Edit and format header or footer text as usual.

6 When you're done, click the Close button on the Header And Footer toolbar.

Did You Know?

There are default tab stops used to align header and footer text. Headers and footers have two default tab stops. The first, in the middle, centers text. The second, on the far right, aligns text on the right margin. To left align text, don't press Tab. You can add and move the tab stops as needed. In addition, you can use the alignment buttons on the Formatting toolbar.

Most books, including this one, use headers and footers to help you keep track of where you are. A **header** is text printed in the top margin of every page within a document. **Footer** text is printed in the bottom margin. Commonly used headers and footers contain your name, the document title, the file name, the print date, and page numbers. If you divide your document into sections, you can create different headers and footers for each section.

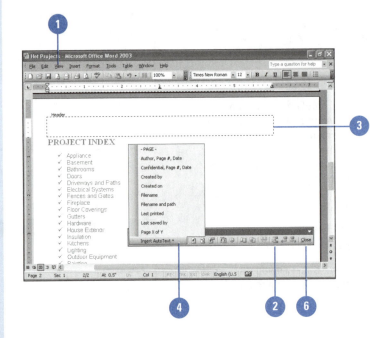

This header text is printed on every page.

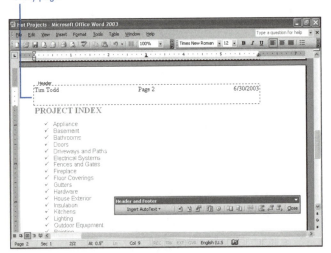

Create Different Headers and Footers for Different Pages

1. Click the View menu, and then click Header And Footer.

2. Click the Page Setup button on the Header And Footer toolbar.

3. Click the Layout tab.

4. To create different headers or footers for odd and even pages, select the Different Odd And Even check box.

   To create a unique header or footer for the document's first page, select the Different First Page check box.

5. Click OK.

6. Click the Show Previous and Show Next buttons to move from one header to the next. To move between the header and footer, click the Switch Between Header And Footer button.

7. Click the Close button on the Header And Footer toolbar.

Did You Know?

There is a format difference between even and odd pages. As in books, odd pages appear on the right, and even pages appear on the left.

You can add a graphic to either a header or footer, such as a company logo. Click the header or footer to position the insertion point, click the Insert menu, click Picture, and then click the type of file and the location of the file on the submenus that follow.

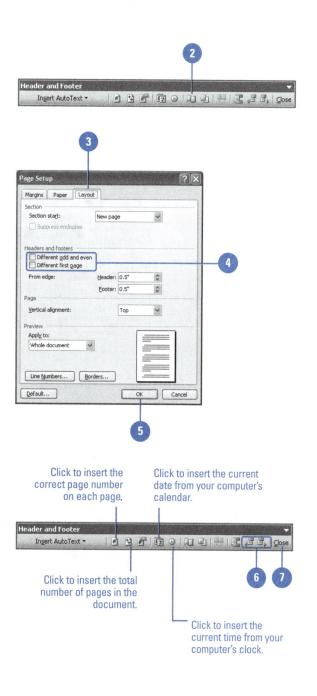

Click to insert the correct page number on each page.

Click to insert the current date from your computer's calendar.

Click to insert the total number of pages in the document.

Click to insert the current time from your computer's clock.

Inserting Cross References

WW03E-3-4

Cross references direct the reader to related information located elsewhere in the document. Cross references can refer to figures or illustrations, sidebars, section headings, even individually marked paragraphs. Without distracting the reader of the document, cross references can be an easy tool to help navigate through a larger document. You can cross-reference only items in the same document. To cross-reference an item in another document, you need to first combine the documents into a master document.

Create a Cross Reference

1. Select the text that starts the cross reference in the document.

2. Click the Insert menu, point to Reference, and then click Cross-Reference.

3. Click the Reference Type list arrow, and then select the type of item to which you will refer (heading, footnote, bookmark, etc.).

4. Click the Insert Reference To list arrow, and then select the type of data (page, paragraph number, etc.) that you will be referencing.

5. Click the specific item, by number, to which you want to refer.

6. To let users move to the referenced item, select the Insert As Hyperlink check box.

7. If the Include Above/Below check box is selected, click it to include data regarding the relative position of the referenced item.

8. Click Insert.

9. Repeat the steps for each additional cross reference that you want to insert into the document, and then click either Close or Cancel.

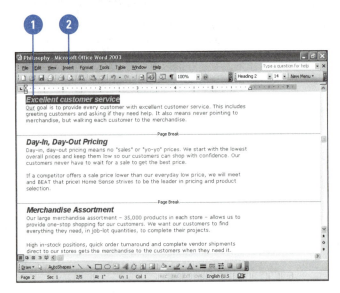

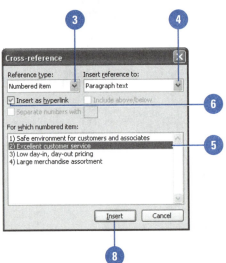

Preparing for a Bound Document

If your finished document will be bound in some fashion, but especially if you will use a form of binding such as is found in books, you must allow additional margin space for the binding process; otherwise some of your text can be in the binding fold and therefore unreadable. If you open a book, the crease between the two facing pages is referred to as the gutter. You must take care to ensure that nothing except white space is in the gutter.

Change the Gutter Margin Setting

1 Click the File menu, and then click Page Setup.

2 If necessary, click the Margins tab.

3 Enter a value for the gutter margin.

4 Click the Gutter Position list arrow, and then click Left or Top depending on the orientation of your intended binding, (Left would be for a normal book, Top would be for a book that flips open from top to bottom).

5 Click OK.

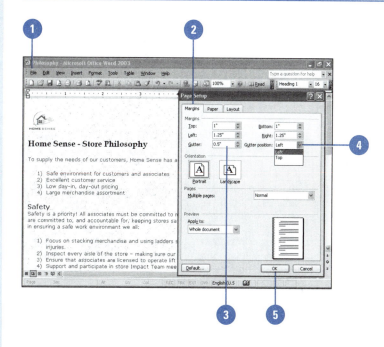

Did You Know?

You can set aside a gutter for printing. The size of the gutter you should use varies greatly depending on the binding process that will be used. Check with your printer before finalizing this setting to ensure that you allow the correct amount of space.

You can use a gutter even if you are printing on both sides. Remember that, if you are using double-sided printing, the gutter will be to the left on odd-numbered pages and to the right on even-numbered pages.

Finding Topics in a Long Document

Instead of searching through pages of text in your document for that certain paragraph, bookmark, tables, footnote or endnote, caption, or other object, you can navigate a lengthy document using the Find and Replace dialog box. Providing that you have set up your long document with bookmarks, captions, object numbers and the like, you will be able to use those as "clues" in which to locate the specific items you are looking for.

Move to a Specific Page or Other Document Item

1. Click the Edit menu, and then click Go To.

2. If necessary, click the Go To tab.

3. Click the type of item to which you want to move (page, table, etc.).

4. Use one of the following methods:

   ◆ To move to a specific item, type the name or number of the item in the Enter box, and then click Go To.

   ◆ To move to the next or previous item of the same type, leave the Enter box empty, and then click Next or Previous.

5. Click Close.

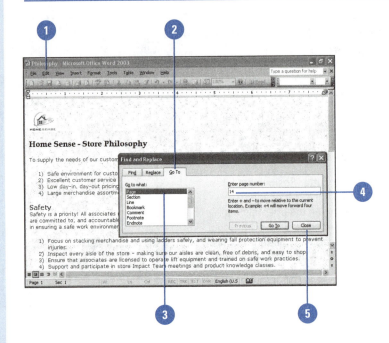

Navigating a Document

WW03S-1-3

Word also includes a very unobtrusive, but powerful tool on the vertical scroll bar, the Select Browse Object button. Now that you might be working with a large document and need to navigate through pages of text, multiple graphics and tables, numerous footnotes, reviewer comments and the like, the Select Browse Object button becomes a useful tool. You can navigate through pages easily, instead of relying on all the various menu commands that are available to locate similar elements of your long document.

Select a Browse Object

1. Click the Select Browse Object button on the vertical scroll bar.

2. Click the icon that represents the browse command you want to activate:

   ◆ **By Field**. Click to browse by field.

   ◆ **By Endnote**. Click to browse by Endnote.

   ◆ **By Footnote**. Click to browse by Footnote.

   ◆ **By Comment**. Click to browse by comment.

   ◆ **By Section**. Click to browse by section.

   ◆ **By Page**. Click to browse by page.

   ◆ **Go To**. Click to go to a specific item.

   ◆ **Find**. Click to find an item.

   ◆ **By Edits**. Click to browse by edits.

   ◆ **By Heading**. Click to browse by heading.

   ◆ **By Graphic**. Click to browse by graphic.

   ◆ **By Table**. Click to browse by table.

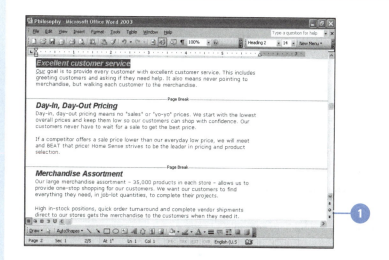

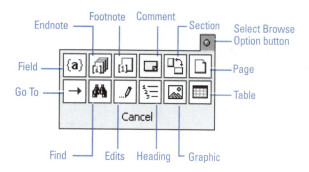

7

Inserting a Table of Contents

WW03E-3-3

A **table of contents** provides an outline of main topics and page locations. Word builds a table of contents based on the styles in a document that you choose. By default, Heading 1 is the first-level entry, Heading 2 the second level, and so on. In a printed table of contents, a **leader**, a line whose style you select, connects an entry to its page number. In Web documents, entries become hyperlinks. Hide nonprinting characters before creating a table of contents so text doesn't shift to other pages as you print.

Insert a Table of Contents

1. Click the Insert menu, point to Reference, and then click Index And Tables.

2. Click the Table Of Contents tab.

3. Select the Show Page Numbers and the Right Align Page Numbers check boxes.

4. Click the Tab Leader list arrow, and then select a leader style.

5. Click the Formats list arrow, and then select a table of contents style.

6. Enter the number of heading levels you want.

7. Click Options.

8. If necessary, delete any numbers, and then type **1** next to the first-level style, **2** next to the second-level style, and so on.

9. Click OK.

10. Click OK.

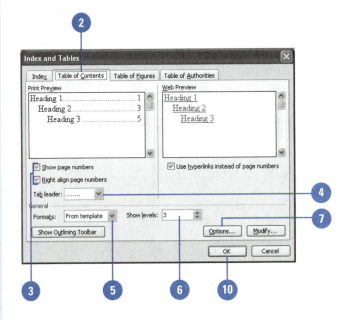

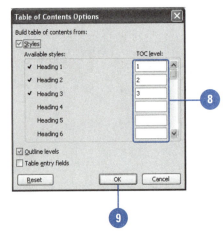

Did You Know?

You can create an index, table of figures and legal notations. Use the Index and Tables dialog box to create an index, table of figures, or table of authorities, which tracks legal notations.

Create a Table of Contents Manually

1. Select the first segment of text you want to include in your table of contents.

2. Press Alt+Shift+O.

3. Enter the index level you want, and then click Mark.

4. To mark additional entries, select the text, click in the Entry box, and then click Mark.

5. When you're done adding entries, click Close.

6. Click the place where you want to insert the table of contents.

7. Click the Insert menu, point to Reference, and then click Index And Tables.

8. If necessary, click the Table Of Contents tab.

9. Click Options.

10. Select the Table Entry Fields check box.

11. Clear the Styles and Outline Levels check boxes.

12. Click OK.

13. Click OK.

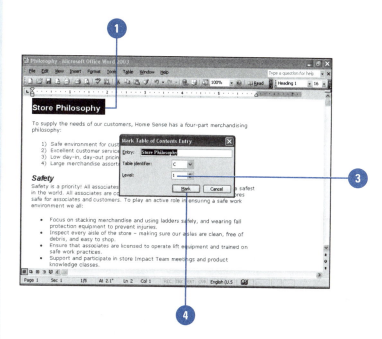

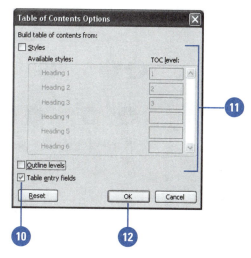

Creating an Index

WW03E-3-3

An index appears at the end of a document and alphabetically lists the main topics, names, and items used in a long document. Each index listing is called an entry. You can create an index entry for a word, phrase, or symbol for a topic. In an index, a cross-reference indicates another index entry that is related to the current entry. There are several ways to create an index. Begin by marking index entries. Some index entries will refer to blocks of text that span multiple pages within a document.

Create an Index

1. To use existing text as an index entry, select the text. To enter your text as an index entry, click at the point where you want the index entry inserted.

2. Press Alt+Shift+X.

3. Type or edit the entry. The entry can be customized by creating a sub-entry or a cross-reference to another entry.

4. To format the text for the index, right-click it in the Main Entry or Sub-entry box, click Font, select your formatting options, and then click OK.

5. To select a format for the page numbers that will appear in the index, select the Bold or Italic check boxes.

6. To mark the index entry, click Mark or Mark All for all similar text.

   Repeat steps 1-6 for additional index entries, and then click Close.

7. Go to the page where you want to display your Index.

8. Click the Insert menu, point to Reference, and then click Index And Tables.

9. Click the Index tab.

10. Click OK.

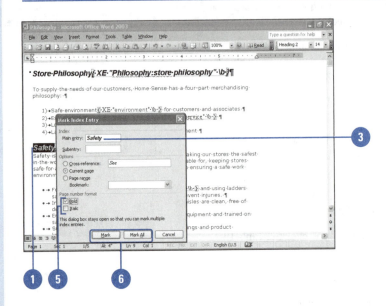

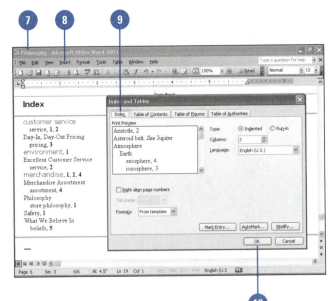

Create Multiple Page Index Entries

1. Select the text in which you want the index entry to refer.

2. Click the Insert menu, and then click Bookmark.

3. Enter a name, and then click Add.

4. Click after the end of the text in the document that you just marked with a bookmark.

5. Press Alt+Shift+X.

6. Enter the index entry for the marked text.

7. To format the text for the index, right-click the Main Entry or Sub-entry box, click Font, select your formatting options, and then click OK.

8. To select a format for the page numbers that will appear in the index, select the Bold or Italic check boxes.

9. Click the Page Range option.

10. Select the bookmark name you entered in Step 3.

11. Click Mark.

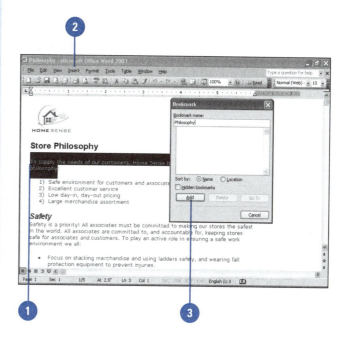

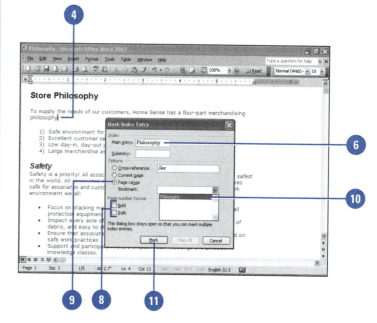

Creating a Summary

WW03E-2-4

Create a Summary of a Document

1. Open the document you want to summarize.

2. Click the Tools menu, and then click AutoSummarize.

3. Select the type of summary you want.

4. Enter the length of your summary. The higher the percentage, the greater the detail.

5. To maintain your existing keywords and comments on the Summary tab in the Properties dialog box, clear the Update Document Statistics check box.

6. Click OK.

   TIMESAVER *Press Esc to cancel a summary in progress.*

If you are preparing an executive summary of a lengthy document for business purposes, or have some other reason to condense the high points of a document for your reader, you can use AutoSummarize to help you get started. AutoSummarize looks through your document and tries to summarize the material based on the type of summary you want and the percentage of the original you specify. After Word summarizes the material, you'll need to review it and make necessary changes.

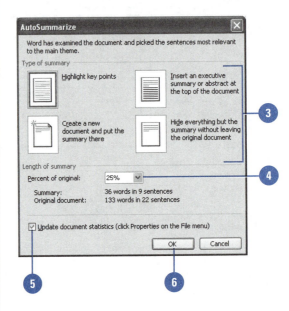

Modifying Document Properties

WW03S-5-2, WW03E-4-6

If you're not sure of the version of a document, or if you need statistical information about a document, such as the number of pages, paragraphs, lines, words, and characters to fulfill a requirement, you can use the Properties dialog box to quickly find this information. You can create custom file properties, such as client or project, to help you manage and track files. If you associate a file property to an item in the document, the file property updates when you change the item.

Display and Modify Document Properties

1. Click the File menu, and then click Properties.

2. Click the tabs (General, Summary, Statistics, or Contents) to view information about the document.

3. To add title and author information for the document, click the Summary tab.

4. To add and modify tracking properties, click the Custom tab.

5. When you are done changing your document properties, click OK.

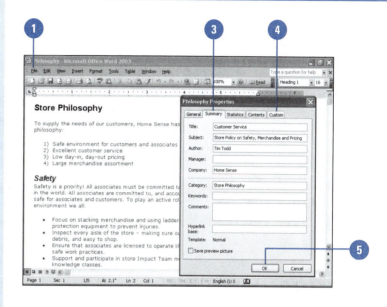

Customize Document Properties

1. Click the File menu, and then click Properties.

2. Click the Custom tab.

3. Type a name for the custom property or select a name from the list.

4. Click the data type for the property you want to add.

5. Type a value for the property that matches the type you selected in the Type box.

6. Click Add.

7. Click OK.

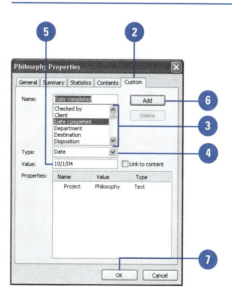

Determining Word Count

WW03S-5-2

Find Out the Word Count

1 Select the text you want to count.

2 Click the Tools menu, and then click Word Count.

3 To display the Word Count toolbar, click Show Toolbar.

4 Click Close.

Did You Know?

You can display the Word Count toolbar quickly. Right-click any toolbar, and then click Word Count.

Producing lengthy documents for business, school or as contract work can often be regulated by the word count. Legal briefs may charge by the line or word, or school papers might need to be a certain length in word count. Either way, if you need to determine your word count, there is an easier way than counting each word manually. You can use the Word count command on the Tools menu or the Word Count toolbar to find out word count statistics.

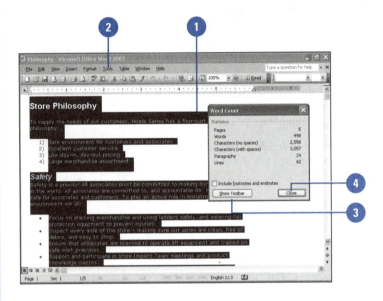

Creating Mail Merge Documents

Introduction

Whether you are looking to personalize your annual Christmas letter to friends and family, or prepare a direct-mail marketing piece to 10,000 customers of your business, Word's new Mail Merge Wizard is up to the task. To perform a mail merge, you need a **form letter** that contains the text you want to send out, plus **merge fields** for the information that you want to use to personalize each letter, such as the recipient's address, first name in the greeting line, and so forth. These fields can be added manually, or as part of the Mail Merge Wizard process.

You must have a **data document** that contains all of this information in either comma or tab delimited format. Most databases, such as Outlook and Access, can automatically export into this format. Alternately, you can manually create a data document if you do not have an existing database of contact information that you can use for the merge. Equipped with these two sources, the Mail Merge Wizard can quickly and easily create thousands of personalized letters, address labels, and envelopes, in a fraction of the time it would otherwise take you to do these tasks.

What You'll Do

Start the Mail Merge

Import Data from a Database

Import Data from Outlook

Import Data from a Document

Edit the Data Source

Sort and Filter Data

Create a Form Letter

Preview the Mail Merge

Complete the Mail Merge

Merge to E-Mail

Create Merged Mailing Labels

Create Merged Envelopes

Address Envelopes and Labels

Starting the Mail Merge

WW03E-2-6

Did you ever send the same letter to several people and spend a lot of time changing personal information, such as names and addresses? If so, form letters will save you time. **Mail merge** is the process of combining names and addresses stored in a data file with a main document (usually a form letter) to produce customized documents. There are four main steps to merging. First, select the document you want to use. Second, create a data file with the variable information. Third, create the main document with the boilerplate (unchanging information) and merge fields. Finally, merge the main document with the data source to create a new document with all the merged information. When you start the mail merge, you need to open the letter that you want to mail merge or type one. Don't worry about addressing the letter or adding a greeting line, you can accomplish that with the Mail Merge Wizard.

Start the Mail Merge Wizard

1. Click the Tools menu, point to Letters And Mailings, and then click Mail Merge.

   The Mail Merge task pane opens, displaying Step 1 of 6 in the Mail Merge Wizard.

2. Select the type of document you are working on (in this case the Letters option).

3. Click Next: Starting Document on the task pane to display Step 2 of 6.

4. Click a starting document option (such as Use The Current Document).

5. Click Next: Select Recipients on the task pane to display Step 3 of 6.

Importing Data from a Database

WW03E-2-6

Import Data from an Existing Database

1. On Step 3 of 6 in the Mail Merge task pane, click the Use An Existing List option.

2. Click Browse on the task pane.

3. Locate and select the database file from which you want to import the recipient data.

4. Click Open.

   The Mail Merge Recipient dialog box opens, displaying the data source for the merge.

5. Edit the recipient data (if necessary), and then click OK.

6. Click Next: Write Your Letter on the task pane to display Step 4 of 6.

Now it is time to specify the recipients for your mail merge. To do so, you must identify a **data document** as the source of the recipient information you will use to personalize the mailing. If you have an existing database of information to work with, this is the easiest method. The mail merge works with most standard database and spreadsheet programs including Microsoft Access, Microsoft FoxPro, and Microsoft Excel. Before you can import data into the Mail Merge Wizard from an external database, you must first export it from the database you are using. Follow the instructions for that database to export a file in either comma or tab delimited format, and remember which format you chose. Export the file to the My Data Sources folder in the My Documents folder.

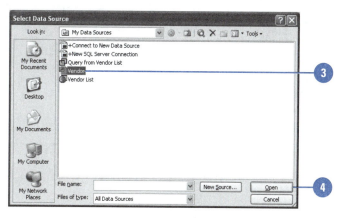

Importing Data from Outlook

WW03E-2-6

If you are already using Outlook to manage your contact database, you can import your Outlook contact records into the Mail Merge Wizard quickly and easily. For example, a contact record for a person or company might contain an address, telephone, e-mail address, and so forth. An item record might contain the part number, description, quantity on hand, and so on. The information in each record is organized by fields. The fields of the database correspond to the merge fields you specify in the Form Letter. Additional fields other than the ones to be used by the merge can exist, and will be ignored by the Mail Merge Wizard. For example, a direct mail piece would use the address field in a record as a merge field and ignore the e-mail address field for that record, whereas an e-mail merge would do exactly the opposite.

Import Data from Outlook

1 On Step 3 of 6 in the Mail Merge task pane, click Select From Outlook Contacts.

2 Click Choose Contacts Folder.

3 If an Outlook profile dialog box opens, select a profile, and then click OK.

The Select Contact List Folder dialog box opens.

4 Select the contacts list you want to use.

5 Click OK.

The Mail Merge Recipients dialog box opens, displaying the data source for the merge.

6 Edit the recipient data (if necessary), and then click OK.

7 Click Next: Write Your Letter on the task pane to display Step 4 of 6.

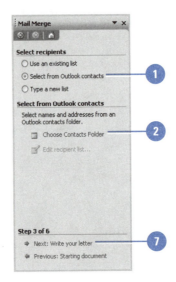

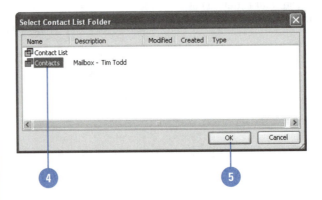

Importing Data from a Document

WW03E-2-6

When you are only doing a limited number of pieces in a mail merge, or you cannot input the records into one of the previously mentioned programs for permanent use and then export them to the Mail Merge Wizard to perform the task at hand, you can use the Wizard to create your recipient list. You can also use Word to manually type a data document. The first line of the document should contain the merge field names separated by commas or tabs (choose one format and be consistent throughout the document). For example, FirstName, LastName, Address, City, State, Zip. Note that field names cannot contain spaces. At the end of the field name line, press Enter. Input all of the data for a given record separated by commas on the lines that follow, press Enter after each record entry. When all entries are entered, save the document as a text file and import it as an existing file in Step 3 of 6 in the Mail Merge Wizard.

Create a Data Document

1. On Step 3 of 6 in the Mail Merge task pane, click the Type A New List option.

2. Click Create.

3. Input your information for the first record, and then click New Entry.

4. Continue to input additional records; click New Entry after each one until all records have been entered, and then click Close.

   The Save Address List dialog box opens, displaying the My Data Sources folder.

5. Enter a name, and then click Save to save your work.

   The Mail Merge Recipients dialog box opens, displaying the data source for the merge.

6. Edit the recipient data (if necessary), and then click OK.

7. Click Next: Write Your Letter on the task pane to display Step 4 of 6.

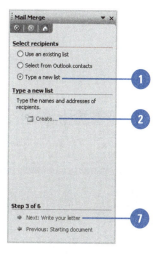

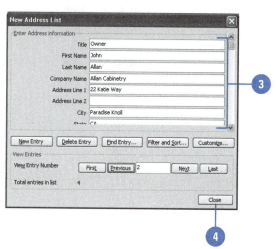

Editing the Data Source

Regardless of the original source of your data, an external database, manually prepared list, Outlook records, or an Address List that you created within the Mail Merge Wizard, periodically you will want to make some changes to the data before completing the merge. The time to do so is in Step 3 of 6 of the Mail Merge Wizard.

Edit a Data Document

1. On Step 3 of 6 in the Mail Merge task pane, click Edit Recipient List.

2. Select any existing record.

3. Click Edit, and then make the changes you want to the fields.

4. To add records to the merge, select any existing record, and then click New Entry.

5. To remove the selected record from the data document permanently, and then click Delete Entry.

6. Click Close.

7. If you want to retain the record in the data document, but exclude it from the merge, clear the check mark next to the record.

   All records begin selected by default and must be manually deselected from the merge.

8. When you're done, click OK.

9. Click Next: Write Your Letter on the task pane to display Step 4 of 6.

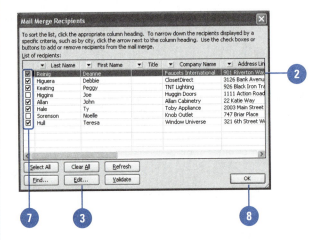

Sorting and Filtering Data

When you are working with large numbers of records, it is often helpful to organize those records in a particular order. For example, if you are doing a bulk mailing via the USPS, they require that the pieces of the mailing be sorted in zip code order for you to receive the savings associated with the bulk mail rate. Word can easily accomplish this task for you so the records are merged and printed in zip code order. You can sort and filter records by any of the merge fields specified in the record.

Sort and Filter Records

1. On Step 3 of 6 in the Mail Merge task pane, click Edit Recipient List.

2. To sort the data in a column, click the field column heading (not the list arrow inside of it).

3. To filter out data in a field column by a specific criterion or value, click the list arrow in the column heading, and then select a filter option or value.

4. To perform advance sorts, where you compare the values of certain fields, click the list arrow for any field, and then click Advanced.

5. If you chose an advanced sort, select or enter filter and sort criteria in the Field, Comparison, and Compare To box, and then click OK.

6. When you're done, click OK.

7. Click Next: Write Your Letter on the task pane to display Step 4 of 6.

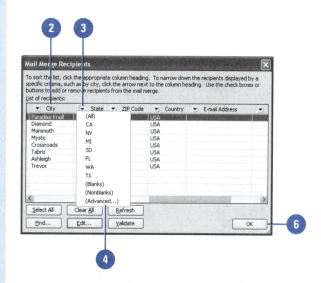

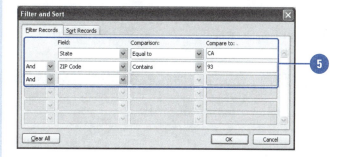

Did You Know?

You can display all the data in a column. In the Mail Merge Recipient dialog box, click the column heading list arrow used for a filter, and then click All.

8

Creating a Form Letter

WW03E-2-6

The only difference between a normal letter and a **form letter** is the presence of merge fields in the latter. Merge fields can exist anywhere in the document, and correspond to any field in the data document. For example, you can insert the FirstName field periodically in a document to reaffirm to the reader that you are speaking directly to them, and minimize the negative reactions that many people feel when they receive a form letter. The most commonly used fields in a form letter are the address block and the greeting line. Each merge field corresponds to a piece of information in the data source and appears in the main document with the greater than and less than characters around it. For example, the <<Address Block>> merge field corresponds to name and address information in the data source. Word incorporates insert commands for each of these in the Mail Merge Wizard.

Create a Form Letter

1. On Step 4 of 6 in the Mail Merge task pane, position the insertion point in the letter where you want the address block to appear.

2. Click Address Block on the task pane.

3. Select the Address Block options you want.

4. Click OK to insert the block in the document.

5. Position the insertion point where you want the greeting to appear.

6. Click Greeting Line.

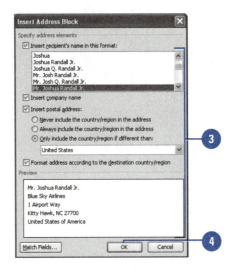

Did You Know?

Word supports international languages in Mail Merge. Mail Merge chooses the correct greeting format based on the gender of the recipient if the language requires it. Mail Merge can also format addresses based on the geographical region of the recipient.

7 Select the format you want for the greeting line.

8 Click OK to apply the style to the merge field.

9 If you want to add other merge fields in the body of the form letter, position the insertion point where you want the information, and then click More Items on the task pane.

10 Select the merge field you want to place, click Insert, and then click Close.

11 When you're done, click Next: Preview Your Letters on the task pane to display Step 5 of 6.

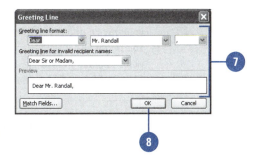

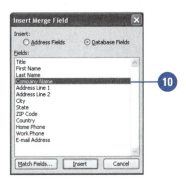

Did You Know?

You can edit the style of a field. Right click on the field to bring up a menu of options, and then click Edit.

You can have common words used as field names. Information in a data file is stored in merge fields, labeled with one-word names, such as FirstName, LastName, City, and so on. You can insert merge field names in the main document as blanks, or placeholders, for variable information. When you merge the data file and main document, Word fills in the blanks with the correct information.

You should beware of those extra spaces. Don't press the Spacebar after entering data in a field. Extra spaces will appear in the document between the data and the next word or punctuation, leaving ugly gaps or floating punctuation. Add spaces and punctuation to your main document instead.

Letter with merged fields.

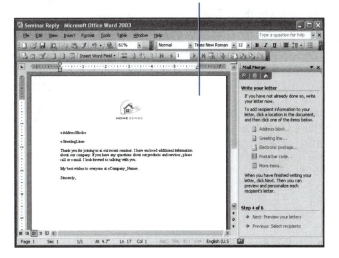

Previewing the Mail Merge

Although Word has automated much of the mail merge process for you, it is always a good idea to review the merged letters before printing them. You might find changes to the body text or even the merge fields that you want to make before the merge is final. The preview process occurs in Step 5 of 6 in the Mail Merge task pane.

Preview the Mail Merge

1. On Step 5 of 6 in the Mail Merge task pane, click the double arrows on the task pane to scroll through the merge letters one at a time.

2. To find a given recipient or group of recipients quickly, click Find A Recipient on the task pane.

3. If you chose Find, enter search criterion, click the All Fields option, or This Field option, and then select a field.

4. Click Find Next to proceed to the next matching record.

5. When you're done, click Close.

6. Click Next: Complete The Merge on the task pane to display Step 6 of 6.

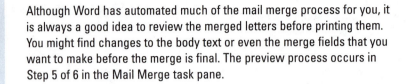

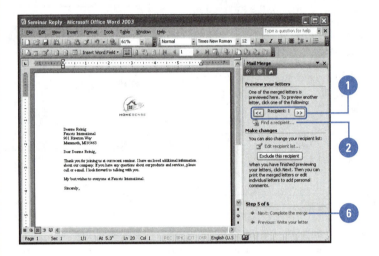

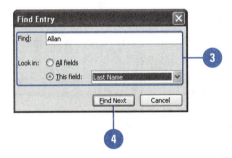

> ### Did You Know?
>
> *You can exclude a recipient from the merge.* Click the Exclude This Recipient button on the task pane on Step 5 of 6.

Completing the Mail Merge ▶

After you set up a data document and enter merge fields into the main document, you are ready to merge the document to create a new document with all the merged information. The new document contains individualized copies of the main document for each record in the data source. You can edit the new document to personalize individual copies in the main document, and then print the end result.

Personalize and Print the Mail Merge

① Proceed to Step 6 of 6 in the Mail Merge task pane.

② If you want to make additional changes to the letters, click Edit Individual Letters.

③ Specify the settings you want to use for the merged records and the selected range of the records are saved to a separate file for editing.

④ Click OK.

⑤ When you're ready to print, click Print on the task pane.

⑥ Click the All option to print the entire merge or click another option to print only a selected portion of the merge.

⑦ Click OK.

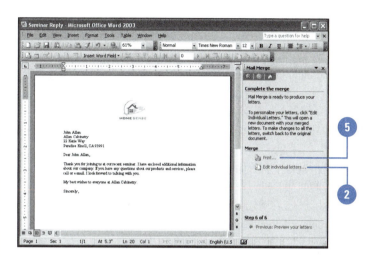

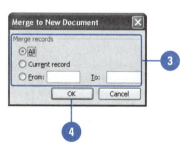

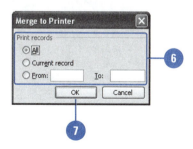

8

Merging to E-Mail

Instead of merging data to create a form letter you can print, you can merge data to an e-mail document. The steps to merge an e-mail document rather than a letter are essentially the same, but there are a few small differences.

Mail Merge to E-Mail

1. On Step 1 of 6 in the Mail Merge task pane, click the E-Mail Messages option.

2. Click Next: Starting Document on the task pane to display Step 2 of 6.

3. Click a starting document option (such as Use The Current Document).

4. Click Next: Select Recipients on the task pane to display Step 3 of 6.

5. Click a recipient option (such as Use An Existing List or Type A New List).

6. Click Browse, double-click a data document, and then click OK to select the mail recipients.

7. Click Next: Write Your E-Mail Message on the task pane to display Step 4 of 6.

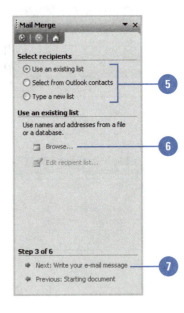

8. Type your e-mail, click a location in the document, and then click one of the field items on the task pane (such as Address Block or Greeting Line), select the options you want, and then click OK.

9. Click Next: Preview Your E-Mail Message on the task pane to display Step 5 of 6.

10. Preview the data in the letter, and then make any changes.

11. Click Next: Complete The Merge on the task pane to display Step 6 of 6.

12. Click Electronic Mail.

13. Select the mail format you want to use, normal text, HTML mail, or sending the document as an attachment.

14. Specify the range of records you want to send, and then click OK.

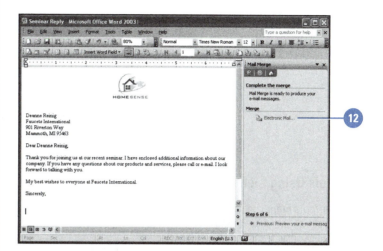

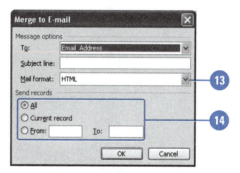

Creating Merged Mailing Labels

WW03E-2-7

You can use a data document to create more than one kind of merge document. For example, you can use a data document to print mailing labels or envelopes to use with your mailing. The process for creating mailing labels is similar to the mail merge process for form letters, except that you insert the merge field into a main document that contains a table with cells in a specific size for labels. During the process for creating mailing labels, you can select brand-name labels in a specific size, such as Avery Standard 1529. After you merge the data into the main document with the labels, you can print the labels on a printer.

Create Labels Using Mail Merge

1. Click the Tools menu, point to Letters And Mailings, and then click Mail Merge.

   The Mail Merge task pane opens. Step 1 of 6 appears on the task pane.

2. Click the Labels option.

3. Click Next: Starting Document on the task pane to display Step 2 of 6.

4. Click a starting document option (such as Change Document Layout).

5. Click Label Options.

6. Select the label options you want.

7. Click OK.

8. Click Next: Select Recipients on the task pane to display Step 3 of 6.

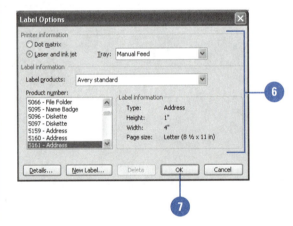

9. Click a recipient option (such as Use An Existing List or Type A New List).

10. Click Browse, double-click a data document, and then click OK.

11. Click Next: Arrange Your Labels on the task pane to display Step 4 of 6.

12. Click in the first label of the document, and then click one of the field items on the task pane (such as Address Block or Greeting Line), select the options you want, and then click OK.

13. Click Update All Labels, and then click Next: Preview Your Labels on the task pane to display Step 5 of 6.

14. Preview the data in the letter, make any changes, and then click Next: Complete The Merge on the task pane to display Step 6 of 6.

15. Click Print.

16. Click a Print Records option.

17. Click OK.

18. When you're done, click the Close button on the task pane, and then save the form letter.

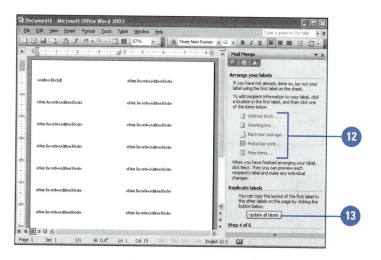

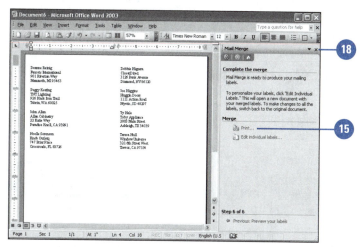

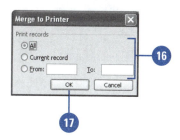

Creating Merged Envelopes

If your printer is set up to accept a batch feed of blank envelopes, you can skip the steps required to create mailing labels, and merge the addresses from the data document directly onto the envelopes. To determine if your printer supports this function, consult the documentation that accompanied your hardware.

Create Envelopes

1. Click the File menu, click New, and then click Blank Document on the New Document task pane.

2. Click the Tools menu, point to Letters And Mailings, and then click Mail Merge.

3. Click the Envelopes option.

4. Click Next: Starting Document on the task pane to display Step 2 of 6.

5. If necessary, click the Use The Current Document option.

6. Click Envelope Options.

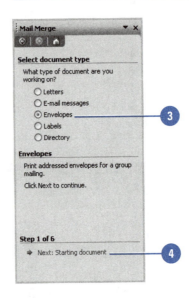

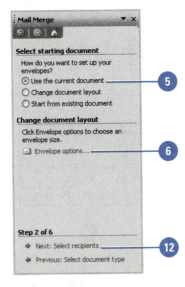

7 Click the Envelope Options tab.

8 Select the appropriate envelope size and layout.

9 Click the Printing Options tab.

10 Select the printer, feed type, and tray to use for printing.

11 Click OK.

12 Click Next: Select Recipients on the task pane to display Step 3 of 6.

13 If necessary, click the Use An Existing List option, and then choose the same list you used mail merge to print the letters.

14 Click Next: Arrange Your Envelope on the task pane to display Step 4 of 6.

15 If you want to include a return address on the mailing, type it now, position the insertion point where you want the recipient's mailing address to appear, click Address Block on the task pane to insert the merge field, select your options, and then click OK.

16 Complete the remaining steps just as you would with creating mailing labels.

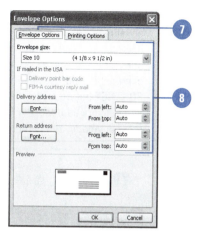

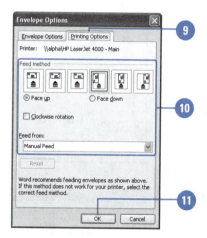

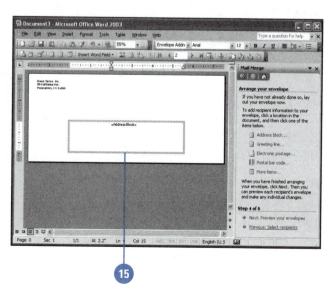

Addressing Envelopes and Labels

Microsoft® Office Specialist
Approved Courseware   WW03S-5-5

Address and Print Envelopes

1 Click the Tools menu, point to Letters And Mailings, and then click Envelopes And Labels.

2 Click the Envelopes tab.

3 Type the recipient's name and address in the Delivery Address box., or click the Insert Address button to search for it.

4 Type your name and address in the Return Address box.

5 Click Options.

6 Select a size, placement, bar code, and font as necessary.

7 Click OK.

8 Insert an envelope in your printer, and then click Print.

When you write a letter, you can use Word to print an address on an envelope or mailing label. Word scans your document to find a delivery address. You can use the one Word finds, enter another one, or select one from your Address Book. You can specify a return address, or you can omit it. Addresses can contain text, graphics, and bar codes. The POSTNET bar code is a machine-readable depiction of a U.S. zip code and delivery address; the FIM-A code identifies the front of a courtesy reply envelope. You can print a single label or multiple labels.

Insert Address button

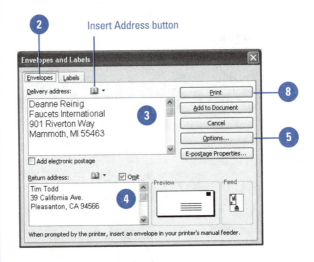

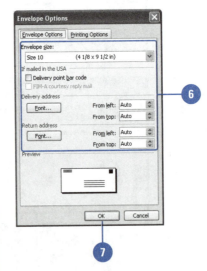

Address and Print Mailing Labels

1. Click the Tools menu, click Letters And Mailings, and then click Envelopes And Labels.

2. Click the Labels tab.

3. Type the recipient's name and address, or click the Insert Address button to search for it.

4. Select what you want to print on the labels.

5. Click Options.

6. Select a type or size.

7. Click OK.

8. Insert labels in your printer, and then click Print.

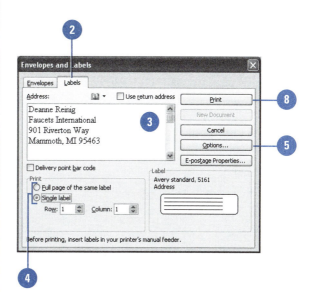

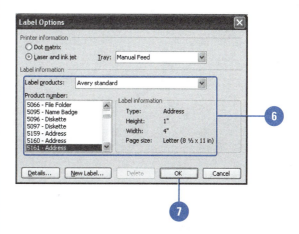

8

Proofing and Printing Documents

Introduction

After finalizing your document, there are some necessary steps you should do prior to printing. You can check for inconsistent formatting in your document. If you have established a certain style, checking your formatting can ensure that your document is formatted correctly. You might find that a certain word or phrase needs to be replaced. With Microsoft Office Word 2003, you can find and replace your text.

You can also look up and use synonyms and antonyms to make your document more interesting. Under the Tools menu, you can use a Thesaurus, translate a word or document into another language, or even use multiple languages with the Word program. Of course, no document should be printed without first going through the spell checker to check your spelling and grammar usage. You can add personalized names, terms, company information to your spell checker, so that when you are using the spell checker, it won't make unnecessary stops on words that are spelled and used correctly.

If your document is larger, page numbers might be necessary to help your reader follow along. You can insert page numbers for single or double sided printing, and you can even add chapter numbers. When getting ready to print, you might want to preview your document to make sure that your margins are appropriate for your text and printing. If, after previewing your document, you find that some text should be on a different page, you can insert page breaks to end the page early, so that common text stays together on a page. You can also insert a whole new page in your document.

When it's finally time to print, you can print all or part of a document, change your page orientation to print landscape or portrait, or even print a two-sided document.

Checking for Inconsistent Formatting

By default, Word does not automatically check for inconsistent formatting as you create documents. To instruct Word to mark the document for inconsistent formatting, and also to check documents that you have already prepared for inconsistent formatting, you need to change editing options in the Options dialog box. Word will automatically detect any inconsistent format elements and mark them with a blue wavy underline.

Change Editing Options

1. Click the Tools menu, and then click Options.

2. Click the Edit tab.

3. Select the Keep Track Of Formatting check box.

4. Select the Mark Formatting Inconsistencies check box.

5. Click OK.

   The formatting inconsistencies are indicated by a blue wavy underline.

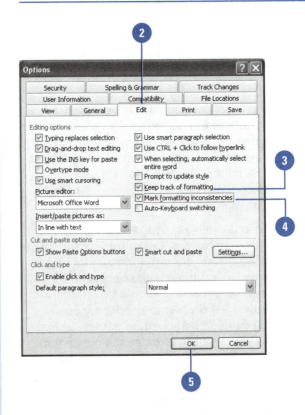

Change Inconsistent Formatting

1. In the document, right-click any wavy, blue line to open a list of Formatting commands.

2. Click the appropriate choice based on the error in the text to make the necessary correction.

   ◆ Replace Direct Formatting With Style... or Replace List Formatting With Style...

   ◆ Ignore Once

   ◆ Ignore Rule

Did You Know?

You can find similar inconsistent formatting quickly. You can also click Select Text With Similar Formatting on the shortcut menu to facilitate global changes of mistakes that have been repeated throughout the document.

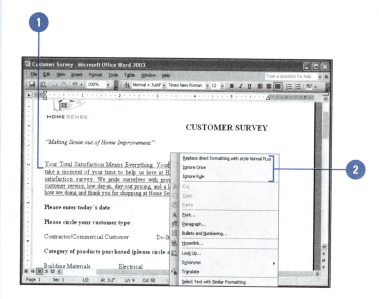

9

Finding and Replacing Text

 WW03S-1-3

In the editing process, it is sometimes helpful to find and replace a particular word or phrase, either because you know you need to address text that you created in proximity to that word or phrase, or because the word or phrase needs to be changed, either locally or globally throughout the document. The Find and Replace commands make it easy to locate or replace specific text in a document. Any word or words located with the Find command can be automatically replaced.

Find Text

1. Click at the beginning of the document, or select the text you want to find.

2. Click the Edit menu, and then click Find.

3. Type the text you want to find.

4. Click More to display the additional options, and then select other options as appropriate.

5. Click Find Next until the text you want to find is highlighted.

   You can click Find Next repeatedly to locate each instance of the text.

6. If a message box opens when you reach the end of the document, click OK.

7. When you're done, click Close or Cancel.

You might need to drag the dialog box out of the way to see the selected text.

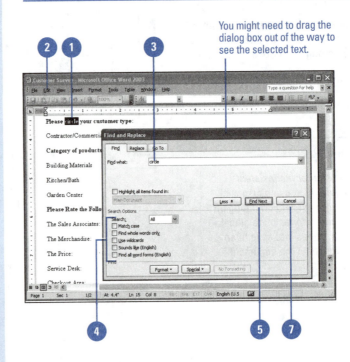

Did You Know?

You can use wildcards to help you search. When you select the Use Wildcards check box, click the Special button to see the wildcards you can use. To enter a wildcard in the Find What or Replace What box, click Special, and then click a wildcard. For example, enter "ran*" to find "ranch", "ranger", and so on.

Replace Text

1 Click at the beginning of the document, or select the text you want to replace.

2 Click the Edit menu, and then click Replace.

3 Type the text you want to find.

4 Type the text you want to replace.

5 Click More to display the additional options, and then select other options as appropriate.

6 Click Find Next to begin the search and select the next instance of the search text.

7 Click Replace to substitute the replacement text, or click Replace All to substitute text throughout the entire document.

You can click Find Next to locate the next instance of the search text without making a replacement.

8 If a message box appears when you reach the end of the document, click OK.

9 When you're done, click Close or Cancel.

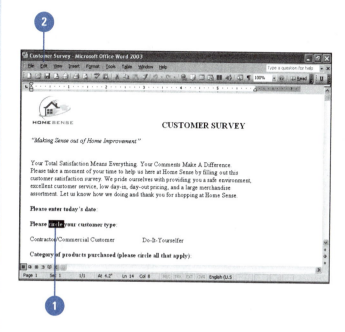

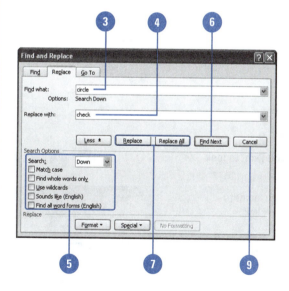

9

Finding the Right Words

WW03S-1-1

Repeating the same word in a document can reduce a message's effectiveness. Instead, replace some words with **synonyms**, words with similar meanings. Or find **antonyms**, words with opposite meanings. If you need help finding exactly the right word, use the shortcut menu to look up synonyms quickly or search Word's Thesaurus for more options. This feature can save you time and improve the quality and readability of your document. You can also install a thesaurus for another language.

Find a Synonym

1. Right-click the word for which you want a synonym.

2. Point to Synonyms.

3. Click the synonym you want to substitute.

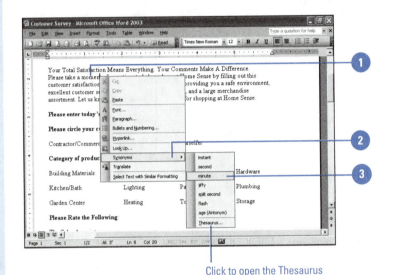

Click to open the Thesaurus and find other synonyms.

Use the Thesaurus

1. Select the word you want to look up.

2. Click the Tools menu, point to Language, and then click Thesaurus.

3. Click a word to find other synonyms.

4. Point to the word you want to use, click the list arrow, and then click Insert.

5. When you're done, click the Close button on the task pane.

Translating Words

Word offers basic translation capabilities with the Translate task pane. With the right bilingual dictionary installed on your computer, you can translate specific words or short phrases, selected text, or an entire document. If you need more extensive translation capabilities, you can connect to translation services on the World Wide Web directly from the Translate task pane.

Translate a Word

1. Select the word you want to translate.

2. Click the Tools menu, and then click Research.

3. Click the Reference list arrow, and then click Translation.

4. Select the language you want the word translated to.

5. Copy and paste the translated word into your Office document.

6. When you're done, click the Close button on the task pane.

Word to translate

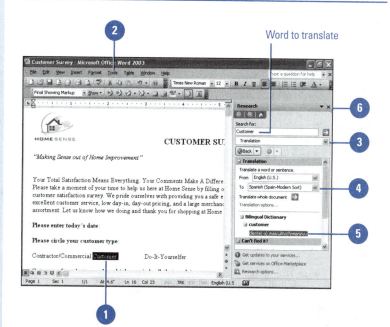

Using Multiple Languages

International Microsoft Office users can change the language that appears on their screens by changing the default language settings. Users around the world can enter, display, and edit text in all supported languages, including European languages, Japanese, Chinese, Korean, Hebrew, and Arabic, just to name a few. You'll probably be able to use Office programs in your native language. If the text in your document is written in more than one language, you can automatically detect languages or designate the language of selected text so the spelling checker uses the right dictionary.

Add a Language to Office Programs

1 Click Start on the taskbar, point to All Programs, point to Microsoft Office, point to Microsoft Office Tools, and then click Microsoft Office 2003 Language Settings.

2 Click to select the languages you want to use.

3 Click Add.

4 Click OK, and then click Yes to quit and restart Office.

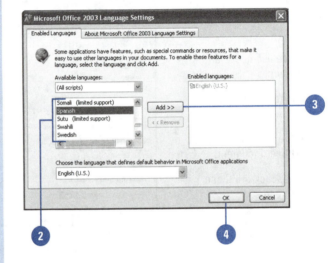

Did You Know?

There is a Multilingual AutoCorrect. Office supports an AutoCorrect list for each language. For example, the English AutoCorrect list capitalizes all cases of the single letter "i;" in Swedish however, "i" is a preposition and is not capitalized.

You can check your keyboard layout. After you enable editing for another language, such as Hebrew, Cyrillic, or Greek, you might need to install the correct keyboard layout so you can enter characters for that language. In the Control Panel, double-click the Regional And Language icon, click the Language tab, and then click Details to check your keyboard.

Detect Languages Automatically

1. Click the Tools menu, point to Language, and then click Set Language.

2. Select the Detect Language Automatically check box.

3. If you want, select the Do Not Check Spelling Or Grammar check box to skip other language words while checking spelling and grammar.

4. Click OK.

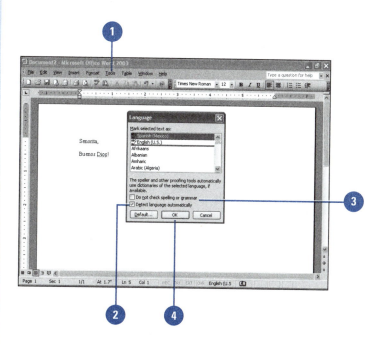

Mark Text as a Language

1. Select the text you want to mark.

2. Click the Tools menu, point to Language, and then click Set Language.

3. Click the language you want to assign to the selected text.

4. Click OK.

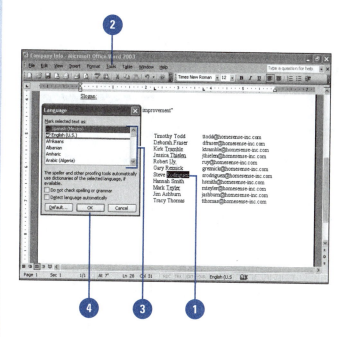

Checking Spelling and Grammar

WW03S-1-1, WW03E-2-4

As you type, a red wavy line appears under words not listed in Word's dictionary (such as misspellings or names) or duplicated words (such as *the the*). A green wavy underline appears under words or phrases with grammatical errors. You can correct these errors as they arise or after you finish the entire document. Before you print your final document, use the Spelling and Grammar checker to ensure that your document is error-free.

Correct Spelling and Grammar as you Type

1. Right-click a word with a red or green wavy underline.

2. Click a substitution, or click Ignore All (or Grammar) to skip any other instances of the word.

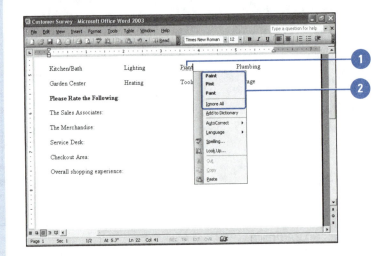

Change Spelling and Grammar Options

1. Click the Tools menu, and then click Options.

2. Click the Spelling & Grammar tab.

3. Select or clear the spelling option check boxes you want.

4. Select or clear the grammar option check boxes you want.

5. If you want, click Settings, select or clear the advanced grammar and style option check boxes, and then click OK.

6. Click OK.

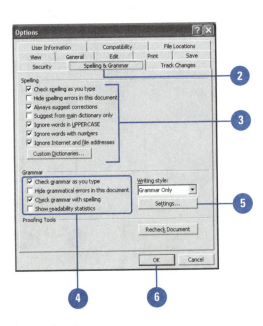

Correct Spelling and Grammar

1 Click at the beginning of the document or select the text you want to correct.

2 Click the Spelling And Grammar button on the Standard toolbar.

As it checks each sentence in the document, Word selects misspelled words or problematic sentences and provides appropriate alternatives.

3 To check spelling only, clear the Check Grammar check box.

4 Choose an option:

◆ Click a suggestion, and then click Change to make a substitution.

◆ Click Ignore Once to skip the word or rule, or click Ignore All or Ignore Rule to skip every instance of the word or rule.

◆ If no suggestion is appropriate, click in the document, and then edit the text yourself. Click Resume to continue.

5 Click OK to return to the document.

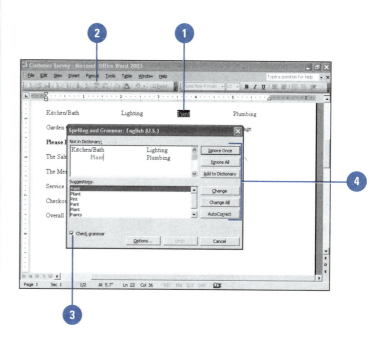

Did You Know?

You can add a familiar word to your dictionary. Right-click the wavy line under the word in question, and then click Add To Dictionary.

You can hyphenate words. Click the Tools menu, point to Language, click Hyphenation, select the Automatically Hyphenate Document check box, and then click OK.

For Your Information

Finding out Document Readability

Word can help you determine the readability of your documents. When you set the readability option and check spelling and grammar, Word displays information and statistics about the reading level of the document, including the Flesch Reading Ease score and the Flesch-Kincaid Grade Level score. The readability scores are based on the average number of syllables per word and words per sentence. To display readability statistics, click the Tools menu, click Options, click the Spelling & Grammar tab, select the Check Grammar With Spelling check box, select the Show Readability Statistics check box, and then click OK.

9

Adding to the Spelling Dictionary

WW03E-5-3

The Word dictionary contains a good selection of common word choices, but it is by no means a comprehensive reference of the English language. You will need to add words that the dictionary does not recognize, including proper names that you use frequently, so that Word doesn't identify the words or names as errors. When you spell a word that Word thinks is misspelled, it selects the word with a red wavy underline. Custom dictionaries are appropriate when you are doing a lot of work in a specific field and you would like Word to automatically recognize and spell check terminology associated with that field.

Add Entries to the Main Dictionary

◆ To scan the document and add words to your dictionary, click the Spelling And Grammar button on the Standard toolbar. The spelling and grammar checker scans the document, generating the Spelling And Grammar dialog box every time what is believed to be a spelling or grammatical error. Click Add To Dictionary.

◆ To add an individual word (such as a person's name) to your dictionary, right-click the red wavy line under the word in question, and then click Add To Dictionary.

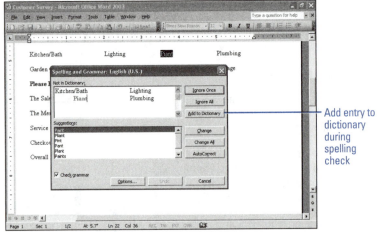

Add entry to dictionary during spelling check

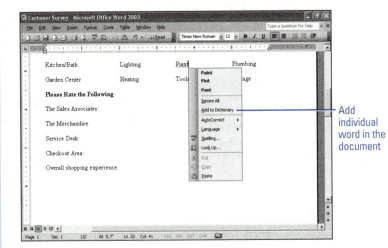

Add individual word in the document

Create a New Custom Dictionary and Add Entries

1. Click the Tools menu, and then click Options.

2. Click the Spelling & Grammar tab.

3. Click Custom Dictionaries.

4. To create a new custom dictionary, click Next, enter a dictionary name, and then click Save.

5. Select the dictionary you want to edit (but don't clear its text box).

6. Click Modify.

7. Perform the tasks you want:

   ◆ To add a word, enter it in the Word box, and then click Add.

   ◆ To delete a word, select it in the Dictionary box, and then click Delete.

   ◆ To edit a word, delete it, enter it with the new spelling, and then click Add.

8. Click OK.

9. Click OK, and then click OK again.

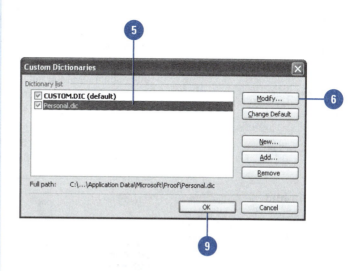

9

Inserting Page Numbers

WW03S-3-4

Page numbers help you keep your document in order or find a topic from the table of contents. Number the entire document consecutively or each section independently; pick a numbering scheme, such as roman numerals or letters. When you insert page numbers, you can select the position and alignment of the numbers on the page. Add page numbers and the date in a footer to conveniently keep track of your work. If you are inserting page numbers for use with double-sided printing and bound printing, you can determine whether the page numbers appear on the inside or outside of facing pages. If you're working on a book, you can include the chapter number in your page numbering (Example 11-1, 11-2, etc.).

Insert Page Numbers

1. Click the Insert menu, and then click Page Numbers.

2. Click the Position list arrow, and then select a location.

3. Click the Alignment list arrow, and then select the horizontal placement.

4. If you want to show a number on the first page, select the Show Number On First Page check box.

5. Click Format.

6. Click the Number Format list arrow, and then select a numbering scheme.

7. Select the starting number.

8. Click OK.

9. Click OK.

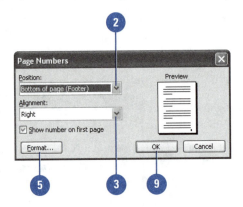

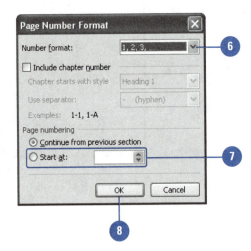

Did You Know?

You can format page numbers in headers and footers. Click the View menu, click Header And Footer, select the text you want to format in the header or footer, and then use the formatting tools on the Formatting toolbar to customize the text.

Change Page Numbers for a Two-Sided Document

1. Click the Insert menu, and then click Page Numbers.

2. Click the Position list arrow, and then select a location.

3. Click the Alignment list arrow, and then click Inside or Outside.

4. Click OK.

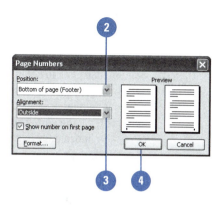

Include Chapter Numbers with Page Numbers

1. Click the Insert menu, and then click Page Numbers.

2. Click Format.

3. Click the Include Chapter Number check box.

4. Click the Chapter Starts With Style list arrow, and then select a style.

5. Click the Use Separator list arrow, and then select a separator.

6. Click OK.

7. Click OK.

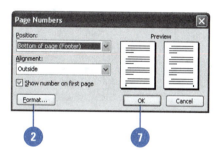

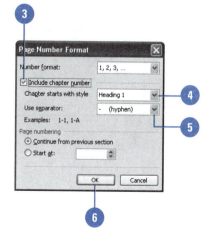

Setting Up the Page Margins

WW03S-3-5

Margins are the blank space between the edge of a page and the text. The default setting for Word documents is 1.25 inches on the left and right, and 1 inch on the top and bottom. You can use the mouse pointer to adjust margins visually for the entire document, or you can use the Page Setup dialog box to set precise measurements for an entire document or a specific section. You can also select the page orientation (portrait or landscape) that best fits the entire document or any section. **Portrait** orients the page vertically (taller than it is wide) and **landscape** orients the page horizontally (wider than it is tall). When you shift between the two, the margin settings automatically change. If you need additional margin space for binding pages into a book or binder, you can adjust the left or right gutter settings. Gutters allow for additional margin space so that all of the document text remains visible after binding. Unless this is your purpose, leave the default settings in place.

Adjust Margins Visually

1 Click the Print Layout View button.

2 Position the pointer over a margin boundary on the horizontal or vertical ruler.

3 Press and hold Alt, and then click a margin boundary to display the measurements of the text and margin areas as you adjust the margins.

4 Drag the left, right, top, or bottom margin boundary to a new position.

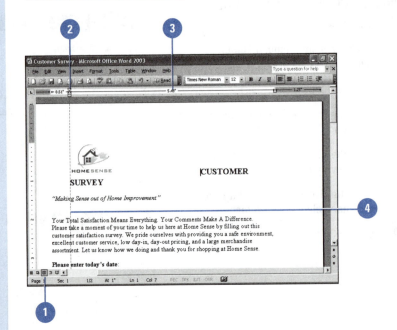

Did You Know?

You can turn off features not otherwise viewable in older versions. Click the Tools menu, click Options, click the Compatibility tab, click the Recommended Options For list arrow, and then click the version you want. Select the option check boxes you don't want, and then click OK.

Adjust Margins and Page Orientation Using Page Setup

1. Click the File menu, and then click Page Setup.

2. Click the Margins tab.

3. Type new margin measurements (in inches) in the Top, Bottom, Left, or Right boxes.

4. If necessary, enter the gutter size you want, click the Gutter Position list arrow, and then select a position.

5. Click the page orientation you want.

6. Click the Apply To list arrow, and then click Selected Text, This Point Forward, or Whole Document.

7. To make the new margin settings the default for all new Word documents, click Default, and then click Yes.

8. Click OK.

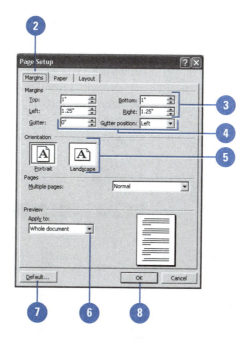

9

For Your Information

Working with Two Page Spreads

If you are working with documents that contain two page spreads, such as a book, you can select printing options for multiple pages: Normal, 2 Pages Per Sheet, Book Fold, or Mirror Margins. The Normal option is the standard setting. The 2 Pages Per Sheet option positions two pages on one page. The Book Fold option offsets the left and right page margins for binding. The Mirror Margins option sets the inside margins of facing pages equal to print both sides of a page. Click the File menu, click Page Setup, click the Margins tab, click the Multiple Pages list arrow, and then click a printing option.

Adjusting Paper Settings

Every document you produce and print might need a different page setup. You can achieve the look you want by printing on a standard paper size (such as letter, legal, or envelope), international standard paper sizes, or any custom size that your printer accepts. The default setting is 8.5 x 11 inches, the most common letter and copy size. You can also print several pages on one sheet. If you want to create a custom paper size, you can input custom settings for special print jobs on odd-sized paper.

Set the Paper Size

1. Click the File menu, and then click Page Setup.

2. Click the Paper tab.

3. Click the Paper Size list arrow, and then select the paper size you want, or specify a custom size.

4. Select the paper source for the first page and other pages.

5. Click the Apply To list arrow, and then click This Section, This Point Forward, or Whole Document.

6. Verify your selections in the Preview box.

7. To make your changes the default settings for all new documents, click Default, and then click Yes.

8. Click OK.

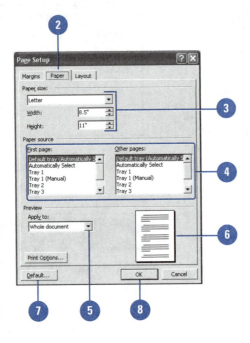

Did You Know?

You can improve printing speed. If printing is slow, you can turn off background printing to speed up the process. In the Page Setup dialog box on the Paper tab, click Print Options, clear the Background Printing check box, and then click OK.

Controlling the Way Pages Break

 WW03E-1-2

When you're creating a document, sometimes a line of text, known as a widow or orphan, in a paragraph doesn't fit on a page and looks out of place on the next page. A **widow** is the last line of a paragraph printed by itself at the top of a page. An **orphan** is the first line of a paragraph printed by it self at the bottom of a page. You can use the Widow/Orphan Control option to automatically correct the problem. If a widow or orphan occurs, Word adjusts the paragraph to make sure at least two lines appear together on the next page. When two paragraphs need to remain grouped to maintain their impact, regardless of where the normal page break would have occurred, you can keep paragraphs together on a page or in a column. If you need to start a paragraph at the top of a page, you can automatically generate a page break before a paragraph.

Control Pagination

1. Select the paragraph in which you want to control.

2. Click the Format menu, and then click Paragraph.

3. Click the Line And Page Breaks tab.

4. Choose an option:

   ◆ Select the Widow/Orphan Control check box to avoid paragraphs ending with a single word on a line or a single line at the top of a page.

   ◆ Select the Keep Lines Together check box to keep paragraph lines together.

   ◆ Select the Keep With Next check box to group paragraphs together.

   ◆ Select the Page Break Before check box to precede a paragraph with a page break.

5. Click OK.

9

Inserting New Pages and Sections

WW03S-3-5, WW03S-5-7, WW03E-1-2

When you fill a page, Word inserts a page break and starts a new page. As you add or delete text, this **soft page break** moves. A soft page break appears as a dotted gray line in Normal view. To start a new page before the current one is filled, insert a **hard page break** that doesn't shift as you edit text. A hard page break appears as a dotted gray line with the text *Page Break* centered in Normal view. A **section** is a mini-document within a document that stores margin settings, page orientation, page numbering, and so on. In Page Layout view, you can show or hide the white space on the top and bottom of each page and the gray space between pages.

Insert and Delete a Hard Page Break

1. Click where you want to insert a hard page break.

2. Click the Insert menu, and then click Break.

   TIMESAVER *Press Ctrl+Enter to insert a page break.*

3. Click the Page Break option.

4. Click OK, and the page break appears.

5. To delete a page break, click the page break in Normal view, and then press Delete.

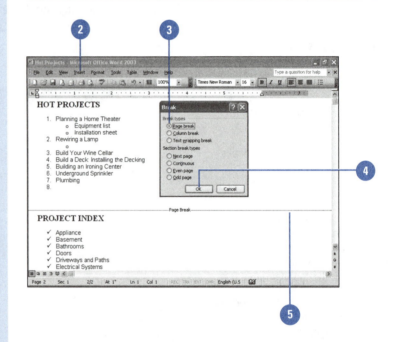

Did You Know?

You can move a page or section break. Click the View menu, click Normal to switch to Normal view, select the break you want to move, and then drag the break to its new location and release the mouse button.

You can opt to start a new line, but not a new paragraph. Insert a text wrapping break to force text to the next line in the same paragraph—the perfect tool to make a phrase fall on one line. Press Shift+Enter where you want to insert a text wrapping break.

Insert and Delete a Section Break

1. Click where you want to insert a section break.

2. Click the Insert menu, and then click Break.

3. Click the type of section break you want.

   ◆ **Next Page.** Starts the section on a new page.

   ◆ **Continuous.** Starts the section wherever the point is located.

   ◆ **Even Page.** Starts the section on the next even-numbered page.

   ◆ **Odd Page.** Starts the section on the next odd-numbered page.

4. Click OK.

5. To delete a section break, click the section break in Normal view, and then press Delete.

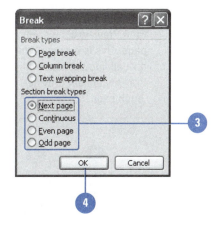

Show or Hide White Space Between Pages

1. Click the Print Layout View button.

2. Scroll to the bottom of a page, and then point to the gap between two pages. (The Hide White Space cursor or Show White Space cursor appears.)

3. Click the gap between the pages to show or hide the white space.

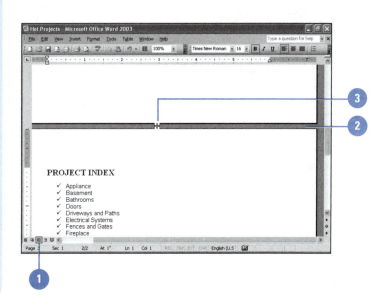

9

Previewing a Document

WW03S-5-6

Before printing, you should verify that the page looks the way you want. You can save time, money, and paper by avoiding duplicate printing. Print Preview shows you exactly how your text will look on each printed page. This is especially helpful when you have a multi-page document divided into sections with different headers and footers. The Print Preview toolbar provides the tools you need to proof the look of each page.

Preview a Document

1. Click the Print Preview button on the Standard toolbar.

2. Preview your document.

    ◆ To view one page at a time, click the One Page button.

    ◆ To view multiple pages, click the Multiple Pages button, and then select the number of pages to view at a time.

    ◆ To change the view size, click the Zoom list arrow to select a magnification percentage.

    ◆ To shrink to fit a page, click the Shrink To Fit button to reduce the document to one page.

    ◆ To display the full screen, click the Full Screen button to hide everything but the toolbar.

3. When you're done, click the Close Preview button on the Print Preview toolbar.

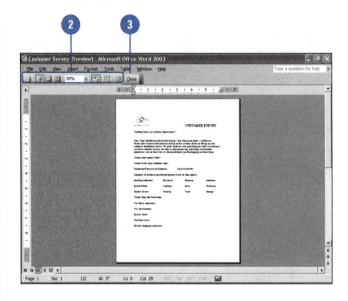

Did You Know?

You can edit while in Print Preview. Zoom the document to a closer view. Click the Magnifier button on the Print Preview toolbar, click the document, and then edit as usual.

Printing a Document

WW03S-5-5

Printing a paper copy is the most common way to share your documents. You can use the Print button on the Standard toolbar to print one copy of your document using the current settings, or you can open the Print dialog box to print your document and set how many copies to print, specify a series of pages to print, and choose what to print. Besides a document, you can also print comments, a list of styles used in the document, and AutoText entries. To review a long document on fewer pages, print multiple pages on one sheet with print zoom. The quality of print you achieve will be limited only by the quality of your printer or other output device, not by the limitations of the program itself.

Print All or Part of a Document

1. Click the File menu, and then click Print.

2. If necessary, click the Name list arrow, and then click the printer you want.

3. Type the number of copies you want to print.

4. Specify the pages to print:

   ◆ All prints the entire document.

   ◆ Current Page prints the page with the insertion point.

   ◆ Selection prints the selected text.

   ◆ Pages prints the specified pages.

5. Specify what you want to print.

6. Specify how many pages to print per sheet of paper, and then select the paper size to which to scale pages.

7. Click OK.

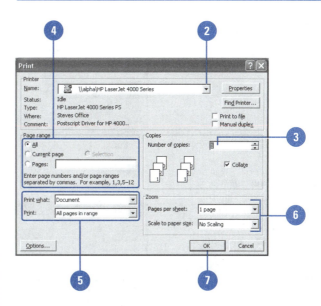

Printing a Double-Sided Document

Two-sided printing is appropriate for bound reports, pamphlets, brochures and many other types of Word documents. Not all printers support automatic two-sided printing. If your printer does not support two-sided printing, you can use the Manual Duplex option in the Print dialog box to help you complete the process.

Print a Two-Sided Document

1. Click the File menu, and then click Print.

2. Click Options.

3. Select the Front Of The Sheet and the Back Of The Sheet check boxes.

4. Click OK.

5. Click OK.

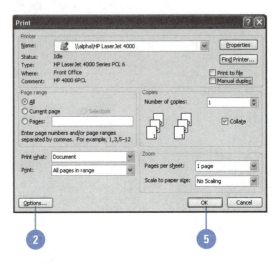

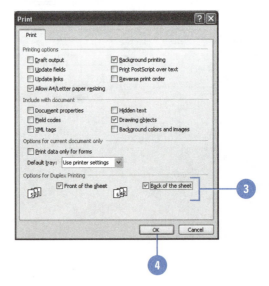

Did You Know?

You can print two-sided documents manually. The first side of each alternate page will be printed. Then you will be prompted to reinsert the pages into the printer so that the second side can be printed.

Creating Desktop Publishing Documents

10

Introduction

Adding some extra flair to an ordinary document can really make it appear more like a Newsletter or Flyer, than a regular document. There are many elements that Microsoft Office Word 2003 offers you in order to create a document that goes the extra mile.

The Drawing Canvas is a virtual working canvas that is placed in your document so as you work with the Drawing toolbar in creating and styling objects, you have a working area that doesn't affect your document. You can resize the Drawing Canvas, just as you would an object, by going to the resize handles and dragging in or out.

When working with objects, it might be helpful to have them grouped together, so that when you move or resize them, you are doing it consistently with the group of objects, instead of having to modify each one individually. Of course, if you need to change just one, you can ungroup, make the change, and then regroup them. Objects are not just AutoShapes or Clip Art, they can be lines and arrows too. All of the objects that you are inserting into your document, can be modified in a number of ways. You can change the color of the objects or lines, apply pattern fills, create shadows, and even apply a 3-D effect, or extra lighting, to your objects. You can rotate or flip them, or you can have text wrap around them in your document.

If you decide that you have a layout of your document where you are using text boxes, you can connect the text boxes together by linking them. Linked text boxes allow you to add text to a section and have it continue into another text box. You can also set up your document in column form. And for that extra touch, you can add a border around a page, or your whole document for that finished look.

Drawing and Resizing Shapes

WW03E-1-3

Word supplies AutoShapes ranging from hearts to lightening bolts to stars. The two most common AutoShapes, the oval and the rectangle, are available directly on the Drawing toolbar. When you select an AutoShape, the Drawing Canvas appears on the document, along with the Drawing Canvas toolbar. When you are done inserting your AutoShape, you can resize it using the sizing handles. Many AutoShapes have an **adjustment handle**, a small yellow diamond located near a resize handle that you can drag to alter the shape of the AutoShape. For precision when resizing, use Word's Format command to specify the new size of the shape. In addition to drawing AutoShapes, you can insert AutoShapes, such as computers and furniture, from the Clip Art task pane.

Draw an Oval or Rectangle

1 Click the Oval or Rectangle button on the Drawing toolbar.

2 Drag the cursor on the document where you want to place the oval or rectangle.

To draw a perfect circle or square, hold down Shift as you drag the cursor.

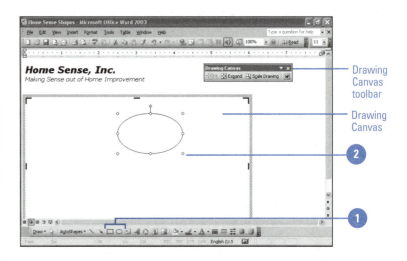

Drawing Canvas toolbar

Drawing Canvas

Draw an AutoShape

1 Click the AutoShapes button on the Drawing toolbar, and then point to the AutoShape category you want to use.

2 Click the symbol you want.

3 Drag the pointer on the document until the drawing object is the shape and size that you want.

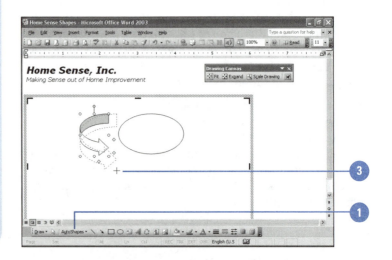

Resize an AutoShape

1. Click the AutoShape you want to resize.

2. Drag one of the sizing handles.

   ◆ To resize the object in the vertical or horizontal direction, drag a sizing handle on the side of the selection box.

   ◆ To resize the object in both the vertical and horizontal directions, drag a sizing handle on the corner of the selection box.

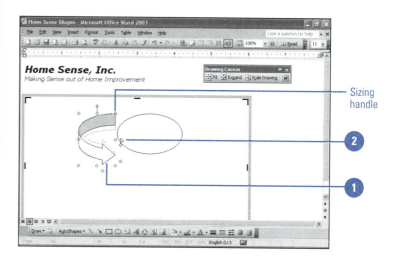

Sizing handle

Adjust an AutoShape

1. Click the AutoShape you want to adjust.

2. Click one of the adjustment handles (small yellow diamonds), and then drag the handle to alter the form of the AutoShape.

Did You Know?

You can draw a circle or square.
To draw a perfect circle or square, click the Oval or Rectangle button on the Drawing toolbar, and then press and hold Shift as you drag.

You can replace an AutoShape.
Replace one AutoShape with another, while retaining the size, color, and orientation of the AutoShape. Click the AutoShape you want to replace, click the Draw button on the Drawing toolbar, point to Change AutoShape, and then click the new AutoShape you want.

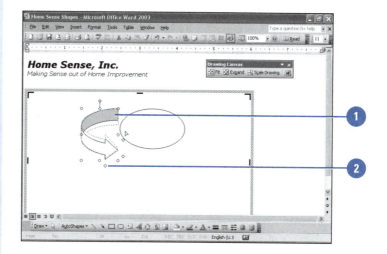

10

Working with Objects

As you learn to use Word, you'll want to enhance your documents beyond just text. You can insert many different types of objects. An **object** is a picture or graphic image you can create with a drawing program or insert from an existing file of another program. Once you have an object in your document, you can resize or move it. Use an objects' **handles** (the little circle that appear on the edges of the selected object) to move the object. The remaining sections of this chapter discuss how to insert objects into your documents.

Select and Deselect an Object

◆ Click an object to display its handles.

◆ To select more than one object at a time, hold down Shift as you click each object. You can also drag a selection rectangle around the objects, and then release the mouse button.

◆ Click elsewhere within the document window to deselect a selected object.

Handles

Click outside the document to deselect the object

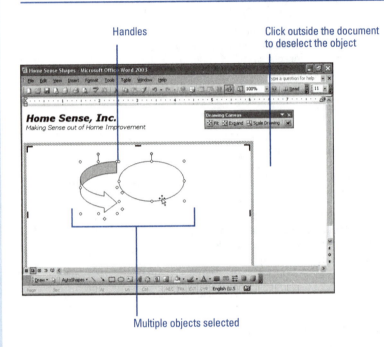

Multiple objects selected

Move an Object

1. Click an object to select it.

2. Drag the object to a new location indicated by the dotted outline of the object.

3. Release the mouse button to drop the object in the new location.

Delete an Object

1. Click the object you want to delete.

2. Press Delete.

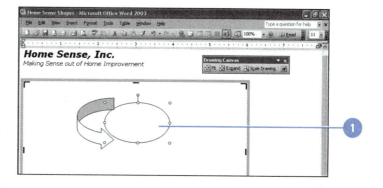

10

For Your Information

Grouping Objects

You can insert multiple objects in a drawing canvas. If one or more objects in a drawing canvas are related (such as a circle and a text box), you can group them in order to move, resize, or copy them as a single unit. To group objects together, hold down the Shift key while you click the objects that you want to group, click the Draw button on the Drawing toolbar, and then click Group.

Inserting AutoShapes from Clip Art

In addition to drawing AutoShapes, you can insert AutoShapes, such as computers and furniture, from the Clip Art task pane. These AutoShapes are called **clips**. The Clip Art task pane gives you a miniature of each clip. You can click the clip you want to insert onto your document or click the clip list arrow to select other options, such as previewing the clip or searching for similar clips. After you insert an AutoShape, you can add text to it. You can format the text in an AutoShape in the same way you format all other text in Word.

Insert an AutoShape from Clip Art

1. Click the AutoShapes button on the Drawing toolbar, and then click More AutoShapes.

2. If necessary, use the scroll arrows to display more AutoShapes.

3. Click the shape you want to insert.

4. When you're done, click the Close button on the task pane.

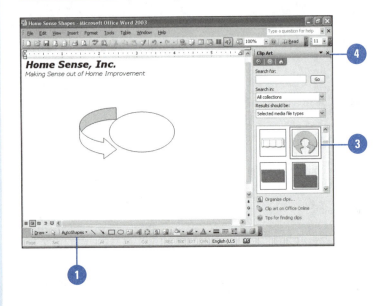

Find Similar AutoShapes in Clip Art

1. Click the AutoShapes button on the Drawing toolbar, and then click More AutoShapes.

2. Point to the AutoShape in which you want to find a similar one.

3. Click the list arrow, and then click Find Similar Style.

   The similar AutoShape styles appear in the results box.

4. When you're done, click the Close button on the task pane.

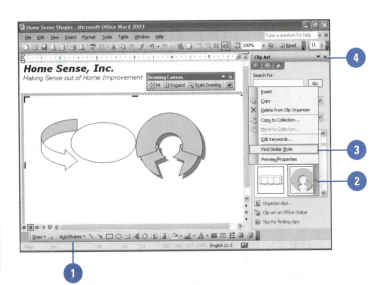

Add Text to an AutoShape

1 Click the Text Box button on the Drawing toolbar, and then drag a box across the AutoShape.

2 Type the text you want.

3 Click outside the text box to quit typing.

Did You Know?

You can edit text in an AutoShape.
Click the AutoShape to select it, click the text in the AutoShape to place the insertion point, and then edit the text.

You can align text in an AutoShape.
Click the AutoShape to select it, and then use the alignment buttons on the Formatting toolbar.

Change Text Orientation

1 Click the text box in the drawing object that you want to be oriented.

2 Click the Text Direction button on the Text Box toolbar.

3 Click the Text Direction button until the text is oriented as you like.

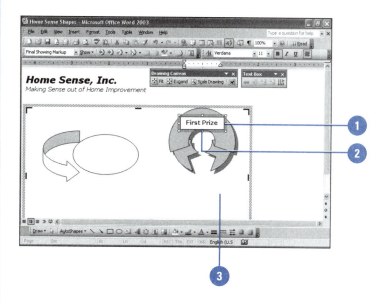

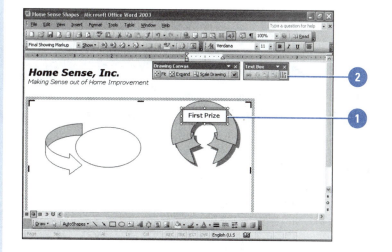

10

Drawing Lines and Arrows

The most basic drawing objects you can create on your documents are lines and arrows. Use the Line tool to create line segments. The Drawing toolbar's Line Style and Dash Style tools let you determine the type of line you can draw—solid, dashed, or a combination. You can add arrowheads to any lines on your document. Use the Arrow tool to create arrows that emphasize key features of your document. You can edit the style of the arrow using the Arrow Style tool.

Draw a Straight Line

1. Click the Line button on the Drawing toolbar.

2. Drag the pointer to draw a line. The endpoints of the line are where you start and finish dragging.

3. Release the mouse button when the line is the correct length. Sizing handles appear at both ends of the line. Use these handles to resize your line or move an endpoint.

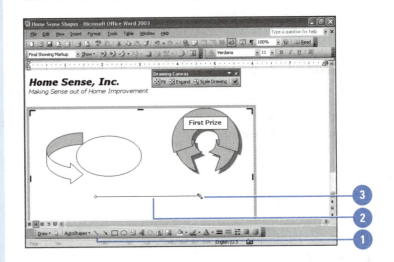

Edit a Line

1. Click the line you want to edit.

2. Click the Line Style button on the Drawing toolbar to select a line thickness.

3. Click the Dash Style button on the Drawing toolbar to select a style.

4. Click the Line Color button list arrow on the Drawing toolbar to select a color.

5. Drag a sizing handle to change the size or angle of the line.

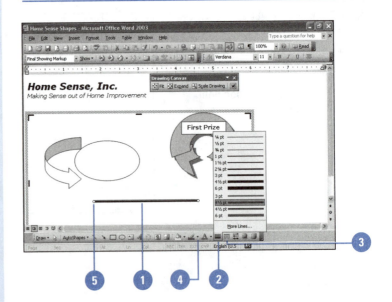

Draw an Arrow

1. Click the Arrow button on the Drawing toolbar.

2. Drag the pointer from the base of the arrow to the arrow's point.

3. Release the mouse button when the arrow is the correct length and angle.

Did You Know?

You can change the default size of an arrow. Click an arrow object, click the Arrow Style button, click More Arrows, change the line and arrow settings to the default format you want. Right click the arrow, and then click Set AutoShape Defaults.

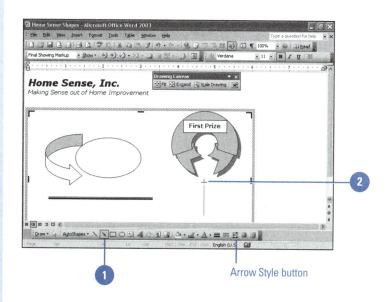

Arrow Style button

Edit an Arrow

1. Click the arrow you want to edit.

2. Click the Arrow Style button on the Drawing toolbar.

3. Click the arrow type you want to use, or click More Arrows.

4. If you click More Arrows, modify the arrow type in the Format AutoShape dialog box as necessary, and then click OK.

Did You Know?

You can increase the size of an arrow. Click the Arrow Style button, click More Arrows, and then increase the Weight setting or End Size setting.

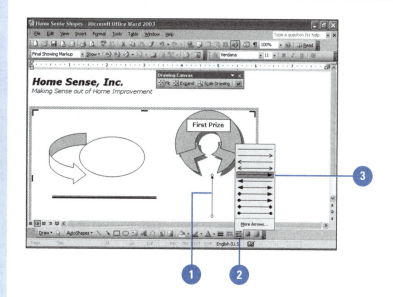

10

Choosing Shape Colors and Fill Effects

When you create a closed drawing object such as a square, it uses two colors from the color scheme: the Fill color and the Line color. When you create a line drawing object, it uses the color scheme Line color. You can change the Fill and Line color settings for drawing objects using the same color tools for changing a document's background or text color. An easy way to apply the current fill color to any object is to select the object and then click the Fill Color button.

Change a Drawing Object's Fill Color

1 Click the drawing object whose fill color you want to change.

2 Click the Fill Color button list arrow on the Drawing toolbar.

3 Select the fill color you want.

4 Click Fill Effects if you want to change the fill effect.

Remove a Fill

1 Click the drawing object whose fill you want to change.

2 Click the Fill Color button list arrow on the Drawing toolbar.

3 Click No Fill.

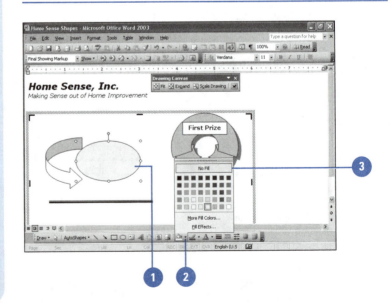

Create a Fill Effect

1. Click the drawing object whose fill you want to change.

2. Click the Fill Color button list arrow, and then click Fill Effects.

   ◆ Click the Gradient tab to select a gradient color and shading style.

   ◆ Click the Texture tab to select a texture.

   ◆ Click the Pattern tab to select a pattern, foreground, and background color.

   ◆ Click the Picture tab to select a picture.

3. Select the fill pattern you want.

4. Click OK.

Click a tab to select a fill effect style.

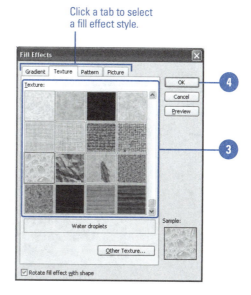

Change Colors and Lines in the Format Dialog Box

1. Click the drawing object you want to modify.

2. Click the Format menu, and then click AutoShape.

3. Click the Colors And Lines tab.

4. Set fill, line, and arrow options.

5. Click OK.

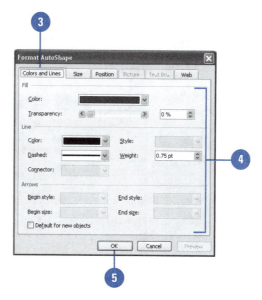

Did You Know?

You can set the color and line style for an object as the default. Right-click the object, and then click Set AutoShape Defaults. Any new objects you create will use the same styles.

10

Applying Fill Effects

Applying a fill effect to a drawing object can add emphasis or create a point of interest in your document. Word offers fill effects such as gradients, patterns, textures, and even clip art pictures. Spend a few minutes in the Fill Effects dialog box to create the right look for your drawing object.

Apply a Picture Fill

1 Select the object you want to fill, click the Fill Color button list arrow on the Drawing toolbar, and then click Fill Effects.

2 Click the Picture tab.

3 Click Select Picture.

4 Locate the picture you want, and then double-click it.

5 Click OK.

Apply a Gradient Fill

1 Select the object you want to fill, click the Fill Color button list arrow on the Drawing toolbar, and then click Fill Effects.

2 Click the Gradient tab.

3 Click the color or color combination you want.

4 Click the shading style option you want.

5 Click the variant you want.

6 Click OK.

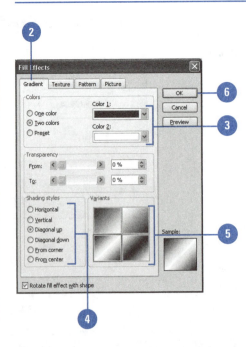

Apply a Pattern Fill

1. Select the object you want to fill, click the Fill Color button list arrow on the Drawing toolbar, and then click Fill Effects.

2. Click the Pattern tab.

3. Click the Foreground list arrow to select the color you want in the foreground.

4. Click the Background list arrow to select the color you want in the background.

5. Click the pattern you want.

6. Click OK.

Did You Know?

You can apply fill effects to other objects. Apply fill effects to objects such as lines and WordArt to enhance your document.

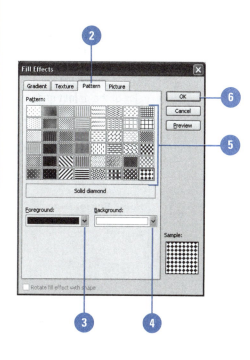

Creating Shadows

You can give objects on your documents the illusion of depth by adding shadows. Word provides several preset shadowing options, or you can create your own by specifying the location and color of the shadow. If the shadow is falling on another object in your document, you can create a semitransparent shadow that blends the color of the shadow with the color of the object underneath it.

Use a Preset Shadow

1. Click the drawing object to which you want to add a preset shadow.

2. Click the Shadow Style button on the Drawing toolbar.

3. Click a shadow style.

Did You Know?

You can remove a shadow. Click the drawing object with the shadow, click the Shadow button on the Drawing toolbar, and then click No Shadow.

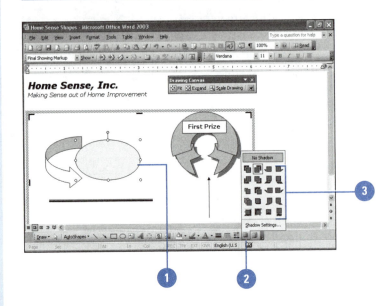

Change the Location of a Shadow

1. Click the drawing object with the shadow.

2. Click the Shadow Style button on the Drawing toolbar, and then click Shadow Settings.

3. Click the tool that creates the effect you want. The Nudge buttons move the shadow location slightly up, down, right, or left.

4. Click the Close button on the Shadow Settings toolbar.

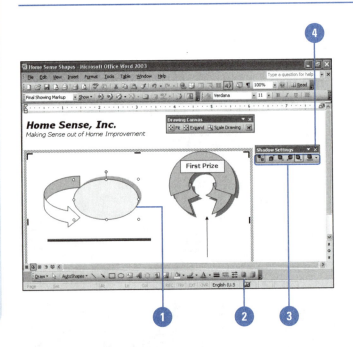

Change the Color of a Shadow

1. Click the drawing object with the shadow.

2. Click the Shadow Style button on the Drawing toolbar, and then click Shadow Settings.

3. Click the Shadow Color button list arrow on the Shadow Settings toolbar, and then select a new color.

4. Click the Close button on the Shadow Settings toolbar.

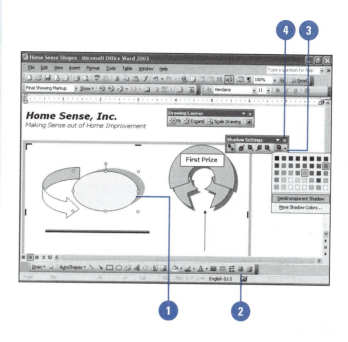

Add a Shadow to Text

1. Click the text object to which you want to add a shadow.

2. Click the Shadow Style button on the Drawing toolbar.

3. Click a shadow style.

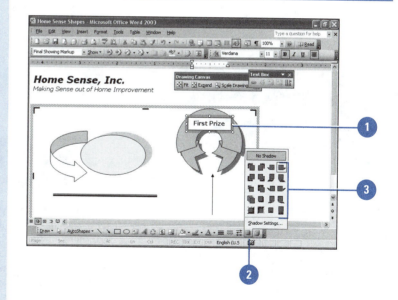

Aligning and Distributing Objects

You can align a group of objects to each other. The Align or Distribute command aligns two or more objects relative to each other vertically to the left, center, or right. You can also align objects horizontally to the top, middle, or bottom. To align several objects to each other evenly across the document, either horizontally or vertically, you select them and then choose a distribution option.

Distribute Objects

1. Select the objects you want to distribute.

2. Click the Draw button on the Drawing toolbar, and then point to Align Or Distribute.

3. Click the distribution option you want.

   ◆ Click Distribute Horizontally to evenly distribute the objects horizontally.

   ◆ Click Distribute Vertically to evenly distribute the objects vertically.

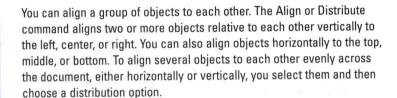
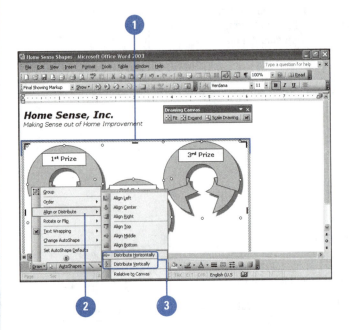

For Your Information

Aligning Objects on a Grid

When working with objects, you can also align them on a grid. To use this feature, click the Draw button on the Drawing toolbar, and then click Grid. There are two methods of alignment that appear. The first, Snap Objects To Grid, automatically aligns the drawing objects on an invisible grid. The second, Snap Objects To Other Objects, automatically aligns objects with gridlines that penetrate the vertical and horizontal edges of other objects. You can use the one that best meets your alignment needs.

Align Objects with Other Objects

1 Select the objects you want to align.

2 Click the Draw button on the Drawing toolbar, and then point to Align Or Distribute.

3 Click the alignment command you want.

◆ Click Align Left to line up the objects with the left edge of the selection or document.

◆ Click Align Center to line up the objects with the center of the selection or document.

◆ Click Align Right to line up the objects with the right edge of the selection or document.

◆ Click Align Top to line up the objects with the top edge of the selection or document.

◆ Click Align Middle to line up the objects vertically with the middle of the selection or document.

◆ Click Align Bottom to line up the objects with the bottom of the selection or document.

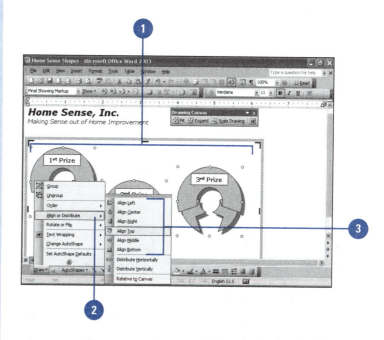

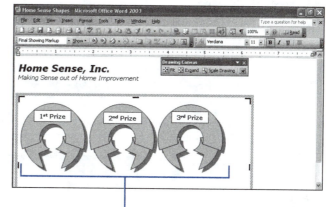

Objects aligned to their tops.

10

Connecting Shapes

Word makes it easy to draw and modify flow charts and diagrams. Flow charts and diagrams consist of shapes connected together to indicate a sequence of events. With Word, you can join two objects with a connecting line. Once two objects are joined, the connecting line moves when you move either object. The connecting line touches special connection points on the objects. When you position the pointer over an object, small blue handles, known as connection sites, appear, and the pointer changes to a small box, called the connection pointer. You can drag a connection end point to another connection point to change the line or drag the adjustment handle to change the shape of the connection line.

Connect Two Shapes

1. On the Drawing toolbar, click AutoShapes, point to Connectors, and then click a connector.

2. Position the cursor over an object handle, and then click the object to select a connection point.

3. Position the cursor over the object handle on another object, and then click the object to select another connection point.

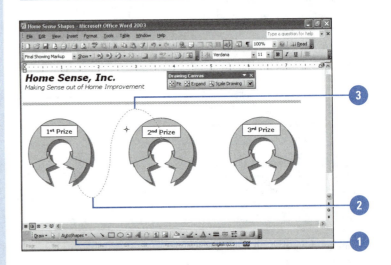

Change and Format a Connector Line

1. Click on the connector line you want to modify. To select more than one line, hold down Shift, and then click all the connector lines you wish to modify.

2. On the Drawing toolbar, use buttons such as Line Color, Line Style, Dash Style, and Arrow Style to modify the connector lines.

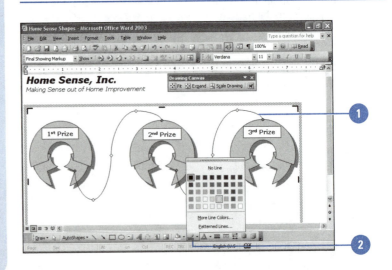

Changing Stacking Order

When a document contains multiple objects, the objects appear on the document in a stacking order. Stacking is the placement of objects one on top of another. The drawing order determines the object stacking order. The first object that you draw is on the bottom, and the last object that you draw is on top. You can change the order of this stack of objects by using the Bring to Front, Send to Back, Bring Forward, and Send Backward commands on the Draw menu on the Drawing toolbar.

Arrange a Stack of Objects

1. Select the object or objects you want to arrange.

2. Click the Draw button on the Drawing toolbar, point to Order, and then click the option you want.

   ◆ Click Bring To Front or Bring Forward to move an object to the top of the stack or up one location in the stack.

   ◆ Click Send To Back or Send Backward to move an object to the bottom of the stack or back one location in the stack.

Did You Know?

You can view a hidden object in a stack. Press the Tab key or Shift+Tab to cycle forward or backward through the objects until you select the object you want.

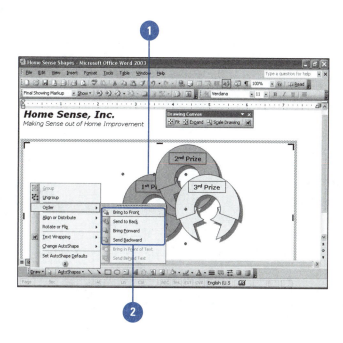

10

Adding 3-D Effects to a Shape

You can add the illusion of depth to your documents by using the 3-D tool. Although not all objects can be turned into 3-D objects, most of the AutoShapes can. You can create a 3-D effect using one of the 20 preset 3-D styles supported by Word, or you can use the 3-D tools to customize your own 3-D style. The settings you can control with the customization tools include the spin of the object, or the angle at which the 3-D object is tilted and rotated, the depth of the object, and the direction of light falling upon the object.

Apply a Preset 3-D Style

1. Click the drawing object you want to change.

2. Click the 3-D Style button on the Drawing toolbar.

3. Click a 3-D style.

> ### Did You Know?
>
> *You can add a different surface to your 3-D object.* Apply interesting surfaces, such as wire frame, matte, plastic, or metal, to your 3-D object by clicking the Surface button on the 3-D Settings toolbar.

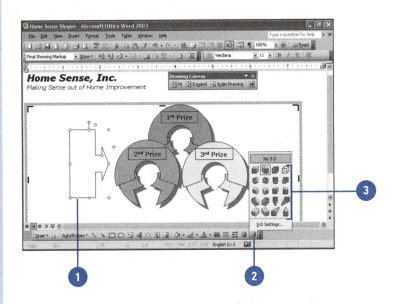

Tilt a 3-D Object

1. Click the 3-D object you want to change.

2. Click the 3-D Style button on the Drawing toolbar, and then click 3-D Settings.

3. Click the tilt setting you want.

4. Click the Close button on the 3-D Settings toolbar.

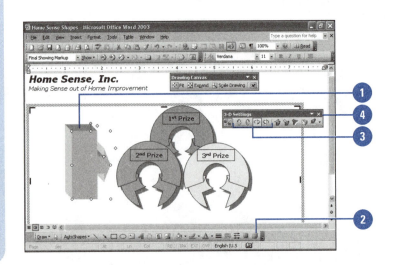

Set Lighting

1 Click the 3-D object, click the 3-D Style button on the Drawing toolbar, and then click 3-D Settings.

2 Click the Lighting button on the 3-D Settings toolbar.

3 Click the spotlight that creates the effect you want.

4 Click the Close button on the 3-D Settings toolbar.

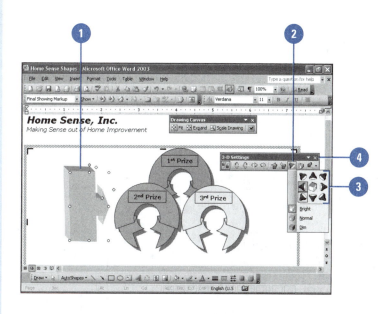

Set 3-D Depth

1 Click the 3-D object, click the 3-D Style button on the Drawing toolbar, and then click 3-D Settings.

2 Click the Depth button on the 3-D Settings toolbar.

3 Click the size of the depth in points, or enter the exact number of points you want in the Custom box.

4 Click the Close button on the 3-D Settings toolbar.

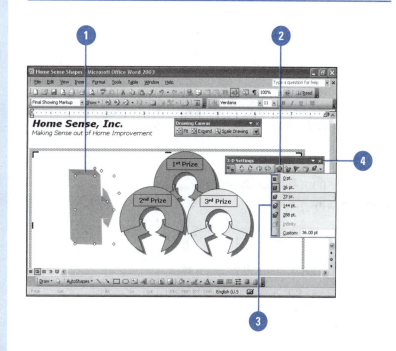

Did You Know?

You can change the direction of a 3-D object. Click the Direction button on the 3-D Settings toolbar. You can also use this button to add perspective to your objects or align them along a parallel.

10

Rotating and Flipping an Object

WW03E-1-3

Once you create an object, you can change its orientation on the document by rotating or flipping it. Rotating turns an object 90 degrees to the right or left; flipping turns an object 180 degrees horizontally or vertically. If you need a more exact rotation, which you cannot achieve in 90 or 180 degree increments, you can drag the green rotate lever at the top of an object to rotate it to any position. You can also rotate and flip any type of picture—including bitmaps—in a document. This is useful when you want to change the orientation of an object or image, such as changing the direction of an arrow.

Rotate an Object to any Angle

1 Click the object you want to rotate.

2 Position the pointer (which changes to the Free Rotate pointer) over the green rotate lever at the top of the object, and then drag to rotate the object.

3 Click outside the object to set the rotation.

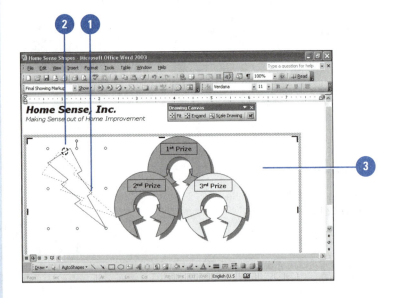

Rotate or Flip an Object Using Preset Increments

1 Click the object you want to rotate or flip.

2 Click the Draw button on the Drawing toolbar.

3 Point to Rotate Or Flip, and then click a rotate or flip option.

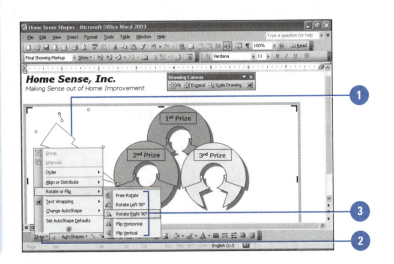

Rotate an Object Around a Fixed Point

1. Click the object you want to rotate.

2. Click the Draw button on the Drawing toolbar, point to Rotate Or Flip, and then click Free Rotate.

3. Click the rotate handle opposite the point you want to rotate, and then press and hold the Ctrl key as you rotate the object.

4. Click outside the object to set the rotation.

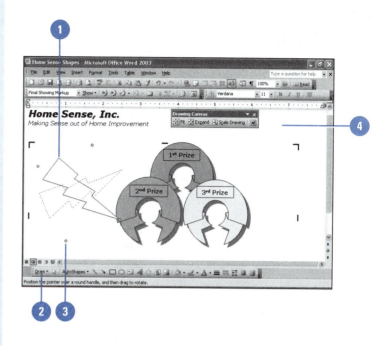

Rotate an Object Precisely

1. Right-click the object you want to rotate, and then click Format AutoShape.

2. Click the Size tab.

3. Enter the angle of rotation, or click the up or down arrows.

4. Click OK.

Did You Know?

You can constrain the rotation in 15-degree increments. Press and hold Shift when you rotate the object.

You cannot rotate or flip some imported objects. Not all imported objects can be rotated or flipped. By ungrouping the imported object and then regrouping its components, you might be able to rotate or flip it.

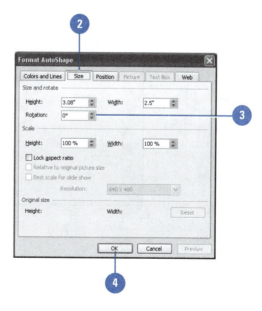

10

Grouping and Ungrouping Objects

Objects can be grouped together, ungrouped, and regrouped in Word to make editing and moving information easier. Rather than moving several objects one at a time, you can group the objects and move them all together. Grouped objects appear as one object, but each object in the group maintains its individual attributes. You can change an individual object within a group without ungrouping. This is useful when you need to make only a small change to a group, such as changing the color of a single shape in the group. You can also format specific AutoShapes, drawings, or pictures within a group without ungrouping. Simply select the object within the group, change the object or edit text within the object, and then deselect the object. However, if you need to move an object in a group, you need to first ungroup the objects, make the change, and then group the objects together again. After you ungroup a set of objects, Word remembers each object in the group and in one step regroups those objects when you use the Regroup command. Before you regroup a set of objects, make sure that at least one of the grouped objects is selected.

Group Objects Together

1. Select the objects you want to group together.

2. Click the Draw button on the Drawing toolbar, and then click Group.

Did You Know?

You can use the Tab key to select objects in order. Move between the drawing objects on your document (even those hidden behind other objects) by pressing the Tab key.

You can use the shortcut menu to select the Order and Grouping commands. Right-click the objects you want to group or reorder, point to Grouping or Order, and then make your selections.

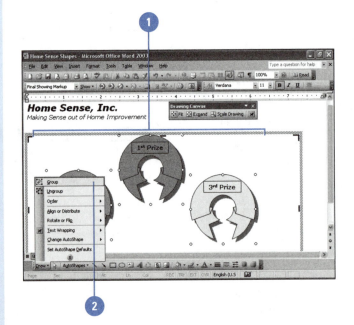

Ungroup a Grouped Object

1 Select the grouped object you want to ungroup.

2 Click the Draw button on the Drawing toolbar, and then click Ungroup.

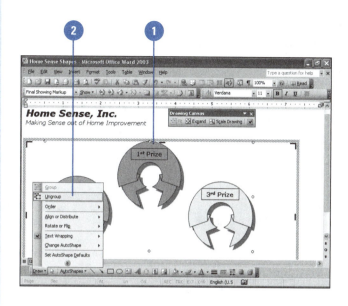

Regroup an Object

1 Select one of the objects in the group of objects you want to regroup.

2 Click the Draw button on the Drawing toolbar, and then click Regroup.

Did You Know?

You can troubleshoot the arrangement of objects. If you have trouble selecting an object because another object is in the way, try moving the first object out of the way temporarily.

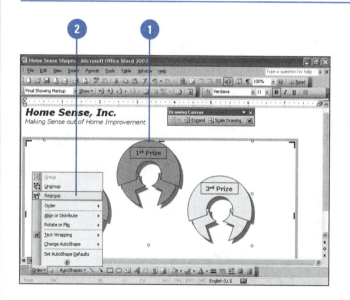

Wrapping Text Around an Object

WW03E-1-3

When integrating pictures, charts, tables, or other graphics with your text, you need to wrap the text around the object regardless of where it is placed on the page. Rather than having to constantly reset margins and make other tedious adjustments, Word simplifies this task with the text wrapping feature. Unless your object or table is large enough to span the entire page, your layout will look more professional if you wrap your text around it instead of leaving excessive white space.

Wrap Text Around an Object or Picture

1. If the picture or object is located on a drawing canvas, click to select that canvas. If the picture or object is not located on a canvas, select the picture or object.

2. Right-click the object, and then click Format Picture or Format AutoShape.

3. Click the Layout tab.

4. Click the wrapping style you want to use, and the horizontal alignment of your choice for the picture (Left, Right, Center, or Other).

5. Click OK.

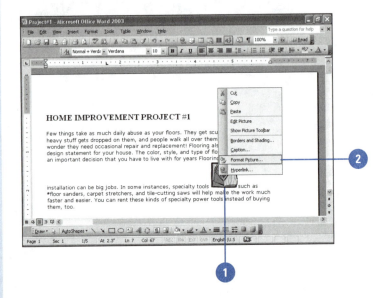

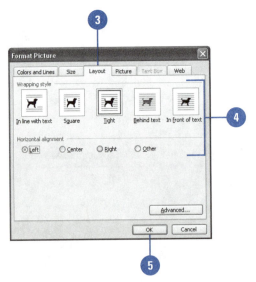

Did You Know?

You can line up objects. To align the drawing canvas quickly, select the drawing canvas, click the Text Wrapping button on the Drawing Canvas toolbar, and then select a text wrapping option.

Wrap Text Around a Table

1. Select the table you want to wrap text around.

2. Click the Table menu, and then click Table Properties.

3. Click the Table tab.

4. If necessary, adjust the Size.

5. Click the Alignment option you want.

6. Click the Text Wrapping option you want to apply.

7. Click Positioning.

8. Select the Horizontal and Vertical positions, set the Distance From Surrounding Text, and then if necessary, choose the Move With Text or the Allow Overlap option.

9. Click OK.

10. If necessary, click the Borders And Shading button to apply a border or shading.

11. Click OK.

Did You Know?

You can reposition a table. Select the table, and then drag it to a new location. You might need to readjust the table positioning and spacing.

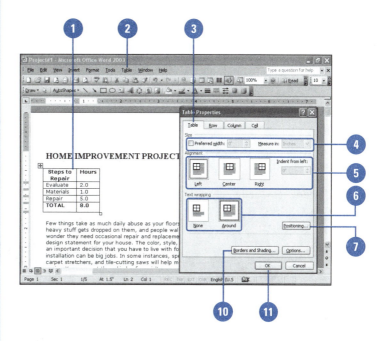

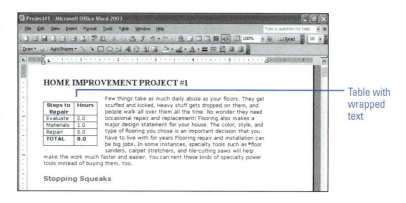

Table with wrapped text

Linking Text Boxes

Linked text boxes can be used to create columns of text that flow side-by-side along the bottom or top of the page in conjunction with either a one-column or two-column layout of the main body text. Using this feature, you can extend a sidebar across a two-page spread. You can link several text boxes together in different parts of a document.

Create a Text Box from Existing Text

1. Select the text in which you want to make into a text box.

2. Click the Insert menu, and then click Text Box.

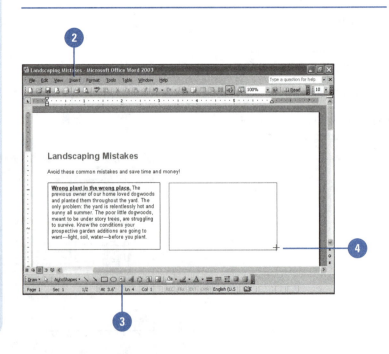

Create an Empty Text Box

1. Position the insertion point where you want the text box to appear.

2. Click the Insert menu, and then click Text Box.

3. Click the Text Box button on the Drawing toolbar.

4. Click and drag inside the drawing canvas where you want the text box to appear, and then enter the text you want.

5. Resize the Drawing Canvas text box so that it surrounds the text box.

Link Text Boxes

1. Select the text box with the text you want to connect with another text box.

2. Click the Text Box button on the Drawing toolbar.

3. Drag where you want the empty text box to appear.

4. Select the first text box with text.

5. Click the Create Text Box Link button on the Text Box toolbar. The cursor changes into the pitcher pointer.

6. Click the second empty text box to create a link. Any overflow text from the first text appears in the second text box.

7. Click anywhere outside the canvas to deselect the text boxes.

Did You Know?

You can move between linked text boxes. Click the Next Text Box button or the Previous Text Box button on the Text Box toolbar.

You can break a link between two text boxes. Select the text box to which you want to break the link, and then click the Break Forward Link button on the Text Box toolbar.

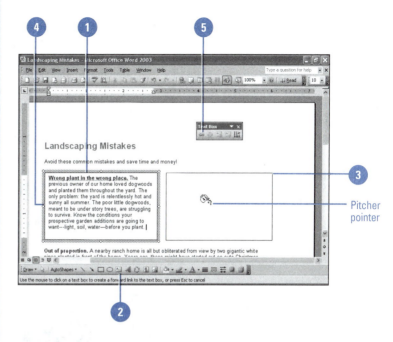

Pitcher pointer

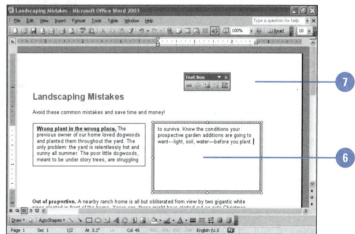

10

Arranging Text in Columns

WW03S-3-3

Newspaper-style columns can give newsletters and brochures a more polished look. You can format an entire document, selected text, or individual sections into columns. You can create one, two, or three columns of equal size. You can also create two columns and have one column wider than the other. Word 2003 fills one column with text before the other, unless you insert a column break. **Column breaks** are used in two-column layouts to move the text after the insertion point to the top of the following column. You can also display a vertical line between the columns. To view the columns side by side, switch to Print Layout view.

Create Columns

1. Click the Print Layout View button.

2. Select the text you want to arrange in columns.

3. Click the Columns button on the Standard toolbar.

4. Drag to select the number of columns you want.

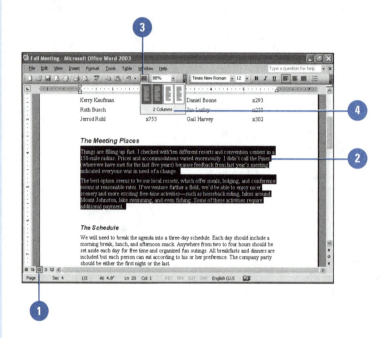

Did You Know?

You can remove columns quickly. Select the columns, click the Columns button on the Standard toolbar, and then click the first column.

You can align text in a column. Click the Align Left, Center, Align Right, or Justify button on the Formatting toolbar to align paragraphs in columns.

Modify Columns

1. Click the Print Layout View button, and then click in the columns you want to modify.

2. Click the Format menu, and then click Columns.

3. Click a column format.

4. If necessary, enter the number of columns you want.

5. Enter the width and spacing you want for each column.

6. To place a vertical line between columns, select the Line Between check box.

7. Click OK.

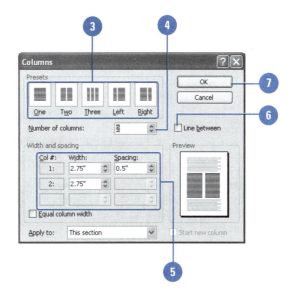

Insert a Column Break

1. Click where you want to insert a column break.

2. Click the Insert menu, and then click Break.

3. Click the Column Break option.

4. Click OK.

5. To delete a column break, click the page break in Normal view, and then press the Delete key.

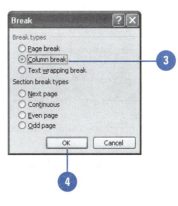

10

Adding a Border to a Page

There may be times when you might want to put a frame around your finished pages with a border. Using Word, you can select from a number of preset options or create custom borders of your own design. You can have either line borders or art borders, or a combination of both.

Add a Border to a Page

1. Click the Format menu, and then click Borders And Shading.

2. Click the Page Border tab.

3. Click a preset border. All remaining steps, except the last one, are optional and completely dependent on the affect you are trying to achieve.

4. Select a line style for the page border.

5. Click the Color list arrow, and then select a color for the page border.

6. Click the Width list arrow, and then select the thickness of the page border.

7. Click the Art list arrow, and then select the border art style you want to apply.

8. Click border edges in the Preview window to deselect and select how many sides will encompass the border. By default, Word will frame borders on four sides.

9. Click the Apply To list arrow, and then select the option you want.

10. Click Options, and then specify the border margins you want.

11. Click OK.

12. Click OK.

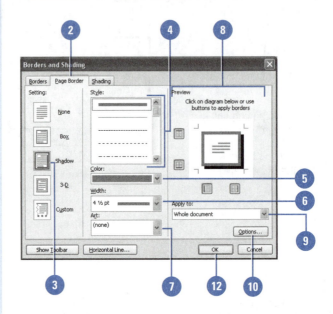

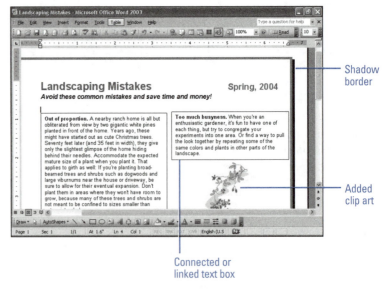

Shadow border

Added clip art

Connected or linked text box

Creating Web Pages

Introduction

If you have something that needs to be said in a public forum, it has never been easier to do so. Microsoft Office Word 2003 can support your efforts by converting your documents into Web pages using HTML, the programming language used by the Web, and also by providing you with numerous Web publishing tools that can be used independently, or in conjunction with other Office programs like Microsoft FrontPage.

You can add **hyperlinks** (graphic objects or text you click to jump to other documents and intranet or Internet pages) to your documents. Word makes it easy to create a Web page without learning HTML, the coding system used to format Web pages. In addition, you can save any document as a Web page to your hard drive just as you would save a document. You can also pre-view how your document will look as a Web page in Word or in your browser. Without ever leaving Word, you can turn a document into a Web page.

What's the most convenient way to meet with sales staff from around the world? NetMeeting—a conferencing program for meeting and collaborating over the Internet or a corporate intranet. Participants share and exchange information as if they were in one room. The host starts the meeting and controls access to the document.

Creating a Blank Web Page from a Template

When you start Word, a blank document opens based on a default template. The default template defines the page margins, default font, and other settings. You can create a new blank Web page based on a default Web Page template. If you want to start a Web page with more than a blank page, you can check the Office Online Web site for templates. When you save a Web page based on the default Web Page template, the file is saved as a single Web page.

Create a Blank Web Page from a Template

1. Click the File menu, and then click New.

2. Click Web Page.

3. Click the Save button on the Standard toolbar.

4. Select the drive and folder in which to store the file.

5. Type a name for the file.

6. Click Save.

See Also

See "Saving Documents as Single File Web Pages" on page 259 for information on saving a Web page based on the default Web Page template.

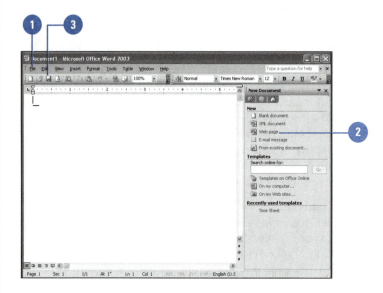

Get Templates on the Web

1. Click the File menu, and then click New.

2. Click Templates On Office Online to open the Microsoft Web site in your browser.

3. Click the link to the template you want.

4. Click Download Now, and then follow the online instructions.

See Also

See Chapter 4, "Using Templates and Applying Styles," on page 83 for information on working with templates.

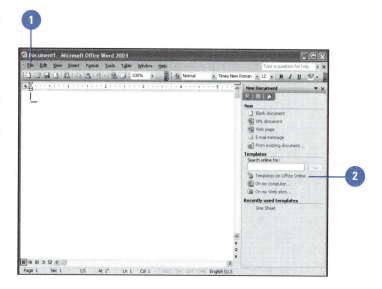

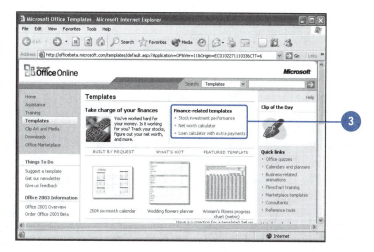

Designing Web Pages

Web pages are multimedia documents that provide information and contain **links** to other documents on the Internet, an intranet, a local network, or a hard disk. These links—also called **hyperlinks**, **hypertext**, or **hypermedia**—are highlighted text or graphics that you click to follow a pathway from one Web page to another. Linked Web pages, often called a **Web site**, are generally related by topic.

Web pages are based on **Hypertext Markup Language** (HTML)—a simple coding system used to format Web pages. A browser program, such as Microsoft Internet Explorer, interprets these special codes to determine how a certain Web page should be displayed. Different codes mark the size, color, style, and placement of text and graphics as well as which words and graphics should be marked as hyperlinks and to what files they link.

As the World Wide Web becomes a household word and many businesses create intranet and Internet Web sites—both of which use HTML documents—the ability to create, read, open, and save HTML documents directly from Office becomes an important time saver.

HTML and Office 2003

Office 2003 uses HTML as a companion file format. That means that Word, Excel, Access, PowerPoint, and Publisher all can save and read HTML documents without any compatibility problems. Additionally, Office recognizes the .html filename extension as accurately as it does those for its own programs (.doc, .xls, .mdb, .ppt, and .pub). In other words, you can use the familiar Office tools and features you use to create printed documents to create and share Web documents. Anyone with a browser can view your Office Web documents.

Converting Documents to Web Pages

In addition to creating Web pages from scratch in Office programs, you can also save any existing document as a Web page to your hard disk, intranet, or Web server. These HTML documents preserve such features as styles, revision marks, PivotTables, linked and embedded objects, and so forth. When the layout or an item in your document can't be converted to HTML in exactly the same way, a dialog box explains what items will be changed and how.

Each Office file saved as HTML creates a handful of individual files. For example, each graphic, worksheet, or slide in an Office document becomes its own file. To make it easy to manage these multiple files, Office creates a folder with the same name, and in the same location, as the original HTML file for the document. Any Office document saved as a Web page consists of an HTML file and a folder that stores supporting files, such as a file for each graphic, worksheet, slide, and so on.

Opening Web Pages

 WW03E-4-2

After saving a document as a Web page, you can open the Web page, in HTML format, in Word. This allows you to quickly and easily switch from HTML to the standard program format and back again without losing formatting or functionality. For example, if you create a formatted chart in Word, save the presentation file as a Web page, and then reopen the Web page in Word, the chart will look the same as the original did when you created it in Word. Word preserves the original formatting and functionality of the file.

Open an Office Web Page

1. Click the Open button on the Standard toolbar.

2. Click the Files Of Type list arrow, and then click All Web Pages.

3. Click one of the icons on the Places bar for access to often used folders.

4. If necessary, click the Look In list arrow, and then select the folder where the file is located.

5. Click the name of the file.

6. Click Open.

   To open an Office Web page in your default Web browser, click the Open button list arrow, and then click Open In Browser.

Did You Know?

You can create a blank Web page in Word. In Web Layout view, the New Blank Document button on the Standard toolbar changes to the New Web Page button.

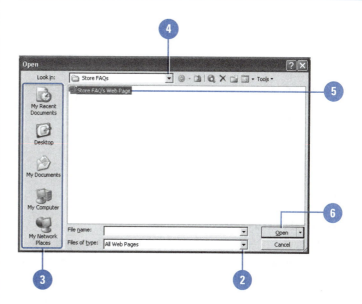

11

Inserting Hyperlinks

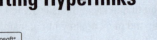

WW03S-2-3

When you reference information included earlier in a document, you had to duplicate material or add a footnote. Now you can create a **hyperlink**—a graphic object or colored, underlined text that you click to move (or **jump**) to a new location (or **destination**). The destination can be in the same document, another file on your computer or network, or a Web page on your intranet or the Internet. Word inserts an absolute link—a hyperlink that jumps to a fixed location—to an Internet destination. Word inserts a relative link—a hyperlink that changes when the hyperlink and destination paths change—between documents. You must move the hyperlink and destination together to keep the link intact.

Insert a Hyperlink Within a Document

1. Click where you want to insert the hyperlink, or select the text or object you want to use as the hyperlink.

2. Click the Insert Hyperlink button on the Standard toolbar.

3. Click Place In This Document.

4. Click a destination in the document.

5. Type the text you want to appear as the hyperlink.

6. Click ScreenTip.

7. Type the text you want to appear when someone points to the hyperlink.

8. Click OK.

9. Click OK.

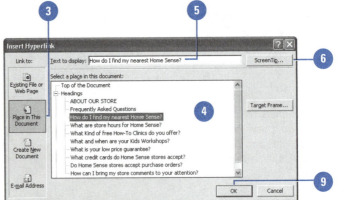

Insert a Hyperlink Between Documents

1. Click where you want to insert the hyperlink, or select the text or object you want to use as the hyperlink.

2. Click the Insert Hyperlink button on the Standard toolbar.

3. Click Existing File Or Web Page.

4. Enter the name and path of the destination file or Web page.

   ◆ Or click the Bookmark button, select the bookmark, and then click OK.

5. Type the text you want to appear as the hyperlink.

6. Click ScreenTip.

7. Type the text you want to appear when someone points to the hyperlink.

8. Click OK.

9. Click OK.

Did You Know?

You can create a hyperlink to send e-mail messages. Click where you want to insert the hyperlink, click the Insert Hyperlink button on the Standard toolbar, click E-Mail Address, enter the recipient's e-mail address, enter a subject, enter the hyperlink display text, and then click OK.

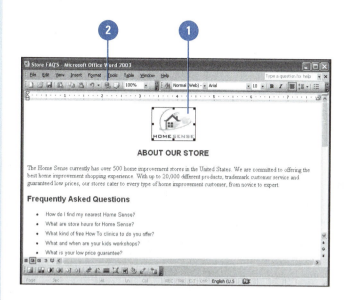

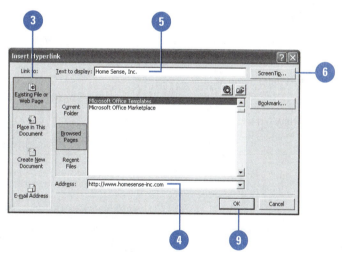

Using and Removing Hyperlinks

WW03S-2-3

Hyperlinks connect you to information in other documents. Rather than duplicating the important information stored in other documents, you can create hyperlinks to the relevant material. When you click a hyperlink for the first time (during a session), the color of the hyperlink changes, indicating that you have accessed the hyperlink. If a link becomes outdated or unnecessary, you can easily revise or remove it. Word repairs broken links. Whenever you save a document with hyperlinks, Word checks the links and repairs any that aren't working. For example, if a file was moved, Word updates the location.

Use a Hyperlink

1. Position the mouse pointer over any hyperlink.

2. Press and hold Ctrl (which changes to a hand pointer), and then click the hyperlink.

   Depending on the type of hyperlink, the screen:

   ◆ Jumps to a new location within the same document.

   ◆ Jumps to a location on an intranet or Internet Web site.

   ◆ Opens a new file and the program in which it was created.

   ◆ Opens Outlook and displays a new e-mail message.

3. Navigate between open hyperlinked documents with the Web toolbar.

   ◆ Click the Back or Forward buttons to move between documents.

   ◆ Click the Start Page button to go to your home page.

   ◆ Click the Search The Web button to go to a search page.

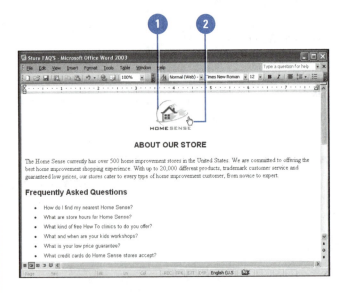

Start Page button

Web toolbar

Search The Web button

Back and Forward buttons

Edit a Hyperlink

1. Right-click the hyperlink you want to edit, and then click Edit Hyperlink.

2. If you want, change the display text.

3. If you want, click ScreenTip, edit the custom text, and then click OK.

4. If necessary, change the destination.

5. Click OK.

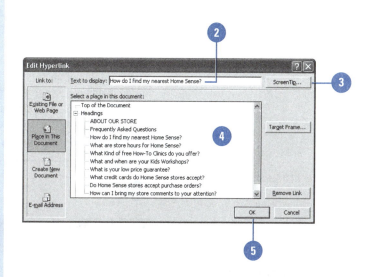

Remove a Hyperlink

1. Right-click the hyperlink you want to remove.

2. Click Remove Hyperlink.

   TIMESAVER *Drag the I-beam pointer across the hyperlink to select it, and then press Ctrl+Shift+F9 to delete a hyperlink.*

3. If necessary, delete the text or object.

Did You Know?

You can display the Web toolbar. Click the View menu, point to Toolbars, and then click Web.

You can format a hyperlink. You can change the look of a hyperlink just as you do other text—select it and apply attributes. Right-click the hyperlink, click Select Hyperlink, and then use the Bold, Italic, Underline, Font, and Font Size buttons on the Formatting toolbar.

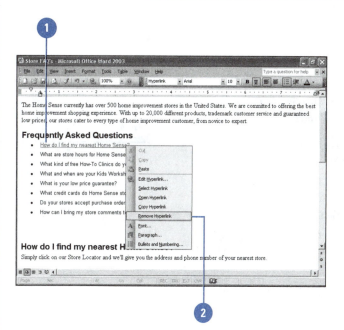

11

Adding a Frame to a Web Page

WW03E-4-2

You can make your Web site easier to navigate by adding **frames**—separate panes that contain unique content and scroll independently. For example, you might place navigation links in one frame and a home page link in another frame. A frame is ideal for a header at the top of a Web page or a table of contents. Word builds a table of contents based on the built-in heading styles (Heading 1, Heading 2, etc.) on the page. After you create a frame, you can create a new page in the frame or set an existing page to display in the frame. You can use Frame Properties to set and name frames as well as modify the frame border.

Add or Remove Frames

1. Open the Word document to which you want to add or remove a frame.

2. Right-click any toolbar, and then click Frames to display the Frames toolbar.

3. Click the appropriate button to add or remove a frame.

    ◆ Click Table of Contents In Frame to create a left frame with a table of contents.

    ◆ Click New Frame Left to create a left frame.

    ◆ Click New Frame Right to create a right frame.

    ◆ Click New Frame Above to create a frame at the top of the page.

    ◆ Click New Frame Below to create a frame at the bottom of the page.

    ◆ Click Delete Frame to delete the frame with the insertion point.

4. If necessary, drag the frame border to resize the frame.

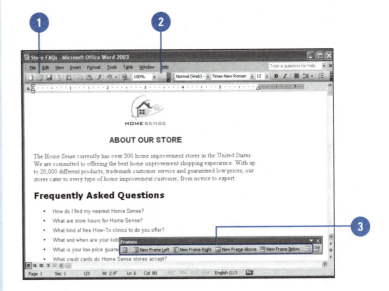

Change Frame Properties

1 Open the Word document or Web page with frames, and then display the Frames toolbar.

2 Click the Frame Properties button on the Frames toolbar.

3 Click the Frame tab.

4 To specify the page you want to display in the frame, click Browse, locate and select the file, and then click Open.

5 To create a dynamic link to the page in the frame, select the Link To File check box.

6 Click the Name list arrow, and then click the name you want.

7 Click OK.

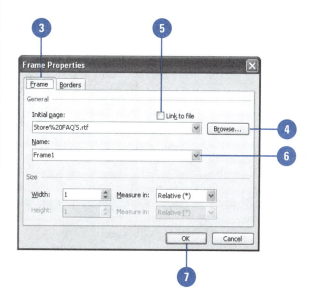

Change Frame Border Properties

1 Open the Word document or Web page with frames, and then display the Frames toolbar.

2 Click the Frame Properties button on the Frames toolbar.

3 Click the Borders tab.

4 Click the No Borders or the Show All Frame Borders option.

5 If you select the Show All Frame Borders option, specify a border width and color, and then select the frame options for the browser you want.

6 Click OK.

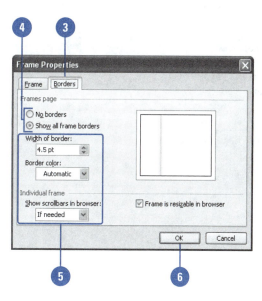

11

Enhancing Web Pages

 WW03E-3-2

Use Themes to Add a Color Scheme

1. Open the Word document to which you want to add a theme.

2. Click the Format menu, and then click Theme.

3. Click a theme to view a sample.

4. Select the check boxes with the options you want.

5. Click OK.

See Also

See "Formatting Text with Special Effects" on page 58 for information on adding text effects, such as Las Vegas Lights and Sparkle Text, to a Web page.

A basic Web page usually includes text, graphics, and hyperlinks. You can change the look of your Web site by selecting a **theme**—a pre-designed visual layout that changes text formatting (such as font type, size, format, and color), as well as bullets, backgrounds, colors, and horizontal lines to create a specific mood. Each theme has two color variations: default and vivid. You can also set the background of the current theme as the background for the Web page or document; otherwise a background color is applied.

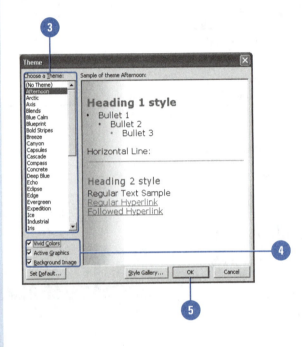

Previewing Web Pages

Microsoft® Office Specialist
Approved Courseware

WW03S-5-6

After you create or enhance a Web page, you should preview it in a Web browser, such as Microsoft Internet Explorer, or Word to make sure others see your Web page the same way you do. **Web Page Preview** displays the open file in your default browser even if you haven't saved it yet. Web Layout view shows you how a document will be displayed on the Web. If the document includes formatting or layouts that cannot be achieved in HTML, Word switches to an HTML layout that closely matches the original look.

Preview a Web Page in a Browser

1. Open the Web page you want to preview.

2. Click the File menu, and then click Web Page Preview.

3. Scroll to view the entire page, click hyperlinks to test them, and so forth.

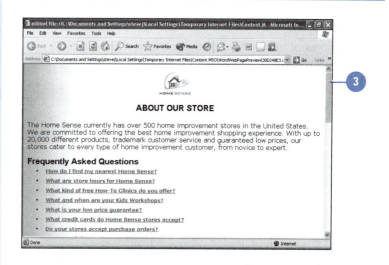

Preview a Web Page in Word

1. Open the Word document you want to preview.

2. Click the Web Layout View button.

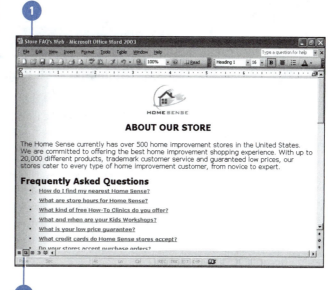

11

Saving Documents as Web Pages

WW03S-5-4, WW03E-4-2

Any existing Word document, or new document that you create, can be saved as a Web Page. When Word saves the document as a Web Page, it automatically converts any Word formatting to **Hypertext Markup Language (HTML)**. HTML is the standard format for posting and viewing data on a Web site. A Web browser, such as Microsoft Internet Explorer, interprets HTML code to determine how to display a Web page. The document that you save as a Web page consists of an HTML file and a folder that stores supporting files, such as graphics. Word selects the appropriate graphic format for you based on the image's content. You can continue to open and work with the file from Word.

Save a Document as a Web Page

1. Open the Office document you want to save as a Web page.

2. Click the File menu, and then click Save As Web Page.

3. Select the drive and folder in which to store the file.

4. Type a name for the file.

5. Click Save.

    The Web page is saved in the selected folder, and the supporting graphics and related files are saved in another folder with the name of the Web page.

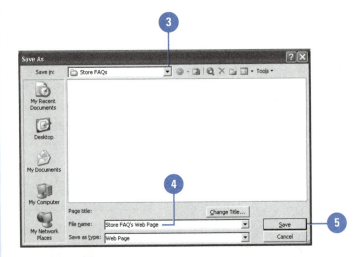

For Your Information

Reducing Web Page Size

You can reduce Web page size by filtering HTML in Word. Filtered HTML reduces the file size of the Web page to make e-mail transmission of the Web page faster or to speed the download and display of the Web page by a browser. To save a Web page in filtered HTML, click the File menu, click Save As Web Page, click the Save As Type list arrow, click Web Page, Filtered, and then click Save. If you save a document as Filtered HTML, and then want to edit the document, you might find that some features of Word are unavailable.

Saving Documents as Single File Web Pages

 WW03S-5-4, WW03E-4-2

A single file Web page saves all the elements of a Web site, including text and graphics, into a single file. When you save a document as a single file Web page, all the Web site elements are stored together in one file in the MHTML format, which is a Microsoft Web page format supported by Internet Explorer 4.0 or later. A single file makes it easy to manage the Web site. When you move the Web site, you don't need to worry about forgetting linked files stored in another folder. A single file also makes it easy to send an entire Web site as an e-mail attachment or transfer it over the Web.

Save a Document as a Single File Web Page

1. Open the Office document you want to save as a Web page.

2. Click the File menu, and then click Save As Web Page.

3. Click the Save As Type list arrow, and then click Single File Web Page.

4. Select the drive and folder in which to store the file.

5. Type a name for the file.

6. Click Save.

    The Web page is saved as a single file.

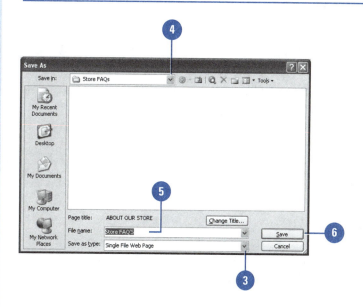

Transferring Files Over the Web

File Transfer Protocol (FTP) is an inexpensive and efficient way to transfer files between your computer and others on the Internet. You can download or receive from another computer any kind of file, including text, graphics, sound, and video files. To download a file, you need an ID and password to identify who you are. Anonymous FTP sites are open to anyone; they usually use *anonymous* as an ID and your full e-mail address as a password. You can also save the FTP site address to revisit the site later.

Add or Modify FTP Locations

① Click the Open button on the Standard toolbar.

② Click the Look In list arrow, and then click Add/Modify FTP Locations.

③ Type the complete address for an FTP site.

④ Type your e-mail address as the password.

⑤ Click Add.

⑥ Click OK.

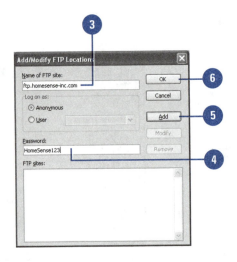

Access an FTP Site

1. Click the Open button on the Standard toolbar.

2. Click the Look In list arrow, and then click the FTP site you want to log in to.

3. Select a Log On As option.

4. Enter a password (your e-mail address or personal password).

5. Click OK.

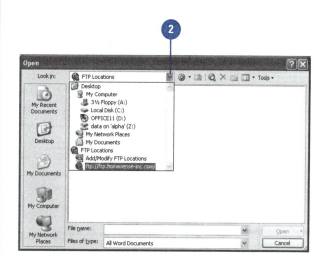

11

Holding an Online Meeting

What's the most convenient way to meet with sales staff from around the world? **NetMeeting**—a conferencing program for meeting and collaborating over the Internet or a corporate intranet. Participants share and exchange information as if they were in one room. The **host** starts the meeting and controls access to the document. When the host allows editing, participants can work on the document one at a time. Otherwise, they cannot make changes, but they can see any changes the host makes. All participants can talk to each other, video conference, share programs, collaborate on documents, send files, exchange messages in Chat, transfer files, and draw on the Whiteboard.

Schedule a Meeting

1. Click the Tools menu, point to Online Collaboration, and then click Schedule Meeting.

2. Enter participants' names or e-mail addresses, a subject, and the meeting location.

3. Click Browse, and then double-click a document you want to send.

4. Select a start and end date and time.

5. Type a message.

6. Click the Send button.

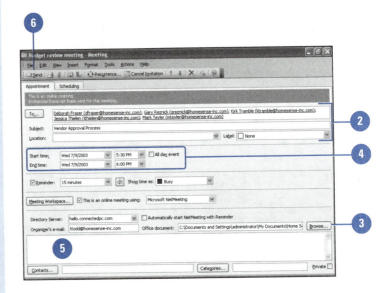

Hold a Meeting

1. Open the document you want to share.

2. Click the Tools menu, point to Online Collaboration, and then click Meet Now.

3. If this is your first meeting, enter your personal information, select a server, and then click OK.

4. Select the participants for the meeting, and then click Call.

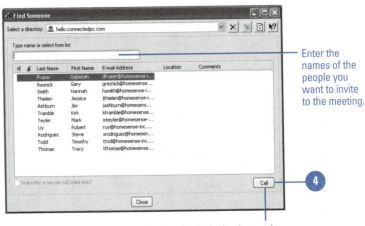

Enter the names of the people you want to invite to the meeting.

Click to start NetMeeting running in the background.

Collaborate in an Online Meeting

1. As the host, click the Allow Others To Edit button on the Online Meeting toolbar.

2. When collaboration is turned on, click anywhere in the document to gain control. If you are a participant, double-click anywhere in the document to gain control.

3. Click the Allow Others To Edit button again to turn off the collaboration, or press Esc if you don't have control of the document.

Participate in an Online Meeting

◆ Use the buttons on the Online Meeting toolbar to participate in an online meeting.

Did You Know?

You can join an online meeting. If you receive an online meeting call, click Accept in the Join Meeting dialog box. If you receive an Outlook reminder for the meeting, click Start This NetMeeting (host), or Join This NetMeeting (participant). To receive an Outlook reminder to join a meeting, you need to have accepted the meeting from an e-mail message.

Online Meeting Toolbar

Button	Description
	Allows the host to invite additional participants to the online meeting
	Allows the host to remove a participant from the online meeting
	Allows participants to edit and control the presentation during the online meeting
	Allows participants to send messages in a Chat session during the online meeting
	Allows participants to draw or type on the Whiteboard during the online meeting
	Allows either the host to end the online meeting for the group or a participant to disconnect

11

Creating a Web Form

WW03E-3-1

Creating forms for online use differs slightly from the normal Word form. To create a Web form, you must work in a Web page in Word and use the Web Tools toolbar rather than the Forms toolbar. Using the Web Tools toolbar, you can insert text boxes, buttons, scrolling text bars that move across the page, background sounds, and movies (including streaming video media, such as Windows Media Player) in a Web form. After you create a Web form, you can save the document as a Web page, and then post it on the Web.

Create an Online Form

1. Click the View menu, point to Toolbars, and then click Web Tools.

2. Position the insertion point where you want to insert controls.

3. Use the Web Tools toolbar to insert online form fields.

   ◆ Click the Checkbox, Option Button, Drop Down Box, List Box, Textbox, Text Area, Submit, Submit with Image, Reset, or Password button to insert the form field.

   ◆ Click the Scrolling Text, Movie, or Sound button to open a dialog box with additional options. Specify the options you want for the control, select a file, and then click OK.

4. Click the Properties button on the Web Tools toolbar.

5. Designate the properties for the form control by using either the Alphabetic or Categorized tab, both of which contain the same information, organized slightly different.

6. After making your modifications, click the Design Mode button on the Web Tools toolbar to apply your choices and test the form.

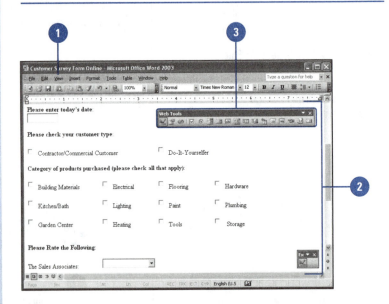

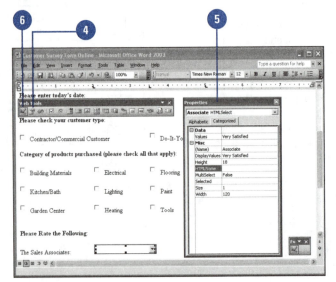

Working with E-Mail and Faxes

Introduction

When you create or edit an e-mail message, Microsoft Office Outlook 2003 takes advantage of the editing and formatting features in Microsoft Office Word 2003. You can use Word as your e-mail editor to lay out the information in your messages and create the exact look and mood you want. You can get the look you want by adding formatting text effects, changing text alignment, adjusting line and paragraph spacing, setting tabs and indents, and creating bulleted and numbered lists. When you're done, your e-mail is sure to demand attention and convey your message in its appearance.

The quickest way to send a copy of a document is to send an electronic copy by e-mail. The E-Mail button on the Standard toolbar opens a new message in your e-mail program and inserts a standard message header at the top of the open file so you can send it as an e-mail message. However, if you need to send the entire file to someone, you can send it as an attachment to your e-mail message. With an attachment, the recipient can open, modify, and save changes to the document. When you add an attachment to a message, an attachment icon appears under the Subject box, identifying the name and size of the attachment.

If e-mail is not an option, and you need to fax, you should have a fax sheet that goes ahead of your document to the recipient. Word offers three template varieties of these basic fax cover sheets—Contemporary, Elegant, and Professional. Each of these can be edited in template form, or used with the Fax Wizard. If you have hardware and software installed on your computer to send and receive faxes, you can fax a document directly from Word using the Fax Wizard. You'll be prompted to create a fax cover sheet to send ahead of your document, all this can be done without leaving Word.

What You'll Do

Use Word for E-Mail Messages

Create an E-Mail Message

Set Default Formatting for E-Mail Messages

Reduce the Size of E-Mail Messages

Send a Document as E-Mail

Send a Document File by E-Mail

Create a Fax Cover Sheet

Send a Document as a Fax

Using Word for E-Mail Messages

When you create an e-mail message in Outlook, the default e-mail editor is Microsoft Word unless you change it to the Outlook editor. With Word as the default editor, you can take advantage of Word's powerful editing and formatting tools, which include AutoCorrect, automatic spelling and grammar checking, automatic bullets and numbering, tables, conversion of e-mail names and Internet addresses, themes, and AutoFormat. If you often receive the message "This message contains formatting that is best viewed with Microsoft Word. Click here to display in Word," you need to set the option to view Rich Text formatted messages.

Use Word for E-Mail Messages

1. In Microsoft Office Outlook 2003, click the Tools menu, and then click Options.

2. Click the Mail Format tab.

3. Select the Use Microsoft Office Word 2003 To Edit E-Mail Messages check box.

4. Select the Use Microsoft Office Word 2003 To Read Rich Text E-Mail Messages check box.

5. Click OK.

6. To create and send a message in Outlook, click the New Mail Message button on the Standard toolbar, compose your message, and then click the Send button.

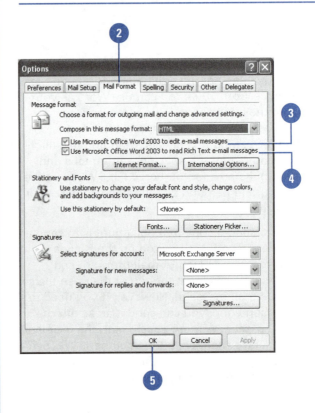

Did You Know?

You can set Word as your e-mail editor for one new message.
In Outlook 2003, click the Actions menu, point to New Mail Message Using, point to Microsoft Office, and then click Microsoft Word Document.

Creating an E-Mail Message

If you're using Microsoft Office Outlook 2003 as your e-mail program, you can start an e-mail message from Word using the New Document task pane, compose the message in an Outlook e-mail message window, and then send it. When you send the message, the e-mail is sent to the Outbox in Outlook. If Outlook is running, the message is sent right away, otherwise the message is sent the next time you start Outlook.

Create an E-Mail Message

1. Click the File menu, and then click New.

2. Click E-Mail Message on the task pane.

   Outlook starts and opens a new e-mail message.

3. Type an e-mail address or click To to select one from your Address Book or Contacts list.

4. Type a subject.

5. Type a message.

6. Click the Send button on the toolbar.

   The message is sent to the Outbox in Outlook. The message is only sent right away when Outlook is running.

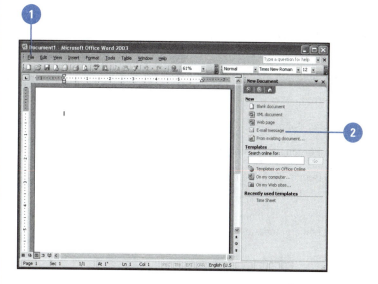

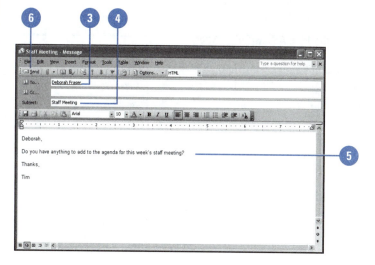

12

Setting Default Formatting for E-Mail Messages

If you're using Word to compose and send messages, you can set the default formatting for your e-mail messages in Word. You can use the E-Mail Options dialog box in Word to set default formatting and add e-mail signatures for your messages. When you set default formatting, you can add a theme and change font styles for new messages. If you need multiple signatures, you can add more than one. When you change settings in the E-Mail Options dialog box in Word, your changes are also set in Microsoft Office Outlook 2003.

Set the Default Format

1. Click the Tools menu, and then click Options.

2. Click the General tab.

3. Click E-Mail Options.

4. Click the Personal Stationery tab.

5. To add a theme, click Theme, select a theme, and then click OK.

6. Click Font to specify font styles for different types of messages.

7. Select the Mark My Comments With check box, and then enter a name, if necessary, to include a name with comments.

8. Select the Pick A New Color When Replying Or Forwarding check box to use a different color when replying or forwarding a message.

9. Click OK.

10. Click OK.

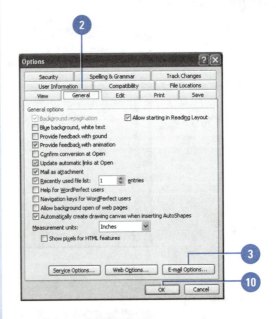

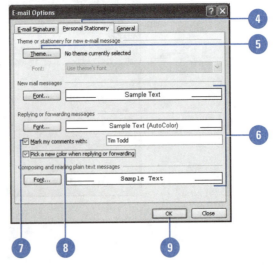

Add a Signature

1. Click the Tools menu, and then click Options.

2. Click the General tab.

3. Click E-Mail Options.

4. Click the E-Mail Signature tab.

5. Type a name for the signature.

6. Type the signature you want.

7. Use the formatting tools to format the signature.

8. Click Add.

9. To create another signature, click New, and follow Steps 5 to 8.

10. Specify the signature you want to use for each type of message or select None.

11. Click OK.

12. Click OK.

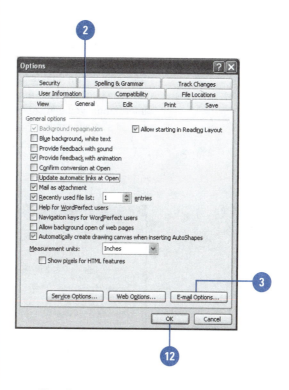

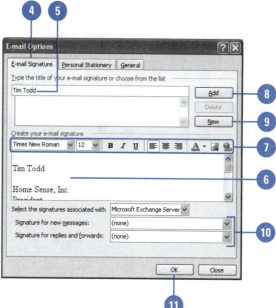

12

Reducing the Size of E-Mail Messages

When you send an Office document in an e-mail, the message includes formatting and smart tag information specific to Office programs. If you or those who receive the document don't plan to edit the material, you can use the high or medium option to reduce the size of your e-mail. Cascading Style Sheets (CSS) provide consistent formatting and layout for Web pages. If your recipients use CSS or need access to smart tag information, you can select the CSS and smart tag options to reduce e-mail size even more.

Reduce the Size of E-Mail Messages

1. Click the Tools menu, and then click Options.

2. Click the General tab.

3. Click E-Mail Options.

4. Click the General tab.

5. Select the HTML Filtering option (None, Medium, or High) you want. If you plan to edit the document in Word, click the None option.

6. Select the Rely On CSS For Font Formatting check box to use cascading style sheets, a Web page formatting feature.

7. Select the Save Smart Tags In E-Mail check box to provide access to smart tag information in the document.

8. Click OK.

9. Click OK.

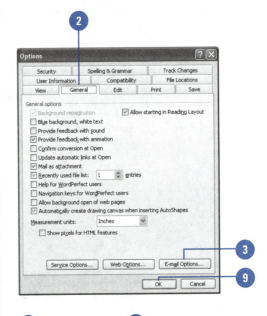

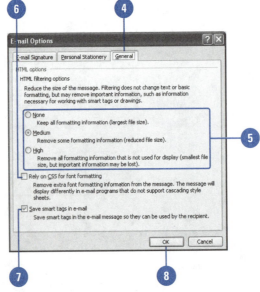

Sending a Document as E-Mail

WW03S-4-1

Send a Document as E-Mail

1 Open the document you want to send as e-mail.

2 Click the E-Mail button on the Standard toolbar.

3 Type an address and subject.

The subject line of the e-mail will contain the file name of the presentation that you are sending.

4 Type an introductory message.

5 Click the Send A Copy button on the toolbar.

Did You Know?

You can select names from your address book or contacts list in Outlook. In the e-mail message window, click the To button, click recipient names in the Name list, and then click To, Cc, or Bcc.

You can cancel the message without sending it. Click the E-Mail button on the Standard toolbar again.

The quickest way to send a copy of a document is to send an electronic copy by e-mail. Without having to open your e-mail program and attach the file, you can send any document to others from within Word. The E-Mail button on the Standard toolbar opens a new message in your e-mail program and inserts a standard message header at the top of the open file so you can send it as an e-mail message. When you send a document in an e-mail message, the recipient can only review the document.

12

Sending a Document File by E-Mail

WW03S-4-1

You can also send the entire document file as an attachment to your e-mail message. With an attachment, the recipient can open, modify, and save changes to the document. When you add an attachment to a message, an attachment icon appears under the Subject box, identifying the name and size of the attachment. Although you can add multiple attachments to a message, you should limit the number and size of the attachments. The size of the attachment affects the time it takes to send the message. The larger the attached file, the longer it takes to send. If an attached file is too large, the message might not be sent; the e-mail server might not be able to transfer it across its network. After you send the message with the attachment, message recipients can double-click the attachment icon to open and view the file.

Send a File by E-Mail

1. Open the document you want to send as an e-mail attachment.

2. Click the File menu, point to Send To, and then click Mail Recipient (As Attachment).

3. Type an address and subject.

   The subject line of the e-mail will contain the file name of the document you are sending.

4. Type a message.

5. Click the Send button on the toolbar.

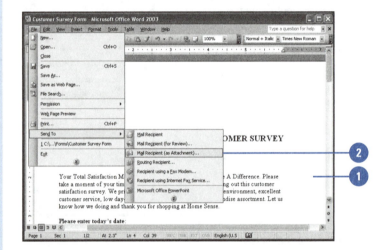

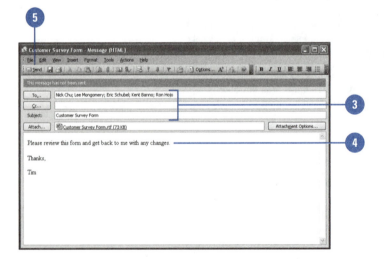

Creating a Fax Cover Sheet

Word offers three varieties of basic fax cover sheets: Contemporary, Elegant, and Professional. Each of these can be edited in template form, or used with the Fax Wizard. If you use the Fax Wizard, you can select the document and fax program you want to use, enter the name and fax number of multiple recipients, select a fax cover template, and specify sender information. If you are sending an individual fax, the basic cover sheets work the best. If you are sending a fax to multiple recipients, the Fax Wizard makes it easy to create multiple cover sheets using mail merge, which saves you time.

Create a Fax Cover Sheet

1. Click the File menu, and then click New.

2. Click On My Computer on the task pane.

3. Click the Letters & Faxes tab.

4. Double-click a fax icon such as: (Contemporary Fax, Elegant Fax, Professional Fax, or Fax Wizard).

5. If you're using the Fax Wizard, step through the dialog boxes, and then click Finish when you're done. Depending on your fax program, your steps will differ.

   ◆ Select a document.

   ◆ Select a fax program.

   ◆ Enter the name and fax number of each recipient.

   ◆ Select the style of the cover sheet.

   ◆ Specify sender information.

6. When the fax template opens, you can modify and print it.

See Also

See "Creating a Form Letter" on page 176 for information on using mail merge fields in a document.

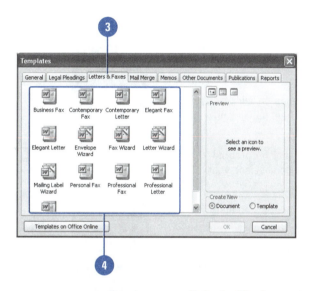

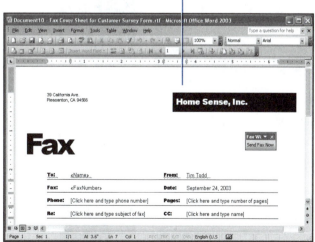

Professional Fax document

12

Sending a Document as a Fax

If you have hardware and software installed on your computer to send and receive faxes, you can fax a document directly from Word using the Fax Wizard. The Fax Wizard makes it easy to create a cover sheet and send a document as a fax. The wizard steps you through the entire process, asking you questions about the document you want to use, fax program, recipients, and cover sheet. If you use Microsoft Fax, the service is typically configured so that you can't use your own cover sheet.

Send a Document as a Fax

1. Open the document you want to send as a fax.

2. Click the File menu, point to Send To, and then click Recipient Using A Fax Modem.

3. Read the introduction, click Next, click a cover sheet option, and then click Next.

   Depending on your fax program and the options you select, your steps will differ.

4. Select a fax program, and then click Next.

5. Specify the recipient's names and fax numbers to whom you want to fax, and then click Next.

6. If necessary, specify the recipients you want to use, and then click Next.

7. If you selected to use a cover sheet, select a style, and then click Next.

8. Specify your name, company, mailing address, phone and fax, and then click Next.

9. When you complete the wizard, click Finish.

10. Modify the fax template, and then send it using your faxing program.

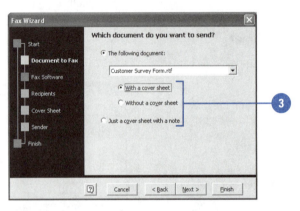

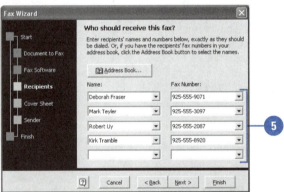

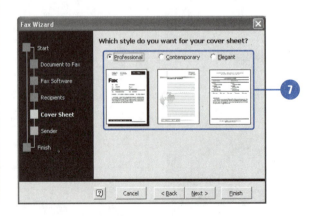

Reviewing and Sharing Documents

Introduction

If you work in an office environment with Microsoft Office Word 2003, or are part of some other group that routinely collaborates in document preparation, learning the basics of document sharing is a must. The greater the number of people that interact with a document before it reaches final form, the more critical it becomes for you to keep track of versions, comments, the source of all editing marks, and adequately manage the process of correcting them.

Forms are an easy way to collect information in a consistent manner, such as a survey, invoice, or order form. With a form you can ask specific questions and get the response in the format that you want, such as yes/no, itemized list, or a brief comment. Forms can be either printed or online documents with instructions, questions, and fields where users can enter their responses.

Because working together on a document may be crucial to the success of it's completion, there might be various levels of security that need to be set for your readers. Some may have full access to read and make changes, while others are limited to just reading the document, and still other may only be able to read part of the document because it contains hidden text.

When sending document files through e-mail and transferring them to others, a new feature called Information Rights Management (IRM) greatly protects your document from getting in the wrong hands. With IRM, you can restrict the document from getting forwarded to others that weren't on your original send to list. In Word, you can send out a document for review using e-mail, from within Word. You can also set up a routing process when you send it out for review. By listing the e-mail addresses of your recipients, the document is transferred to the list, and you receive confirmation each step of the way.

Creating Multiple Document Versions

WW03E-4-3

If you want a record of changes made to a document, you can save different versions of a document within the same document. When you save different versions within Word, you also save disk space because Word saves only the differences between versions, not an entire copy of each document. After you've saved several versions of the document, you can go back and review, open, print, and delete earlier versions. Before you can modify an earlier version, you must open that version and use the Save As command to save it as a separate file. You can also have Word save a version of your document each time you close the document. You cannot access this feature when you save a document as a Web page.

Create Document Versions Automatically

1. Click the File menu, and then click Versions.

2. Select the Automatically Save A Version On Close check box.

3. Click Close.

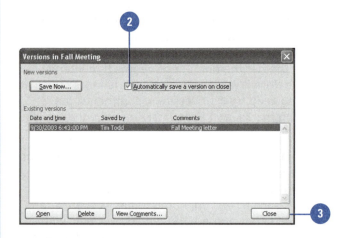

Save a Document Version

1. Click the File menu, and then click Versions.

2. Click Save Now.

3. Type descriptive information about the version you're saving.

4. Click OK.

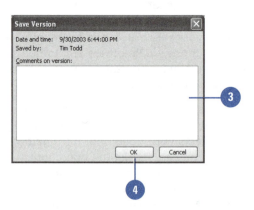

Open a Document Version

1. Click the File menu, and then click Versions.

2. Click the file you want to open.

3. Click Open.

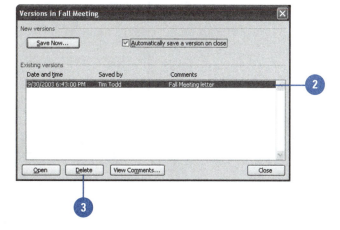

Delete a Document Version

1. Click the File menu, and then click Versions.

2. Click the file you want to delete.

3. Click Delete, and then click Yes to confirm the deletion.

13

Inserting Comments

WW03S-4-3

Comments are useful when someone who is editing the document has queries pertaining to the document. Perhaps a particular passage needs to be clarified, or the formatting of an item is inconsistent and the editor is uncertain what the author's intentions were in applying that formatting. When a comment is inserted in Print Layout view, it opens a dialog balloon where the editor can type the question. When in Normal view, it opens a window at the bottom of the document where comments are inserted and viewed. Each comment includes the name and initials of the person who made the comment, which you can change in the Options dialog box.

Set User Information for Comments

1. Click the Tools menu, and then click Options.

2. Click the User Information tab.

3. Type your name.

4. Type your initials.

5. Click OK.

Insert a Comment

1. Position the insertion pointer where you want to insert a comment.

2. Click the View menu, point to Toolbars, and then click Reviewing.

3. Click the Insert menu, and then click Comment or click the Insert Comment button on the Reviewing toolbar.

4. Type your comment in the balloon, and then click outside the balloon to save it.

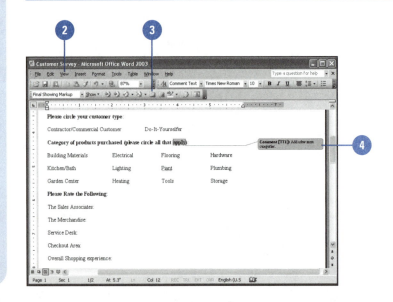

Read a Comment

1️⃣ Click the View menu, point to Toolbars, and then click Reviewing to display the toolbar.

2️⃣ Click the Show button on the Reviewing toolbar, and then click Comments.

3️⃣ Read the comment.

4️⃣ Click the Previous or Next button on the Reviewing toolbar to read another comment.

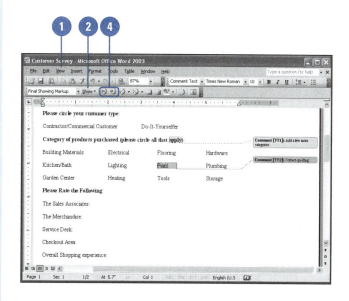

Edit a Comment

1️⃣ Click the View menu, point to Toolbars, and then click Reviewing to display the toolbar.

2️⃣ Click the Show button on the Reviewing toolbar, and then click Comments.

3️⃣ Click the text in the comment, make your changes, and then click outside the balloon to save it.

Did You Know?

You can quickly delete a comment. Right-click the comment, and then click Delete Comment.

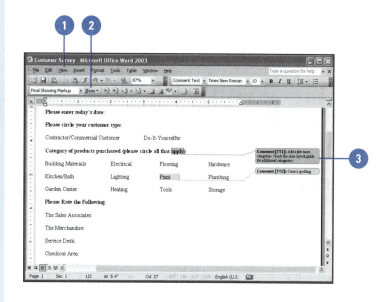

13

Using Track Changes

 WW03S-4-4

Tracking changes in a document allows you to make revisions to a document without losing the original text. Word shows changed text in a different color from the original text and uses revision marks, such as underlines, to distinguish the revised text from the original. You can review changes by using the Reviewing toolbar, which contains buttons that let you accept and reject changes and comments. If you compare and merge two documents, you can review the changes and accept or reject the results.

Track Changes as You Work

1. Open the document you want to edit.

2. Click the Tools menu, and then click Track Changes. The TRK box on the Status bar becomes active.

   TIMESAVER *Double-click TRK on the status bar or press Ctrl+Shift+E to turn tracking on or off.*

3. Make changes to your document. The changes are reflected using alternate color characters, along with comments in balloons at the side of the screen (if you are in Print Layout view) or displayed in a separate window at the bottom of the screen (if you are in Normal view).

4. Click the Track Changes button on the Reviewing toolbar to turn off track changes.

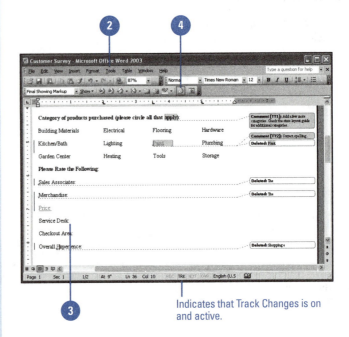

Indicates that Track Changes is on and active.

Did You Know?

You can show or hide balloons.
Click the Tools menu, click Options, click the Track Changes tab, click the Use Balloons list arrow, and then select Always, Never, or Only for Comments/Formatting.

Review Changes

1 Open the document you want to review.

2 Click the View menu, point to Toolbars, and then click Reviewing.

3 Use the buttons on the Reviewing toolbar to review changes:

◆ Click the Next button or the Previous button to view changes one at a time.

◆ Click the Accept Change button or the Reject Change/Delete Comment button to respond to the revisions.

◆ Click the Accept Change button list arrow, and then click Accept All Changes In Document to accept all changes at once.

◆ Click the Reject Change button list arrow, and then click Reject All Changes In Document to reject all changes at once.

Did You Know?

You can display different versions of reviewing marks. Click the Display For Review list arrow on the Reviewing toolbar, and then select an option (Final Showing Markup, Final, Original Showing Markup, or Original).

You can show or hide individual reviewers. Click the Show button on the Reviewing toolbar, point to Reviewers, and then click the reviewer you want to show or hide.

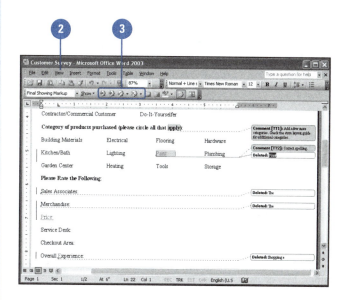

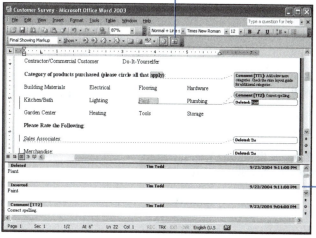

Click to display Reviewing pane

Reviewing pane

Modifying Track Changes Options

WW03E-4-1

You can customize the way track changes marks up a document. When you make insertion, deletion, and formatting changes, you can change the markup text to display the change with a specific color or formatting style, such as bold, italic, underline, double underline, and strikethrough. If you are using balloons in Print and Web Layout views, you can specify a preferred size and location in your document. If you prefer not to use balloons, you can turn the option off.

Modify Track Changes Options

1. Click the Tools menu, and then click Options.

2. Click the Track Changes tab.

3. Specify the markup options you want when you make changes.

   ◆ **Insertions.** Marks inserted text.

   ◆ **Deletions.** Marks deleted text.

   ◆ **Formatting.** Marks formatting changes.

   ◆ **Changed Lines.** Sets the location of vertical line that marks changed paragraphs.

   ◆ **Comments Color.** Sets the color applied to all comments.

4. Specify the balloons options you want.

   ◆ **Use Balloons (Print And Web Layout).** Sets display option for balloons.

   ◆ **Preferred Width.** Sets balloon width.

   ◆ **Margin.** Sets margin location for balloons.

5. Click OK.

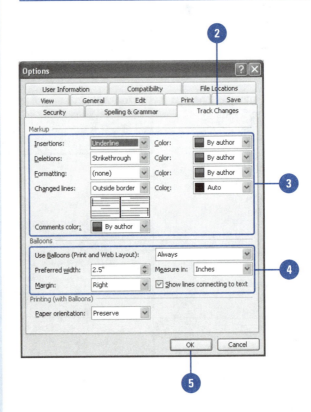

Comparing and Merging Documents

 WW03S-4-2

If you want to compare an earlier version of a document with the current version of a document or if you receive multiple edited versions of the original document back from the recipients, you can compare the documents and merge the changes into one document. The changes can be merged into one document or viewed for comparison. For example, you can compare a newer version of a document with an older one to view the differences. When you compare or merge documents, the text that differs between the two versions will be highlighted in a different color or with track reviewing marks.

13

Compare and Merge Documents

1. Open a document which you want to compare and merge.

2. Click the Tools menu, and then click Compare And Merge Documents.

3. Select the document you want to compare and merge.

4. Click Merge or click the Merge button list arrow, and then click one of the following:

   ◆ Merge to display the results in the original document.

   ◆ Merge Into Current Document to display the results in the newer document that is currently open.

   ◆ Merge Into New Document to display the results in a new document.

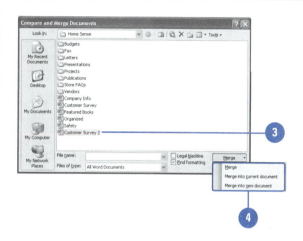

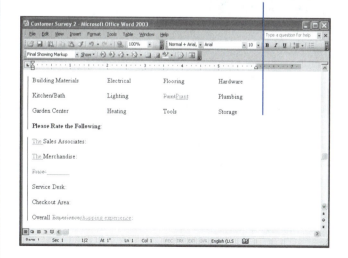

Merged document in Normal view

Creating a Form

WW03E-3-1

Forms are an easy way for you to interact with users of your documents, either online or in print, and gain information and feedback from them in the process. Form fields are predefined places where users enter their answers to the questions on the form. Word includes many different types of form fields: text boxes for typed entries, data fields, time fields, fields that perform calculations, and check boxes, where users can click the box that represents either answer. After you insert the fields you want, you can change field properties to customize the form.

Create a Form

1. Click the View menu, point to Toolbars, and then click Forms.

2. Position the insertion point where you want to insert a form field.

3. Use the Forms toolbar to insert form fields.

   ◆ To insert a fill-in field (where users can enter text), click the Text Form Field button on the Forms toolbar, so that you can specify a default entry the user can either leave as is, or edit.

   ◆ To insert a check box next to an option that users either select or deselect by clicking, click the Check Box Form Field button on the Forms toolbar.

   ◆ Click the Insert Table button or the Draw Table button on the Forms toolbar to create and modify a table using the Tables and Borders toolbar.

   ◆ Click the Insert Frame button on the Forms toolbar to provide boundaries for your form. Drag to create a frame.

   ◆ To provide a shading effect within a form field, click the Form Field Shading button on the Forms toolbar.

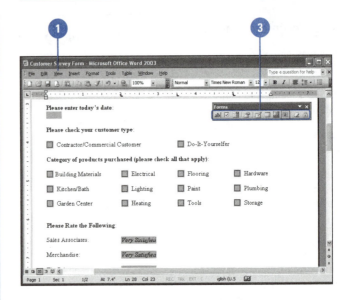

Change Form Field Properties

1. Click the View menu, point to Toolbars, and then click Forms.

2. Select the form field you want to modify.

3. Click the Form Field Options button on the Forms toolbar.

4. Select the new options you want for the form field.

5. Click OK.

Did You Know?

You can reset form fields to default settings. Click the Reset Form Fields button on the Forms toolbar.

You can protect a form. Click the Protect Form button on the Forms toolbar to prevent users of the form from being able to edit its content (not their answers, but the questions and choices themselves).

See Also

See "Creating a Web Form" on page 264 for information on creating other types of forms.

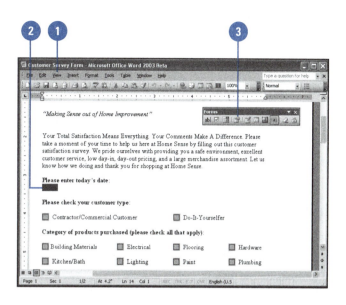

Text Form Field Options dialog box

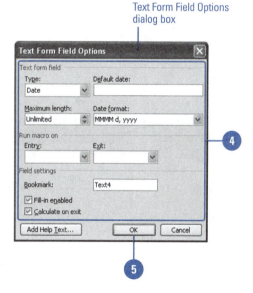

Setting Password Protection

WW03E-4-4

File encryption is additional security you can apply to a document. **File encryption** scrambles your password to protect your document from unauthorized people breaking into the file. You can use the Security tab in the Options dialog box to set password protection using file encryption. If you are aware of file encryption types, you can select the one you want to use. You don't have to worry about the encryption, Word handles everything. All you need to do is remember the password. At times, you will want the information to be used but not changed. Setting a document as read-only is useful when you want a document, such as a company-wide bulletin, to be distributed and read, but not changed. Password protection takes effect the next time you open the document.

Set a File Encryption Password

1 Open the document you want to protect.

2 Click the Tools menu, and then click Options.

3 Click the Security tab.

4 Enter the new password.

5 Click Advanced.

6 Choose your type of encryption, and then click OK.

7 Click OK.

8 Retype the password, and then click OK.

> **IMPORTANT** *Be careful not to forget or lose the password, because a file that is password protected can't be opened again without the password.*

Did You Know?

You can remove file encryption. Click the Tools menu, click Options, click the Security tab, delete the file encryption password, and then click OK.

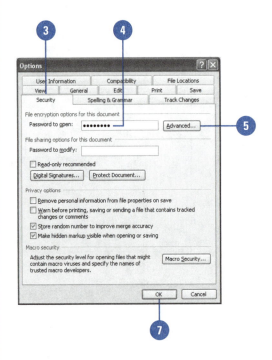

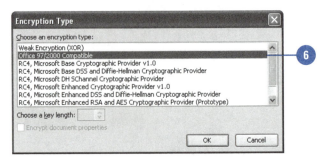

Set a Password to Modify a Document

1. Open the document you want to protect, inputting the previous password to do so.

2. Click the Tools menu, and then click Options.

3. Click the Security tab.

4. Enter the new password.

5. To display a read-only recommendation when the document is opened, select the Read-Only Recommended check box.

6. Click OK.

7. Retype your password, and then click OK.

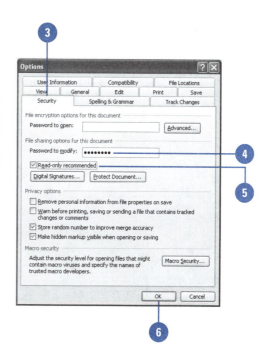

Open a Document with Password Protection

1. Click the Open button on the Standard toolbar, navigate to a document with password protection, and then click Open.

2. Click Read Only if you do not wish to modify the document, or type the password in the Password dialog box.

3. Click OK.

Password dialog box to modify a document.

Click to open read only version.

Adding a Digital Signature

WW03E-4-5

Word uses Microsoft Authenticode technology to help you protect your Office documents and macros by using a **digital signature**, or digital ID. A digital ID protects the sender's identity. It contains a private key, which stays on the sender's computer, and a digital certificate that contains a public key. The certificate is sent with digitally signed documents and it contains the key to decipher messages from the sender. Before you can add a digital signature to a document, you need to get a certificate. You can get a digital signature and more information on security options from microsoft at: *http://office.microsoft.com*.

Add a Digital Signature to a Document

1. Click the Tools menu, and then click Options.

2. Click the Security tab.

3. Click Digital Signatures.

4. If necessary, click Add, select a certificate, and then click OK.

5. Click the certificate you want to attach to your digital signature.

6. Click OK.

7. Click OK.

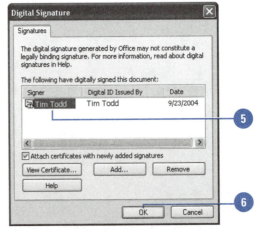

Setting Macro Security

When you open a document, you might be prompted with a security alert. Documents can include additional programming codes called macros, which can contain viruses. You can protect your computer from viruses by running up-to-date antivirus software and setting your macro security level to high for maximum protection or medium for lesser protection. If macro security is set to medium, document users will be prompted to enable macros.

Set Macro Security Options

1 Click the Tools menu, and then click Options.

2 Click the Security tab.

3 Click Macro Security.

4 Click the security option you want.

◆ **High.** Disables all macros except those digitally signed by a trusted source.

◆ **Medium.** Allows you to choose whether or not to run macros.

◆ **Low.** Allows all macros to run in the document.

5 Click OK.

6 Click OK.

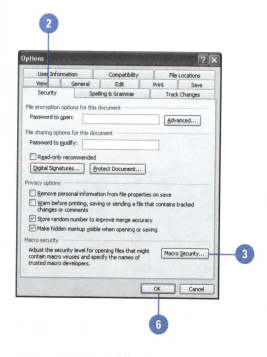

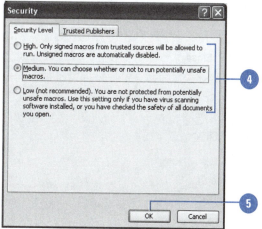

Protecting a Document

 WW03E-4-4

You can use the security options in Word to protect the integrity of your documents as others review it. At times, you will want the information in a document to be used, but not changed; at other times, you might want only specific people in your office to be able to view the document. When you set a password to a document, take a moment to write it down exactly as it was entered; the password is case-sensitive. Word doesn't keep a list of passwords. If you lose or forget the password for a protected document, you will not be able to open it.

Protect a Document

1. Click the Tools menu, and then click Protect Document.

2. Select or clear the Limit Formatting To A Selection Of Styles check box.

3. Select the Allow Only This Type Of Editing In The Document check box.

4. Click the Editing Restrictions list arrow, and then select an editing restriction.

5. Select the groups you want to edit the document and any document area restrictions.

6. Click Yes, Start Enforcing Protection.

7. Type a password, and then type the password again to confirm it.

8. Click OK.

9. When you're done, click the Close button on the task pane.

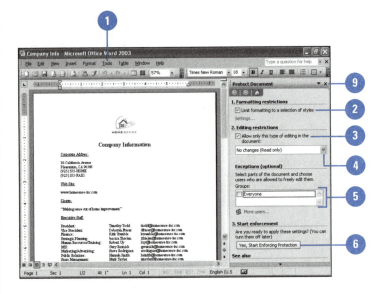

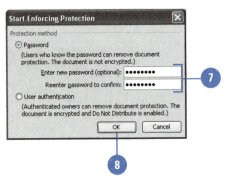

> ### Did You Know?
>
> **You can un-protect a document.** Click the Tools menu, click Un-protect Document, type the password, click OK, clear the Allow Only This Type Of Editing In The Document check box, and then close the task pane.

Hiding Text

WW03S-1-1, WW03S-5-7

If you have confidential information in a document or text that you don't want others to see, you can hide the text. When you hide text, you can't view or print the text unless you select the Hidden Text option in the Options dialog box. When you display or print hidden text, the characters appear with a dotted lined underneath. Hiding text does not protect your text from being seen, but it does conceal it from others.

Hide or Unhide Text

1. Select the text you want to hide or the hidden text.

2. Click the Format menu, and then click Font.

3. Click the Font tab.

4. Select or clear the Hidden check box.

5. Click OK.

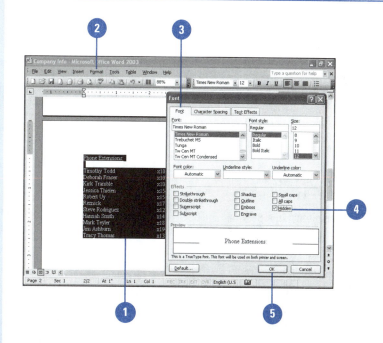

Display or Print Hidden Text

1. Click the Tools menu, and then click Options.

2. Click the View tab.

3. Select the Hidden Text check box.

4. Click the Print tab.

5. Select the Hidden Text check box.

6. Click OK.

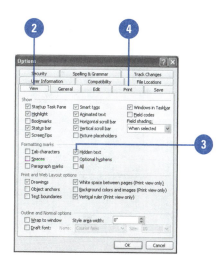

Restricting Document Access

You can use Information Rights Management (IRM) in Office 2003 programs to provide restricted access to Office documents. In Outlook, you can use IRM to create messages with restricted permission to help prevent documents from being forwarded, printed, copied, or edited by unauthorized people. If you attach a document to an Outlook message, the document also contains the restriction. IRM uses a server to authenticate the credentials of people who create or receive documents or e-mail with restricted permission. For Microsoft Office users without access to one of these servers, Microsoft provides a free trial IRM service, which requires a .NET Passport.

Set Up Information Rights Management

1. Click the File menu, point to Permission, and then click Restrict Permission As.

2. Click Yes to download and install IRM. Follow the wizard instructions.

   Upon completion, the Service Sign-Up Wizard opens.

3. Click the Yes, I Want To Sign Up For This Free Trial Service From Microsoft option.

4. Click Next, and then follow the remaining instructions to create a .NET Passport and complete the service sign-up.

5. Click Cancel.

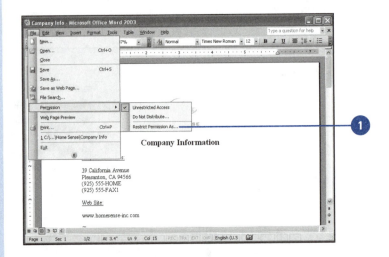

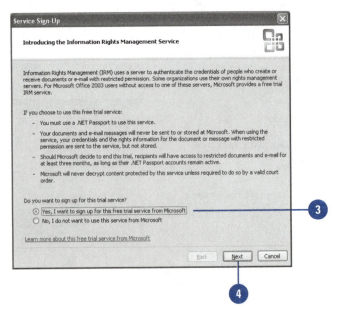

Create a Document with Restricted Permission

1. Open the document you want to restrict permission.

2. Click the File menu, point to Permission, and then click Restrict Permission As.

3. Click the user with the permissions to create or open restricted content.

4. Click OK.

5. Select the Restrict Permission To This Document check box.

6. Enter e-mail addresses of users in the Read and Change boxes or click the Read or Change button to select users from your Address Book.

7. Click More Options.

8. Select the check boxes with the specific permissions you want.

9. Click OK.

   A restricted message appears above the address name.

Did You Know?

You can unrestrict a document. Click the File menu, point to Permission, and then click Unrestricted Access.

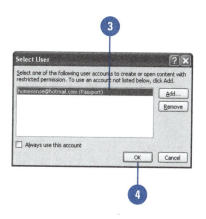

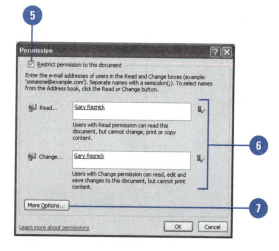

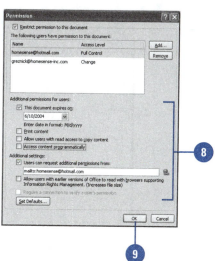

Sending a Document for Review

 Microsoft Office Specialist Approved Courseware

WW03S-4-1

Send a Document for Review

1. Open the document you want to send for review.

2. Click the File menu, point to Send To, and then click Mail Recipient (For Review).

3. Type the e-mail addresses of the recipients you want to receive the document, or click To, select names from the address book, and then click OK.

4. If you want, type a message in the message box.

5. Click Send.

The message includes the text "Please review the attached document.". The subject line of the e-mail will contain the file name of the document that you are sending.

After you finish making changes to a document, you can quickly send it to another person for review using e-mail. Word allows you to send documents out for review using e-mail from within the program so that you do not have to open your e-mail program. However, you need to have an e-mail program installed, such as Microsoft Office Outlook, Outlook Express, Microsoft Exchange, or some 32-bit e-mail program that's compatible with the Messaging Application Programming Interface (MAPI), on your computer and an e-mail account set-up.

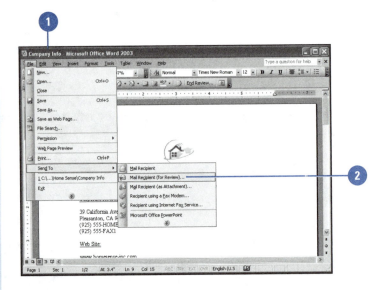

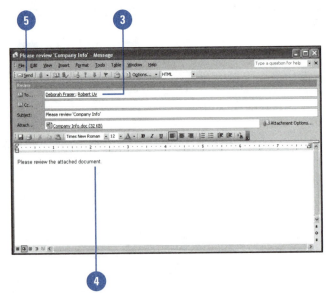

Routing a Document

WW03S-4-1

Most groups who collaborate on documents have a routing process already established. A routing process defines the sequence in which various individuals review, edit, or comment on a document before it reaches its final form. You can define this order when you send a document out for review.

13

Route a Document for Review

1. Open the document you want to route.

2. Click the File menu, point to Send To, and then click Routing Recipient.

3. If necessary, click the Profile Name list arrow to select the e-mail profile you want to use to mail the document, and then click OK.

4. Click Address.

5. Enter a name, and then click To. Repeat this step to enter each recipient in sequence, and then click OK.

6. Determine whether recipients receive the routed document in sequence or all at once, and whether to track changes throughout the process.

7. Follow one of these scenarios:

   ◆ Click Route to route the file immediately.

   ◆ Click Add Slip to add the routing slip and close the dialog box without routing the file.

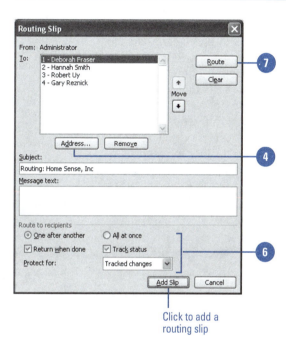

Click to add a routing slip

Reviewing a Routed Document

When you receive a routed document by e-mail, the document either comes as an attachment or the review request e-mail contains a link where you can retrieve the file. When you open the document, the Reading Layout view appears where you can read the document. When you close the Reading Layout view, the Reviewing toolbar opens and track changes is enabled. All edits that you perform to the document are noted in dialog balloons (like comment balloons) in the right margin of the document (in Page Layout view). You can also use the Reviewing toolbar to insert comments. When you have completed the review, either return the document to the originator or forward it to the next person on the routing list, as appropriate, using the document mailing procedures previously described.

As the originator, when the document is routed, you receive an e-mail message indicating who currently has the document. When you receive files returned from reviewers, you are automatically prompted to merge changes. You can then use the reviewing tools to accept or reject the changes. When you've received all the feedback from the reviewers, or when you decide to stop accepting feedback, you can choose to end the review cycle.

Review routed document

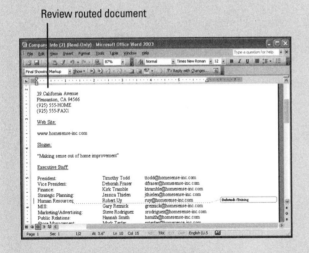

E-mail routing slip confirmation

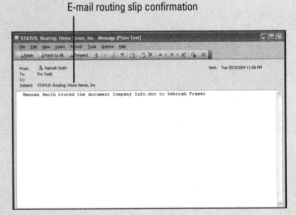

Working Together on Office Documents

Introduction

Microsoft SharePoint technology, known as SharePoint Team Services, is a collection of products and services which provide the ability for people to engage in communication, document and file sharing, calendar events, sending alerts, tasks planning, and collaborative discussions in a single community solution. SharePoint enables companies to develop an intelligent application which connects their employees, teams, and information so that users can be part of a Knowledge Community.

Before you can use SharePoint Team Services, SharePoint needs to be set up and configured on a Windows 2003 Server by your network administrator or Internet service provider.

SharePoint is integrated into Office 2003 and enables you to share data and documents using the Shared Workspace task pane directly from Office Word 2003, Office PowerPoint 2003, or Office Excel 2003. The Shared Workspace task pane allows you to see the list of team members collaborating on the current project, find out who is online, send an instant message, and review tasks and other resources. You can use the Shared Workspace task pane to create one or more document workspaces where you can collect, organize, modify, share, and discuss Office documents. The Shared Workspace task pane displays information related to the document workspaces stored on SharePoint Team Services.

What You'll Do

View SharePoint Team Services

Administer SharePoint Team Services

Store Documents in the Library

View Team Members

Set Up Alerts

Assign Project Tasks

Create an Event

Create Contacts

Hold Web Discussions

Work with Shared Workspace

Install Windows 2003 and SharePoint Server 2003

Viewing SharePoint Team Services

Microsoft SharePoint displays the contents of its home page so you can work efficiently with your site. The available pages are: The Home Page, Manage Content Page, Manage Users Page, Change Portal Site Navigation Page, Change Settings Page, and Site Settings Page. You can navigate within the site by clicking on each of the links within the home page. Certain Administrative Access rights are needed in order to view these pages.

Home Page view is the first page your users see when they access the URL for Microsoft SharePoint Server. If you are within a Windows 2003 Active Domain and have a Domain Account, you will not be prompted to type in your user credentials and password. If you do not have an account you will be asked to type in your credentials to have the page display your SharePoint Site. Please contact your Systems Administrator if you do not have access to the SharePoint Server.

Documents and Lists Page view allows you to manage content to your SharePoint Site. You can create Portal sites, a Document Library, Upload Graphic Images in an Image Library Site, Create Calender Events, Create an Address Book of Contents, setup Project Events, Create a Web Discussion site, and setup Surveys. Within your Document and Lists page you will be able to administer your content to provide users with content management capabilities.

Manage Users Page view allows you to add users to your SharePoint Site. If their e-mail address is located within their Domain Account on Windows 2003, SharePoint will e-mail the users you created, and then invite them to join in to the SharePoint Server. From the Manage Users page you can add, delete, and change the permissions of a user for your site.

Home Page

Manage content on SharePoint

Change the main page look and feel

Documents and Lists Page

Adds a new portal site

Adds documents
to the site

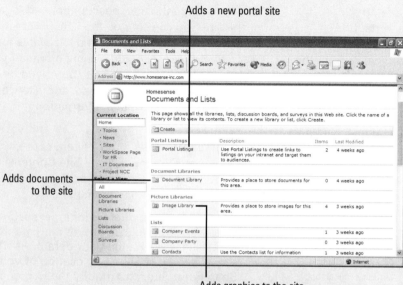

Adds graphics to the site

Manage Users Page

Adds new
users

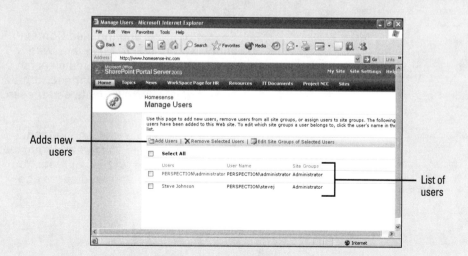

List of
users

Administering SharePoint Team Services

Administering Microsoft SharePoint is easy within the site settings. The available pages are: The Home Page, Manage Content Page, Manage Users Page, Change Portal Site Navigation Page, Change Settings Page, and Site Settings Page. You can navigate within the site by clicking on each of the links within the home page. Certain Administrative Access rights are needed in order to view these pages.

Change Portal Site Navigation Page gives you a hierarchy structure to make changes to other portal sites within SharePoint. If you want to move your site to the top-level within SharePoint or modify your sub-level pages, you can do so with the SharePoint Portal Site Navigation Page.

Change Settings Page allows you to swiftly customize the look and feel of your portal site. You can change the title, description, and logo for the site. You can change the URL for creating sites based on the published templates for your site. You can also add a change management process by having the site approved by a manager before being published, and allowing you to change your contact information for your site.

Site Settings Page has four different categories: General Settings, Portal Site Content, Search Settings and Indexed Content, and User Profile, Audiences, and Personal Sites.

◆ **General Settings** offers additional security features, which allows you to manage the alerts settings, change your default SMTP e-mail server, change the location of your SharePoint Site, and modify the Regional Language Settings to your site.

◆ **Portal Site Content** allows you to manage the site structure, view your site lists and document libraries, import data into your SharePoint Server, and add link listings to your site.

◆ **Search Settings and Indexed Content** allows you to create Meta tags within your SharePoint Server, create search crawlers to investigate your site for new key words which will create better search results within your site.

◆ **User Profile, Audiences, and Personal Sites** allows you to change and manage your user profiles within your site. You can also manage your audiences and personal settings.

Quick Launch bar

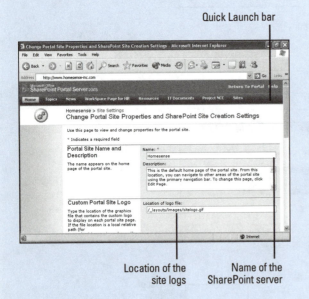

Location of the site logs

Name of the SharePoint server

Change Settings Page

Change publishing settings

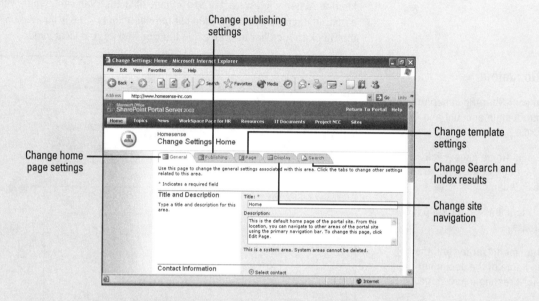

Change home page settings

Change template settings

Change Search and Index results

Change site navigation

Site Settings Page

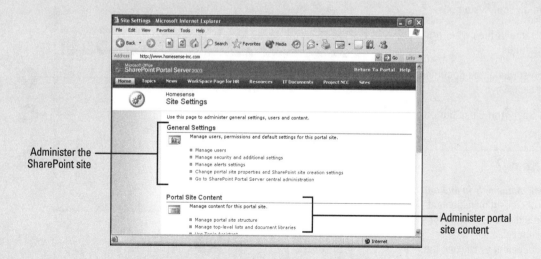

Administer the SharePoint site

Administer portal site content

Storing Documents in the Library

A SharePoint **Document Library** is a central depository of files you can share with company employees, team members and permissible members with access. Within the Document Library you can create a list of common documents for a project, documented procedures, and company wide documents for departments such as human resources or finance. When you first install SharePoint 2003, the Web site comes with a built-in document library called **shared documents**. This is located on the Quick Launch bar as well as on the Documents And Lists page.

Upload a Document

1. Log into your SharePoint server with your domain account and password.

2. On the main Home page, click Create Manage Content under the Actions Sidebar.

3. On the Documents And Lists page, click Create.

4. Click Document Library, and then type the name of the document library for creating a new page.

5. Click Upload Document.

6. Type the location of the document, or click Browse to search for the document on your system.

7. Type the name of the owner and a brief description.

8. Select the status of the document, and then click Save.

9. Click the Save And Close button.

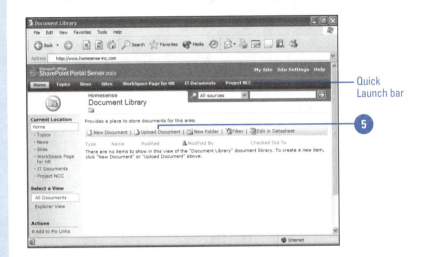

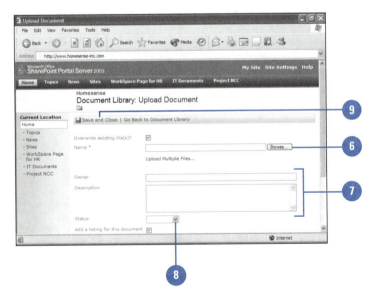

Did You Know?

You can check documents in and out. SharePoint's document management system ensures that only one person at a time can access a file. You can check out a document by clicking the Content menu in the document library, and then clicking Check Out.

Viewing Team Members

After you have setup a portal page, you need to specify a user access list to the site. Specifying a user access list controls who can access the site, as well as who has administrative privileges. With integration to Microsoft Active Directory, users can be managed with the same groups as your domain. The access will allow your users to perform a specific action in your site by assigning them to the appropriate groups.

Add New Members to the Site

1. Log into your SharePoint server with your domain account and password.

2. On the main Home page, click Give User Access To The Portal.

3. On the Manage Users page, click Add Users.

4. Type the name of their domain account.

5. Click the type of permissions you want to give this user:

   ◆ **Reader.** Gives the user read-only access to the portal site.

   ◆ **Contributor.** Gives the user write access to the document libraries and lists.

   ◆ **Web Designer.** Gives the user the ability to create lists and document libraries and customize the overall look and feel of the site.

   ◆ **Administrator.** Gives the user full access of the portal site.

   ◆ **Content Manager.** Gives the user the ability to manage lists, libraries, sites and moderate the discussions.

   ◆ **Member.** Gives the user the ability to personalize the portal site content and create lists.

6. Click Next, fill out any additional information, and then click Finish.

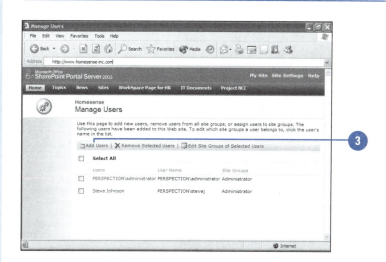

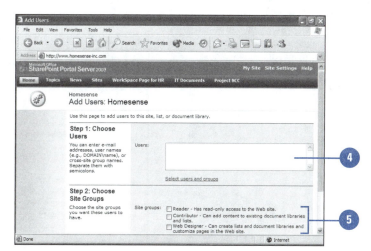

Setting Up Alerts

An Alert notifies you when there is new information which has been changed on the portal site. You can customize your areas of interests and define when you want to be notified after the site has been updated. You can define an alert to track new matches to a search query, changes to the site page, or a new site addition.

Create Your E-Mail Alert

1 Log into your SharePoint server with your domain account and password.

2 In a Portal Site, click Alert Me.

3 Define your delivery options, and then click Next.

4 Click Advanced Options if you want to set up filters.

5 Click OK.

Did You Know?

You can use the following filter categories to be alerted with: Search queries, document and listings, areas, new listings, sites added to the site directory, sharepoint lists and libraries, list items, portal site users, and backward compatible document library folders.

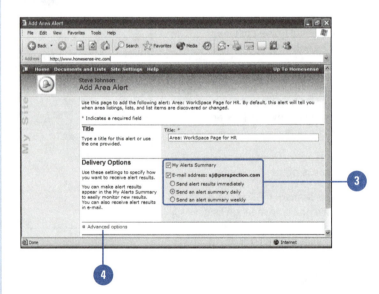

Assigning Project Tasks

Assigning a project task is another way you can use SharePoint to collaborate on the site. By creating a task, you can manage your team with status updates. You can also provide a central way to manage the effectiveness of a project. Since this is a Web based system, everyone can access this with a simple Web browser.

Add a Task Item to Your Site

1. Log into your SharePoint server with your domain account and password.

2. On the main home page, click Create Manage Content under the Actions Sidebar.

3. Click Create, and then click Tasks.

4. Type the name of the task, add in an optional description, click Yes if you want to add the task to the menu bar, and then click Create.

5. Click New Item.

6. Type the title, set the priority, status, and completion percentage, assign your resource, add a description, and then set your due date.

7. Click the Save And Close button.

Did You Know?

You can use the Upload button to add an attachment. A general rule of thumb would be to keep your attachments under 1 MB, however, unless your administrator has set rights on your site, you are free to upload as much as you want.

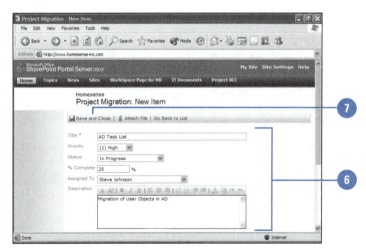

Creating an Event

Creating an event allows you to send out notices on upcoming meetings, deadlines, and other important events. This is helpful if you need to send out information to a wide range of people or in a project you are working on. If you are looking to set up a meeting to a large group of people, you may want to set up an event which is seen by everyone who logs in.

Setup New Events

1. Log into your SharePoint server with your domain account and password.

2. On the main Home page, click Create Manage Content under the Actions Sidebar.

3. Click Create, and then click Events.

4. Type the name of the event, add in an optional description, click Yes, if you want to add the event to the menu bar, and then click Create.

5. Click New Item.

6. Type the event title, select a begin and end event time, a description, the location, and then select an recurrence option.

7. Click the Save And Close button.

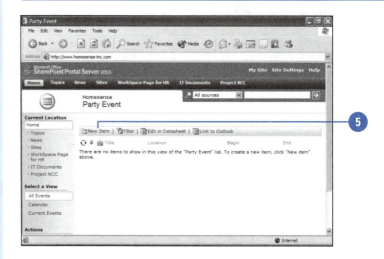

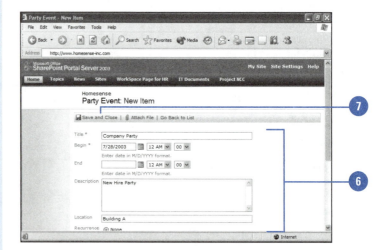

Did You Know?

You can use a new collaboration feature in Outlook 2003 called Meeting Workspace. Meeting Workspace allows you to gather information and organize everyone when you create a scheduled meeting event. To create a Meeting Workspace in Outlook 2003, prepare a calender event and set up your attendees for the event. Then click Meeting Workspace to link this to your SharePoint Server. You may need to type in the URL of your SharePoint server. Please get this from your System Administrator.

Link to Events in Outlook

① On the Events page, click Link To Outlook.

② If a security dialog box appears asking for your approval prior to adding a folder, click Yes.

You will be prompted to type in the credentials of your user account.

③ Type in your Domain User credentials and password, and then click OK.

④ Click Other Calendars to view your SharePoint calendar.

Did You Know?

You will not be able to change the events in your SharePoint calendar folder within Outlook 2003. You will only have read access rights within Outlook 2003. To change the SharePoint calendar information, return to your SharePoint Site, and then modify the information under your Events Site.

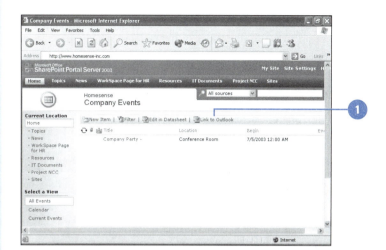

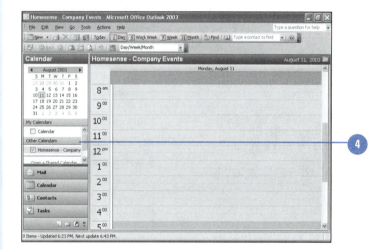

14

Creating Contacts

You can create a contact list when you want to have a central database of your team information. You will have the ability to manage information about sales contacts, vendors, and employees that your team has involvement with.

Create a Contact List

1. Log into your SharePoint server with your domain account and password.

2. On the main Home page, click Create Manage Content under the Actions Sidebar.

3. Click Create, and then click Contacts.

4. Type the name of the contact, add an optional description, click Yes, if you want to add the contacts list to the menu bar, and then click Create.

5. Click New Item.

6. Type the contact name, and then add in all the appropriate information on your contact.

7. Click the Save And Close button.

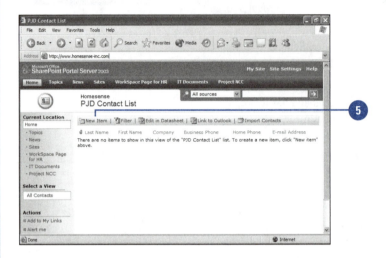

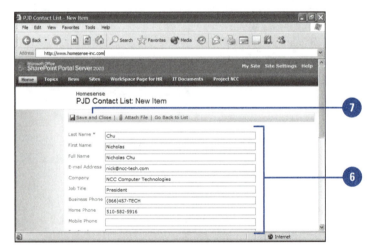

Link to Contacts in Outlook

1. On the Contacts page, click Link To Outlook.

2. If a security dialog box appears asking for your approval prior to adding a folder, click Yes.

   You will be prompted to type in the credentials of your user account.

3. Type your Domain User credentials and password, and then click OK.

4. Click Other Contacts to view your SharePoint contacts.

Did You Know?

You will not be able to change the contact information in your SharePoint contacts folder within Outlook 2003. You will only have read access rights within Outlook 2003. To change the SharePoint contacts information, return to your SharePoint Site, and then modify the information under your Contacts Site.

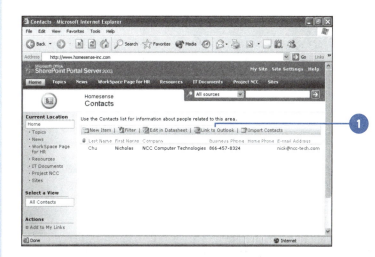

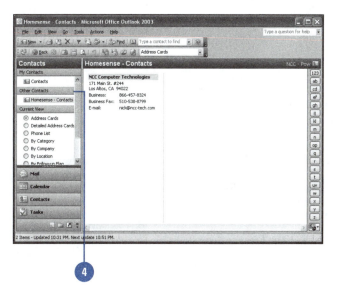

14

Holding Web Discussions

Web discussions are threaded discussions which allow users to collaborate together in a Web environment. Users can add and view discussion items, add in documents during the discussion and carry on conversations. Since the discussions are entered into a different area than the shared document, users can modify the document without effecting the collaborative discussion. Users can add changes to read-only documents and allow multiple users to create and edit discussion items simultaneously.

Hold a Web Discussion

1. Log into your SharePoint server with your domain account and password.

2. On the main Home page, click Create Manage Content under the Actions Sidebar.

3. Click Create, and then click Discussion Boards.

4. Type the name of the Discussion Board, add an optional description, click Yes, if you want to add this to the menu bar, and then click Create.

5. Click New Discussion.

6. Type the subject name, and then add in all the appropriate information on your discussion.

7. Click the Save And Close button.

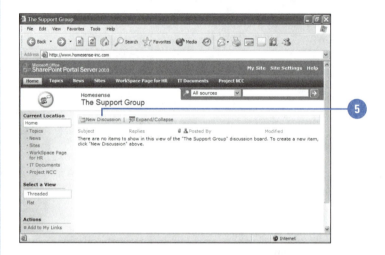

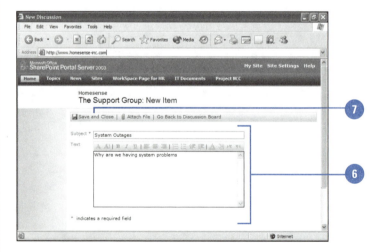

Working with Shared Workspace

Using Shared Workspace icons allow you to connect to your SharePoint Server in an Office 2003 program: Word, Excel and PowerPoint. Each icon displays different information on your document. Users can view the status of a document, see the availability of a document, display properties of a document, and list additional resources, folders, and access rights of a document. You can also show the current tasks which are assigned for your document, display the online team members of your group, and display the workspace information.

Use Shared Workspace in an Office 2003 Program

1. Log into your SharePoint server with your domain account and password.

2. In an Office 2003 program (Word, Excel and PowerPoint), click on the Tools menu, and then click Shared Workspace.

   If you open Shared Workspace for the first time you may be prompted to create a new workspace area.

3. Use the Shared Workspace Navigation bar tools.

   ◆ **Status.** Displays the checked-in/checked-out status of your current document.

   ◆ **Members**. Shows you who is online from your Team Members Group.

   ◆ **Tasks**. Shows you the current tasks assigned for this current document and the completion status.

   ◆ **Documents**. Displays the name and workspace of the selected document.

   ◆ **Links**. Displays additional resources, folders, and lists the access of files.

   ◆ **Document Info**. Displays the author of the document and the properties of the document.

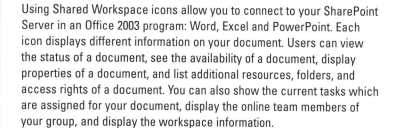

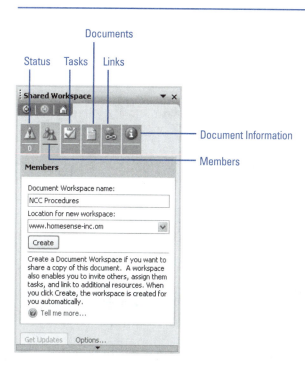

Installing Windows 2003 and SharePoint Server 2003

In order for you to install the new version of SharePoint, you must Install Windows 2003 Server. Windows 2003 Server uses the new .NET Architecture Internet Information Server (IIS) 6.0, Microsoft SMTP (Simple Mail Transport Protocol) Service and Microsoft SQL Server 2000 Desktop Engine (MSDE 2000) or Microsoft SQL Server 2000 Enterprise or Standard Edition (64-bit), with Microsoft SQL Server 2000 SP3 or later.

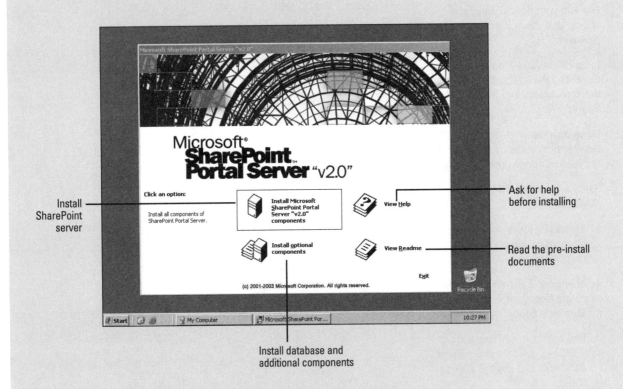

Install SharePoint server

Ask for help before installing

Read the pre-install documents

Install database and additional components

Share Information Between Programs

Introduction

Microsoft Office Word 2003 has the power and flexibility to share information between programs. You can create, store, and manage information in the program that works best for you, and then move that information to another program. You can also import or export data to and from Word to make your Office documents be the best they can be.

Completing a successful project in Word is not always a solitary venture; sometimes you may need to share data with others or obtain data from other programs. In many offices, your co-workers (and their computers) are located across the country or around the world. You can merge information from different programs into a single document, and you can link data between programs.

XML (**Extensible Markup Language**) is a universal language that enables you to create documents in which data is stored independently of the format so you can use the data more seamlessly in other forms. You can work with the familiar Office interface and create and save documents as XML, without ever knowing the language. You can also attach a Word XML Schema (called WordML) or XML Schema (created by a developer)—a set of rules that defines the elements and content used in an XML document—and validate the data against it. Word allows you to open, view, modify, and save XML files and data.

You can create one seamless document that includes data from several programs. Imagine being able to include Excel data, some PowerPoint slides, an Access database into your document—it's easy with Microsoft Office Word 2003.

Sharing Information Between Programs

Office can convert data or text from one format to another using a technology known as **object linking and embedding** (OLE). OLE allows you to move text or data between programs in much the same way as you move them within a program. The familiar cut and paste or drag and drop methods work between programs and documents just as they do within a document. In addition, all Office programs have special ways to move information from one program to another, including importing, exporting, embedding, linking, and hyperlinking.

Importing and Exporting

Importing and exporting information are two sides of the same coin. **Importing** copies a file created with the same or another program into your open file. The information becomes part of your open file, just as if you created it in that format. Some formatting and program-specific information such as formulas may be lost. **Exporting** converts a copy of your open file into the file type of another program. In other words, importing brings information into your open document, while exporting moves information from your open document into another program file.

Embedding

Embedding inserts a copy of a file created in one program into a file created in another program. Unlike imported files, you can edit the information in embedded files with the same commands and toolbar buttons used to create the original file. The original file is called the **source file**, while the file in which it is embedded is called the **destination file**. Any changes you make to an embedded object appear only in the destination file; the source file remains unchanged.

Linking

Linking displays information from one file (the source file) in a file created in another program (the destination file). You can view and edit the linked object from either the source file or the destination file. The changes are stored in the source file but also appear in the destination file. As you work, Office updates the linked object to ensure you always have the most current information. Office keeps track of all the drive, folder, and file name information for a source file. However, if you move or rename the source file, the link between files will break.

Once the link is broken, the information in the destination file becomes embedded rather than linked. In other words, changes to one copy of the file will no longer affect the other.

Embedding and Linking	
Term	**Definition**
Source program	The program that created the original object
Source file	The file that contains the original object
Destination program	The program that created the document into which you are inserting the object
Destination file	The file into which you are inserting the object

Hyperlinking

The newest way to share information between programs is hyperlinks—a term borrowed from World Wide Web technology. A **hyperlink** is an object (either colored, underlined text or a graphic) that you click to jump to a different location in the same document or a different document. (See "Creating Web Pages" on page 245 for more information about creating and navigating hyperlinks in Microsoft Office Word 2003 documents.)

Deciding Which Method to Use

With all these different methods for sharing information between programs to choose from, sometimes it is hard to decide which method to use. To decide which method is best for your situation, answer the following questions:

1 Do you want the contents of another file displayed in the open document?

- ◆ **No**. Create a hyperlink. See "Inserting Hyperlinks" on page 250.
- ◆ **Yes**. Go to question 2.

2 Do you want to edit the content of the file from within the open document?

- ◆ **No**. Embed the file as a picture. See "Embedding and Linking Information" on page 318.
- ◆ **Yes**. Go to question 3.

3 Is the source program (the program used to create the file) available on your computer?

- ◆ **No**. Import the file. See "Exporting and Importing Files" on page 316.
- ◆ **Yes**. Go to question 4.

4 Do you want to use the source program commands to edit the file?

- ◆ **No**. Import the file. See "Exporting and Importing Files" on page 316.
- ◆ **Yes**. Go to question 5.

5 Do you want changes you make to the file to appear in the source file (the original copy of the file)?

- ◆ **No**. Embed the file. See "Embedding and Linking Information" on page 318.
- ◆ **Yes**. Link the file. See "Embedding and Linking Information" on page 318.

15

Exporting and Importing Files

WW03S-5-4

Export a File to Another Program

1 Click the File menu, and then click Save As.

2 If necessary, click the Save In list arrow, and then select the drive and folder where you want to save the file.

3 Click the Save As Type list arrow, and then select the type of file you want.

4 If necessary, type a new name for the file.

5 Click Save.

6 Edit the file from within the new program.

Did You Know?

You can use copy and paste to export information. If you want to move only part of a file into your document, just copy the information you want to insert, and then paste the information in the file where you want it to appear.

You can import part of a file into Word. You can insert into a Word document a bookmarked section of a Word document or a specific range in an Excel worksheet. Click Range in the Insert File dialog box, enter a bookmark name or range, and then click OK.

When you **export** data, you save an open document in a new format so that it can be opened in an entirely different program. When you **import** data, you insert a copy of a file (from the same or another program) into an open document. For example, you might import an Excel worksheet into a Word document to create a one-page report with text and a table. Or you might want to export a document as a Web page or export text as XML data or in the standard Rich Text Format to use in another program.

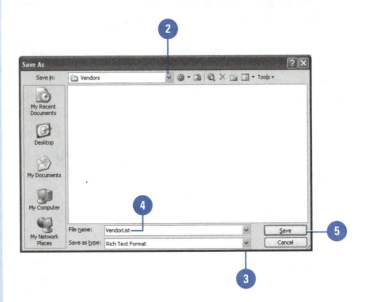

Import a File

1. Click where you want to insert the imported file.

2. Click the Insert menu, and then click File.

3. Click the Files Of Type list arrow, and then click All Files.

4. Select the drive and folder of the file you want to import.

5. Click the name of the file you want to import.

6. Click Insert.

Did You Know?

You can link a file in Word. If you start to import a file into Word, you can link it instead. Click the Insert menu, click Insert File, select the file to link, click the Insert list arrow, and then click Insert As Link.

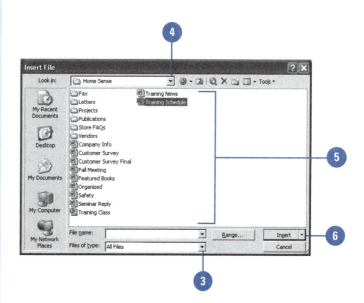

15

Embedding and Linking Information

 WW03E-1-4

Embedding inserts a copy of one document into another. When data is embedded, you can edit it using the menus and toolbars of the program in which it was created (that is, the **source program**). **Linking** displays information stored in one document (the **source file**) into another (the **destination file**). You can edit the linked object from either file, although changes are stored in the source file. For example, you might link an Excel chart or a PowerPoint slide to a Word document so you can update the chart or slide from any of the files. If you break the link between a linked object and its source file, the object becomes embedded. You can use the Links command on the Edit menu to modify a link.

Embed an Existing Object

1. Click where you want to embed the object.

2. Click the Insert menu, and then click Object.

3. Click the Create From File tab.

4. Click Browse, and then double-click the file with the object you want to embed.

5. Click OK.

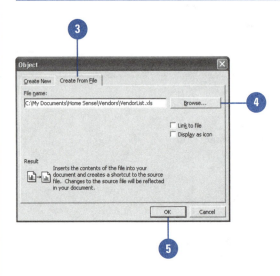

Embed a New Object

1. Click where you want to embed the object.

2. Click the Insert menu, and then click Object.

3. Click the Create New tab.

4. Click the type of object you want to create.

5. Click OK.

6. Enter information in the new object using the source program's commands.

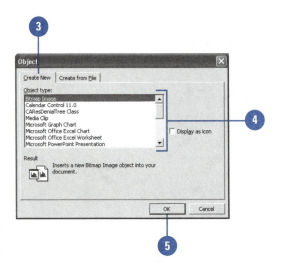

Link an Object Between Programs

1. Click where you want to link the object.

2. Click the Insert menu, and then click Object.

3. Click the Create From File tab.

4. Click Browse, and then double-click the object you want to link.

5. Select the Link To File check box.

6. Click OK.

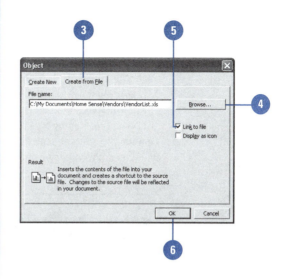

Edit an Embedded or Linked File

1. Double-click the linked or embedded object you want to edit to display the source program's menus and toolbars.

2. Edit the object as usual using the source program's commands.

3. When you're done, click outside the object to return to the destination program.

4. Click the Save button.

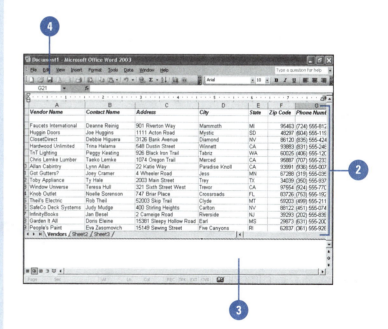

Did You Know?

You can use Paste Special to link or embed. If you want to link or embed only part of a file, copy the information, and then click where you want to link or embed the information. Click the Edit menu, click Paste Special, click the Paste option to embed or the Paste Link option to link, select a format, and then click OK.

Creating an XML Document

 WW03E-2-8

XML (Extensible Markup Language) is a universal language that enables you to create documents in which data is stored independently of the format so you can use the data more seamlessly in other forms. XML is fully supported in Microsoft Office Word 2003. XML allows you to work with the familiar Office interface and create and save documents as XML, without ever knowing the XML language. When you work with XML, you can attach a Word XML Schema (called WordML) or XML Schema (created by a developer)—a set of rules that defines the elements and content used in an XML document—and validate the data against it. Word allows you to open, view, modify, and save XML files and data.

Attach or Separate a Schema

1. Click the Tools menu, and then click Templates And Add-Ins.

2. Click the XML Schema tab.

3. Click Add Schema.

4. Locate and select the XML schema file you want to attach, and then click Open.

5. Select or clear a schema to attach or separate it.

6. Select the Validate Document Against Attached Schemas check box to validate the document.

7. Click OK.

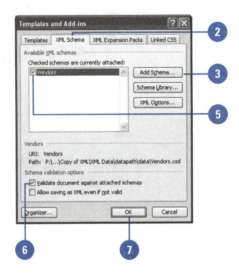

Change XML Options

1. Click the Tools menu, and then click Templates And Add-Ins.

2. Click the XML Schema tab.

3. Click XML Options.

4. Select or clear the check boxes for the validation options.

5. Select or clear the check boxes for the view options.

6. Click OK, and then click OK again.

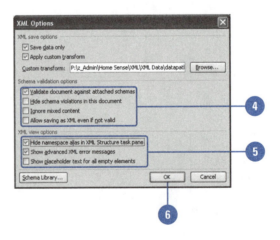

Open, View, and Modify an XML Data File

1 Click the File menu, and then click Open.

2 Click the Files Of Type list arrow, and then click XML Files.

3 Locate the XML file you want to open.

4 Select the XML file.

5 Click Open.

6 To view the XML, click the View menu, click Task Pane (if necessary), click the Other Task Panes list arrow, and then click XML Structure or XML Document.

7 To show XML tags, select the Show XML Tags In The Document check box.

8 To add an XML tag, select the content you want to tag, and then click an element tag in the XML Structure task pane.

9 As necessary, double-click an XML tag to select its contents, and then use common editing techniques to move, copy, and delete it.

10 When you're done, click the Close button on the task pane.

Did You Know?

You can remove an XML tag quickly. Point to the start or end of the tag name, right-click the tag, and then click Remove *Tag Name* tag.

You can locate XML problems quickly. If the structure of the document violates the rules of the schema, a purple wavy line marks the document location.

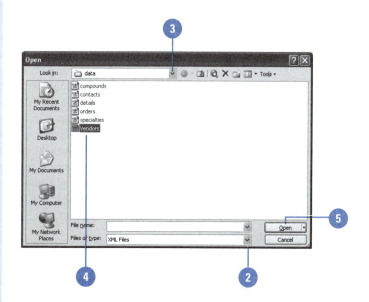

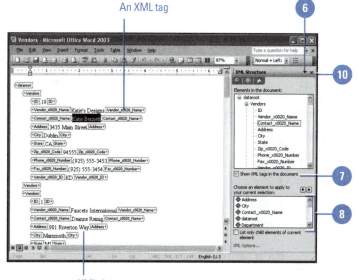

An XML tag

XML data

15

Working with XML Data

WW03E-2-8

The **Schema Library** is a place to manage XML schemas. When you add a schema to the Schema Library, you create a namespace for any XML document in which the schema is attached. A namespace provides a unique identifier for elements defined by a schema. A namespace can also associate other XML related files, such as an XML Transformations file, to the XML document. An **XML Transformations file (XSLT)** is used to save and transform XML documents into other types of documents, such as HTML or XML, in different views. In the Schema Library, you can add, delete, update, and modify schemas and solutions, which are the files associated with the schema, such as XSLT. For example, you can add friendly names (aliases) to schemas and any files associated with the schema. You can add more than one schema to a single document. Word applies both sets of rules and alerts you of any conflicts.

Associate or Modify an XML Transformation with a Schema

1. Click the Tools menu, and then click Templates And Add-Ins.

2. Click the XML Schema tab, and then click Schema Library.

3. Click the schema you want to associate a transformation file (XSLT) with.

4. Click the Use Solution With list arrow, and then click Word.

5. Click Add Solution.

6. Locate and select the XSLT file, and then click Open.

7. Type a name for the XSLT file, and then select the options you want.

8. Click OK.

9. Click the Default Solution list arrow, and then click the default transform you want.

10. To delete a solution or update settings, select the solution, and then click Delete Solutions or Solution Settings.

11. Click OK, and then click OK again.

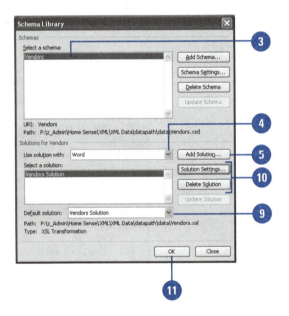

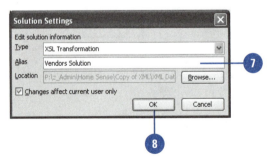

Save an XML Document and Apply a Transformation

1. Open the document you want to save as an XML document.

2. Click the File menu, and then click Save As.

3. Select a location where you want to save the XML data.

4. Click the Save As Type list arrow, and then click XML Document.

5. Type a name for the XML document.

6. To save only XML data (disregard Word formatting), select the Save Data Only check box.

7. To apply a transformation, select the Apply Transform check box, click Transform, select a transformation file (XSLT), and then click Open.

8. Click Save.

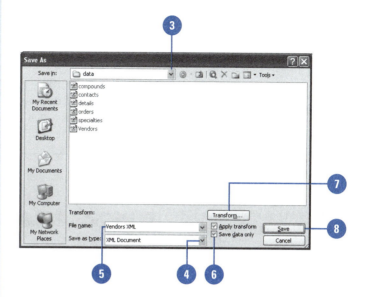

Did You Know?

You can create a Word XML schema. Create a normal Word document, and then save it as an XML document. Word creates the WordML schema.

You can insert XML data. Place the insertion point where you want to insert the data, click the Insert menu, click File, click the Files Of Type list arrow, click XML Files, locate and select the XML file, and then click Insert.

15

Creating a Word Document with Excel Data

 WW03E-1-5

A common pairing of Office programs combines Word and Excel. As you write a sales report, explain a budget, or create a memo showing distribution of sales, you often want to add existing spreadsheet data and charts to your text. Instead of re-creating the Excel data in Word, you can insert all or part of the data or chart into your Word document. You can use the File command on the Insert menu or copy and paste the information from Excel into Word. After you insert data or a chart into your word document, you can double-click the embedded Excel object to modify the data or chart.

Insert an Excel Worksheet Range to a Word Document

1. Click in the Word document where you want to copy the Excel range.

2. Click the Insert menu, and then click File.

3. Click the Files Of Type list arrow, and then click All Files.

4. Locate and select the drive and folder that contains the workbook you want to copy.

5. Double-click the file name of the workbook you want to copy.

6. Click Insert.

7. Click the Open Document In Workbook list arrow, and then select the worksheet you want.

8. Click the Name Or Cell Range list arrow, and then select the range or range name you want to copy.

9. Click OK.

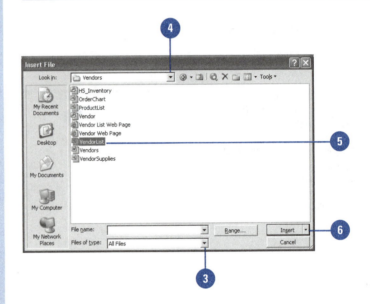

Did You Know?

You can name a range before pairing to make it easier. If you plan to insert part of an Excel worksheet in a Word document, name the range. This is easier to recall than the specific cell references.

Embed an Excel Chart in Word

1. Open the Excel worksheet where the chart you want to use appears.

2. Click the Copy button on the Standard toolbar.

3. Click the Word document where you want to embed the chart.

4. Click the Paste button on the Standard toolbar.

Did You Know?

You can import Excel data as a picture. To save disk space, you can insert Excel data as a picture. Data inserted this way becomes a table that you cannot edit. Select the data you want to import, press Shift as you click the Edit menu, click Copy Picture, and then click OK. Click in the Word document where you want to insert the picture, and then click the Paste button on the Standard toolbar. Drag the picture to a new location, or drag its resize handles to enlarge or shrink it.

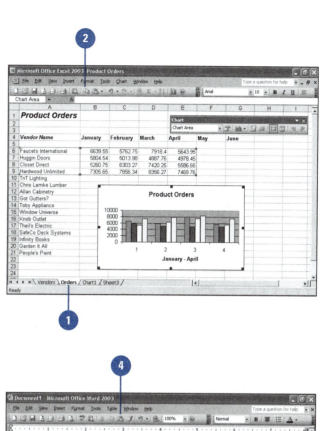

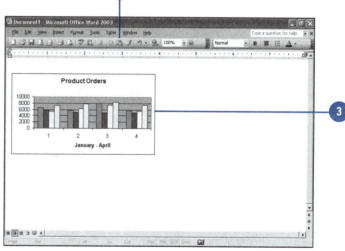

15

Creating a Presentation with Word Text

PowerPoint presentations are based on outlines, which you can create using either PowerPoint, or the more extensive outlining tools in Word. You can import any Word document into PowerPoint, although only paragraphs tagged with heading styles become part of the slides. Each Heading 1 style in a Word document becomes the title of a separate PowerPoint slide. Heading 2 becomes the first level of indented text, and so on. If a document contains no styles, PowerPoint uses the paragraph indents to determine a slide structure. You can edit the slides using the usual PowerPoint commands. You can also copy any table you created in Word to a slide.

Create PowerPoint Slides from a Word Document

1. Open or create a Word document with heading styles.

2. Click the File menu, point to Send To, and then click Microsoft Office PowerPoint.

   PowerPoint opens; each Heading 1 style text becomes the title of a new slide and Heading 2 style text becomes top-level bullets on a slide, and so forth.

3. Save the presentation, and then edit it by adding slides, changing slide layouts, and applying a design template.

Did You Know?

You can create slides from a Word outline and insert them into an existing PowerPoint presentation. In PowerPoint, display the slide after which you want to insert the new slides. Click the Insert menu, click Slides From Outline, and then select the Word document you want.

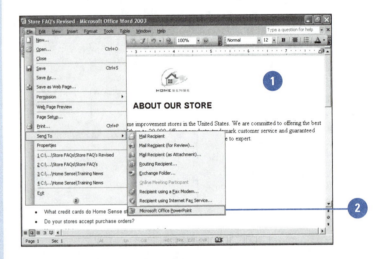

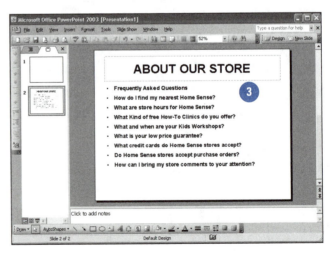

Embed a Word Table in a Slide

1. Click in the Word table you want to use in a slide.

2. Click the table selection box (small black box in the upper-left corner of the table).

3. Click the Copy button on the Standard toolbar.

4. Click the PowerPoint slide where you want to insert the Word table.

5. Click the Paste button on the Standard toolbar.

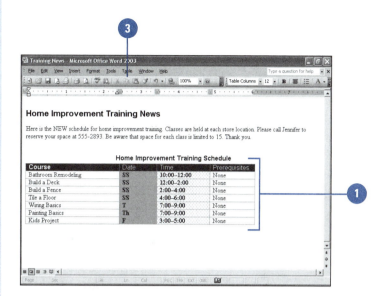

15

Using an Access Database to Create Word Documents

Access is a great program for storing and categorizing large amounts of information. You can combine, or **merge**, database records with Word documents to create tables or produce form letters and envelopes based on names, addresses, and other Access records. For example, you might create a form letter in Word and personalize it with an Access database of names and addresses. Word uses the Mail Merge task pane to step you through the process. Mail merge is the process of combining names and addresses stored in a data file with a main document (usually a form letter) to produce customized documents.

Insert Access Data into a Word Document

1. In the Access Database window, click the table or query you want to use.

2. Click the OfficeLinks button on the Database toolbar.

3. Click Merge It With Microsoft Office Word.

4. Click the linking option you want to use.

   If you choose to link data to an existing document, double-click the name of the file in the Select Microsoft Word Document dialog box.

5. Click OK, and then follow the steps in the Mail Merge task pane.

6. In Word, enter text, and then format it as needed.

7. To add fields, click one or more of the items in Step 4 of 6 in the Mail Merge task pane.

See Also

See "Creating a Form Letter" on page 176 for information on using the Mail Merge task pane.

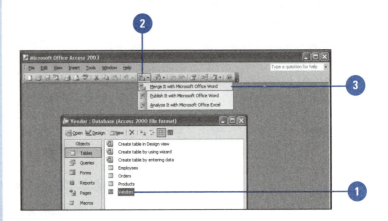

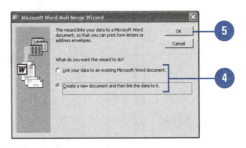

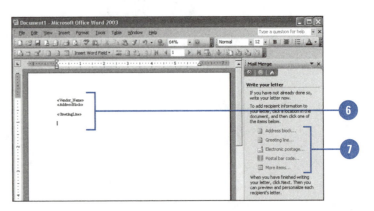

Create a Word Document from an Access Database

1. In the Access Database window, click the table, query, report, or form you want to save as a Word document.

2. Click the OfficeLinks button on the Database toolbar.

3. Click Publish It With Microsoft Office Word to save the data as a Word file, start Word, and then open the document.

4. Edit the document using the usual Word commands.

Did You Know?

Publish It With Microsoft Office Word saves as an RTF. Rich Text Format (RTF) files retain formatting, such as fonts and styles, and can be opened from Word or other word processing programs. When you use the Publish It With Microsoft Office Word command, the output is saved as a Rich Text Format (.rtf) file in the folder in which Access is stored on your computer.

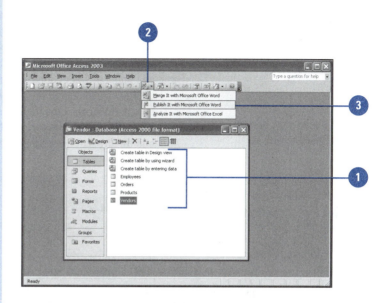

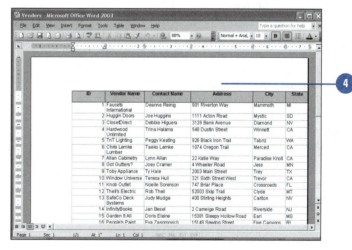

15

Creating a Word Outline from a Presentation

You can send both your notes and slides to Word so that you can use a full array of word processing tools. This is especially handy when you are developing more detailed materials, such as training presentations and manuals. By default, PowerPoint pastes the presentation into the Word document. If you change the presentation after sending it to Word, the changes you make to the presentation are not reflected in the Word document. If you click the Paste Link option in the Send To Microsoft Office Word dialog box, however, you create a link between the Word document and the presentation, so that changes you make in one are reflected in the other.

Create a Word Document from a PowerPoint Presentation

1. Open the PowerPoint presentation you want to use as a Word document.

2. Click the File menu, point to Send To, and then click Microsoft Office Word.

3. Click the Outline Only option.

4. Click the Paste option if you want to make changes to only the Word copy. Click the Paste Link option if you want to make changes to both the Word and PowerPoint copies at one time.

5. Click OK to save the slide text as a Word file, start Word, and then open the file.

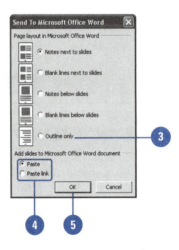

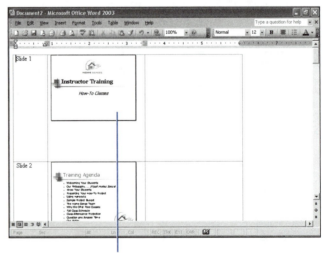

Slides in a Word document

Customizing Word

16

Introduction

Once you've become familiar with Microsoft Office Word 2003 and all the features it contains, you might want to customize the way you work with Word. You can change your view settings so that your Word window looks the way you want. Word comes with set defaults, such as viewing the startup task pane or vertical ruler, how many files you've recently opened, which you can change to a new default. Some of the other Word customization features allow you to set a default font and related attributes to use when you are typing text in text boxes. Other defaults might be the color or line style of an AutoShape that you create.

You can change the configuration of the menus and toolbars that you use. You can also create your own toolbar or menu for just the commands that you use when creating and formatting your documents. There are a variety of shortcut keys that can help you quickly get the job done.

The Language bar performs a variety of functions. The Language bar allows you to control Word with your voice, or execute various commands without having to use the keyboard. Word will need to be trained to your voice in order to perform the voice recognition. You can also dictate text directly into your documents with the speech recognition feature. Or maybe, you want to add handwritten notes to a document.

Macros can simplify common repetitive tasks that you use regularly in Word. Macros can even reside on a Word toolbar for easy access. If a macro has a problem executing a task, Word can help you debug, or fix the error in your macro.

Customizing the Way You Work

You can customize several settings in the Word work environment to suit the way you like to work. You can customize the performance of many Word features including its editing, saving, spelling, viewing, and printing procedures. You can also change security, track changes, user information, and file compatibility settings.

Change General Options

1. Click the Tools menu, and then click Options.

2. Click the General tab.

3. Select or clear the general options you want. Some of the common options include:

   ◆ **Recently Used File List.** Displays most recently used files on the File menu.

   ◆ **Measurement Units.** Selects the default measurement unit for the ruler and dialog boxes.

4. Click OK.

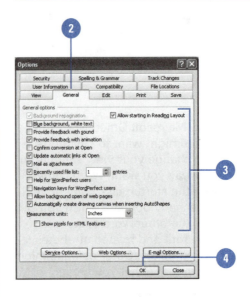

Change View Options

1. Click the Tools menu, and then click Options.

2. Click the View tab.

3. Select or clear the view options you want. Some of the common options include:

   ◆ **ScreenTips.** Displays the toolbar button name when you point to the button.

   ◆ **Startup Task Pane.** Displays the Getting Started task pane when you first start Word.

   ◆ **All.** Displays all formatting characters.

4. Click OK.

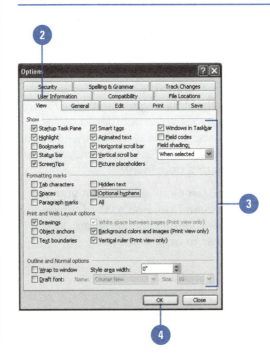

Change Edit Options

1. Click the Tools menu, and then click Options.

2. Click the Edit tab.

3. Select or clear the edit options you want. Some of the common options include:

   ◆ **Show Paste Options Buttons.** Displays the button after you paste with additional options.

   ◆ **Enable Click And Type.** Allows you to insert and format text and graphic while you type.

   ◆ **Use CTRL + Click To Follow Hyperlink.** Allows you to use Ctrl+Click or Click.

4. Click OK.

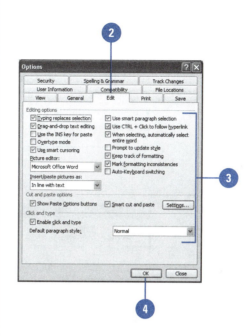

Change Save Options

1. Click the Tools menu, and then click Options.

2. Click the Save tab.

3. Select or clear the save options you want. Some of the common options include:

   ◆ **Allow Background Saves.** Saves document in the background as you work.

   ◆ **Embed Smart Tags.** Saves smart tags in the document.

   ◆ **Save AutoRecover Info Every.** Creates a recovery file every *x* minutes.

4. Click OK.

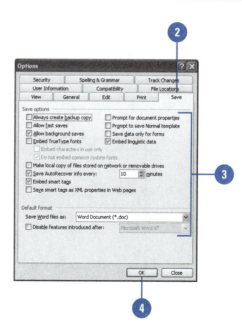

Changing a Default File Location

WW03E-5-3

If you always save documents in a specific folder, you can change the default location where documents are saved. You can change the default file location for documents, clip art pictures, user templates, workgroup templates, AutoRecover files, tools, and startup. Unless you fully understand the internal connects between Word and the clip art, tools, and startup folders, you should not change those default file locations. After you make a change, Word uses the new setting for all subsequent Word sessions until you change the setting again.

Change a Default File Location

1 Click the Tools menu, and then click Options.

2 Click the File Locations tab.

3 Click the file type in which you want to change the default file location.

4 Click Modify.

5 Open the new default folder location you want to use.

6 Click OK.

7 Click OK.

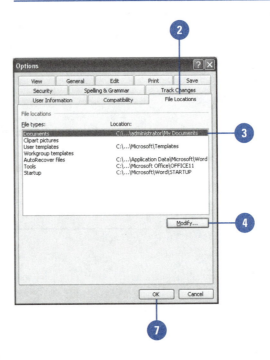

Changing Default Text

 WW03E-5-3

When you type text in a document, Word applies a set of default text attributes. Some examples of Word's font default settings include font style, size, and formatting options, such as bold, italic, and underline. You might find that having your own personalized font style or color setting would really make your documents exciting. To find out the current default settings for your document, you can open a new document, and then type some text.

Change Default Text

1. Click the Format menu, and then click Font.

2. Change the font options to what you want to be the default.

3. Click Default, and then click Yes.

4. Click OK.

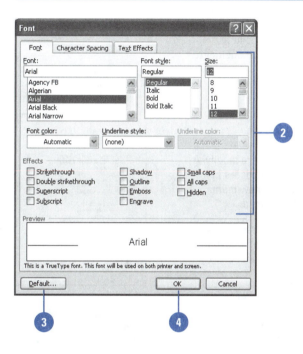

Customizing the Menu Bar

 Microsoft® Office Specialist Approved Courseware

WW03E-5-2

You can customize the existing Word menu bar by adding buttons, commands, and macros that you use frequently. Adding items to the menu bar is a great way to have easy access to features without adding more buttons or toolbars. The ability to drag features from different parts of the program window makes it easy to add items to the menu bar. Imagine, having a menu with all of your most commonly used formatting, sorting, or printing commands.

Customize the Menu Bar

1 Click the View menu, point to Toolbars, and then click Customize.

2 Click the Commands tab.

3 Select a category.

4 To add a button, drag the command to the appropriate place on the menu you want to modify. A solid horizontal line appears below the place where the new menu command will be placed.

5 To remove a button, drag the menu command you want to remove to an empty area in the document workspace.

6 Click Close.

Did You Know?

You can assign an accelerator key to a menu. An accelerator key is the key you press to display a menu or run a menu command. For example, the accelerator key for the File menu is "F." To add an accelerator key to a menu item, type an ampersand (&) before the letter that will be the accelerator key. For example, enter the menu name "&New Menu" to create the menu entry New Menu with the accelerator key "N."

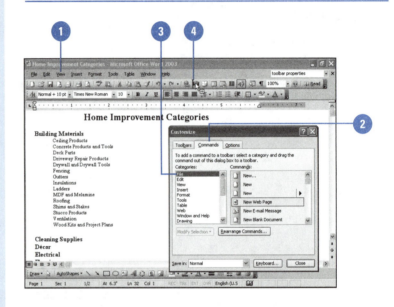

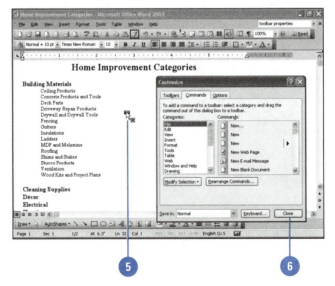

Create a New Menu

1. Click the View menu, point to Toolbars, click Customize, and then click the Commands tab.

2. Click New Menu in the Categories box.

3. Drag New Menu from the Commands list to an empty spot on the menu bar.

4. Click Close.

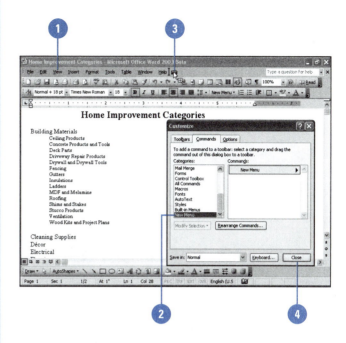

Name a New Menu

1. Click the View menu, point to Toolbars, and then click Customize.

2. Click New Menu on the menu bar.

3. Click Modify Selection.

4. Click the Name box, and then type a new name.

5. Press Enter.

6. Click Close.

Did You Know?

You can copy a command to toolbars and menus. Copy commands from other menus or toolbars to new menus and toolbars by pressing and holding Ctrl as you drag the new command.

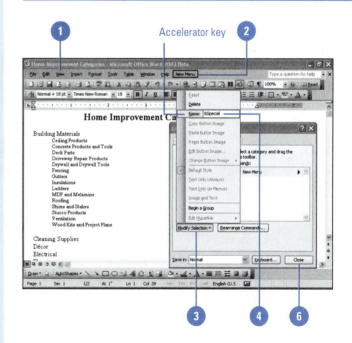

Accelerator key

16

Adding and Removing Toolbar Buttons

WW03E-5-2

Each toolbar initially appears in a default configuration, but many toolbars actually contain many more commands than are displayed. When monitors are set to low resolution, sometimes not all toolbar buttons are visible. You can modify Word's toolbars so that they display only the buttons you want. For example, you can add buttons to a toolbar for commands you frequently use, or you can remove buttons from toolbars that have too many. You can also use the Add Or Remove command on the Toolbar Options menu to quickly show or hide buttons on a toolbar. If a button doesn't appear on the button list for a toolbar, you can add it. If you no longer need a button on the button list, you can remove it.

Show or Hide a Toolbar Button

1. Click the Toolbar Options list arrow on the toolbar.

2. Point to Add Or Remove Buttons.

3. Click to select or clear the check box next to the button you want to show or hide.

4. Click outside the toolbar to deselect it.

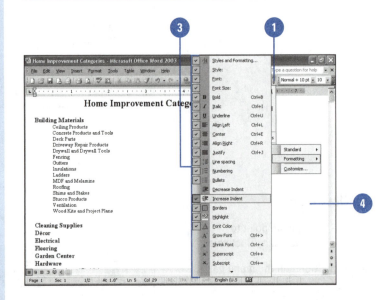

Add or Remove a Toolbar Button

1. Click the Tools menu, and then click Customize.

2. Click the Commands tab.

3. Click the category containing the toolbar button you want to add.

4. Drag a command from the Commands tab to the toolbar to add a button, or drag a button off a toolbar to a blank area to remove it.

5. Click Close.

Did You Know?

You can set options for toolbars and menus. To set some general options for toolbars and menus, click the Tools menu, click Customize, click the Options tab, select the options you want, and then click OK.

A solid vertical line appears to the right of where the new button will be inserted.

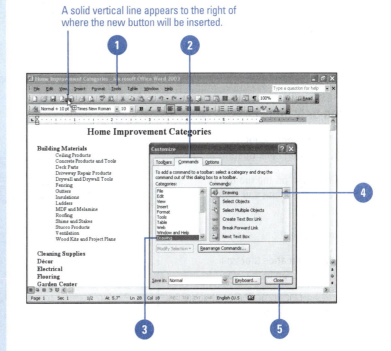

Editing Toolbar Buttons and Menu Entries

Word includes tools that allow you to edit toolbar buttons and menu entries. You can specify whether the button or menu item will display text, an image, or both text and an image. If you choose to display an image, you can edit the image, copy it from another button or use one of Word's predefined images. You can also use the Customize dialog box to makes these and other changes to your buttons and menus.

Edit a Button or Menu Entry

1. Click the View menu, point to Toolbars, and then click Customize.

2. Select the button on the toolbar or command on the menu you want to edit.

3. Click Modify Selection.

4. Choose the commands that will modify the selection in the way you prefer.

   ◆ Click Copy Button Image to copy the button image.

   ◆ Click Paste Button Image to paste the button image.

   ◆ Click Reset Button Image to reset the selected item to its default image.

   ◆ Click Edit Button Image to edit the button image.

   ◆ Click Change Button Image to select from a group of predefined images, as shown.

   ◆ Click Image And Text to paste a button image into the selected item.

   ◆ Click Begin A Group to begin a group of menu items, separated by horizontal lines.

5. Click Close.

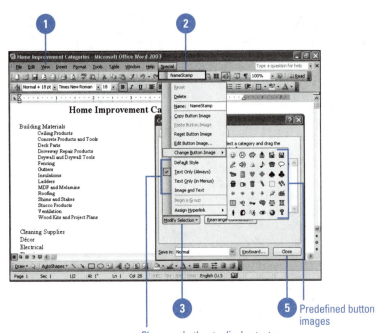

Choose whether to display text, an image, or both text and image.

Predefined button images

Customizing a Toolbar

 WW03E-5-2

You can create your own toolbars to increase your efficiency. You might, for example, create a toolbar that contains formatting and other features that you use most often when you are performing a particular task, such as inserting subdocuments. This will give you a greater workspace, since you will not have to have all the various toolbars up at once. Using one toolbar will help you achieve this.

Create a Custom Toolbar

1 Click the Tools menu, and then click Customize.

2 Click the Toolbars tab.

3 Click New.

4 Type a name for the new toolbar.

5 Click OK.

6 Add buttons to the new toolbar by dragging commands found on the Commands tab.

7 Click Close.

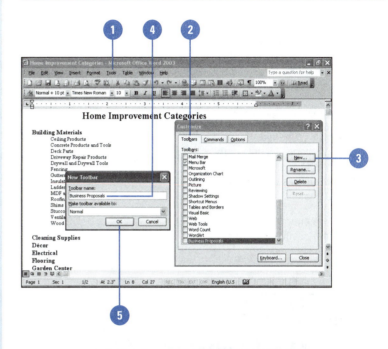

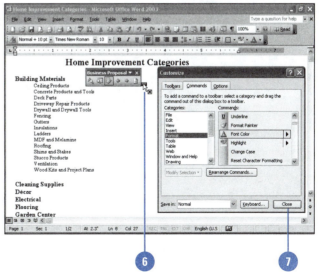

16

Working with Keyboard Shortcuts

As you gain experience and familiarity with Word, you might find it more useful to use keyboard shortcuts for many commands rather than lifting your hands from the keyboard to use your mouse with the toolbars or menus. Most commands are assigned a default shortcut key combination, but you can edit these defaults to make the most frequently used commands easier to remember, or to suit your preferences for typing speed (i.e.: some keystrokes are easier to replicate while maintaining typing speed than others).

Assign Keyboard Shortcuts

1. Click the Tools menu, and then click Customize.

2. Click Keyboard.

3. Click the Save Changes In list arrow, and then select the current document name, or the template that you want to save the keyboard changes.

4. Click the category containing the command that you want your shortcut key to trigger.

5. Click the command you want. Any keys that have already been assigned are displayed in the Current Keys box.

6. Assign the shortcut key combination you want in the Press New Shortcut Key text box.

7. Press Enter or click Assign.

8. Click Close.

9. Click Close.

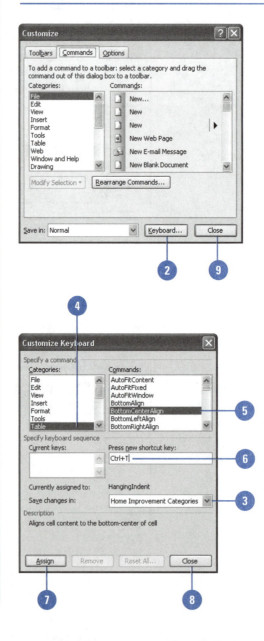

Display Keyboard Shortcuts in ScreenTips

1. Click the Tools menu, and then click Customize.

2. Click the Options tab.

3. Click the Show ScreenTips On Toolbars and the Show Shortcut Keys In ScreenTips check boxes to select them.

4. Click Close.

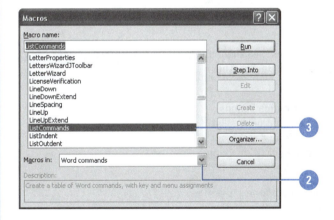

Print a List of Shortcut Keys

1. Click the Tools menu, point to Macro, and then click Macros.

2. Click the Macro In list arrow, and then click Word Commands.

3. Double-click ListCommands.

4. Click the Current Menu And Keyboard Settings option.

5. Click OK.

    A multi-page table appears with all of the keyboard shortcuts.

6. Click the File menu, click Print, choose your printing options, and then click OK.

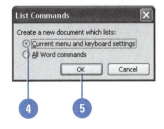

Controlling Word with Your Voice

The Office Language bar allows you to dictate text directly into your document and also to control buttons, menus, and toolbar functions by using the Voice Command option. When you first install an Office program, the Language bar appears at the top of your screen. If you are using English as the default language, the toolbar is denoted by the letters EN. (Other languages have appropriate abbreviations as well.) Before you can use speech recognition, you need to install it first. You can choose the Speech command on the Tools menu in Word, or you can use Add Or Remove Programs in the Control Panel to change the Office 2003 installation. Before you can use the Language bar for either dictation or voice commands, you need to connect a microphone to your computer, and you must train your computer to your voice using the Speech Recognition Wizard.

Work with the Language Bar

◆ **Open.** Right-click a blank area on the taskbar, point to Toolbars, and then click Language Bar.

◆ **Minimize.** Right-click the Language bar, and then click Minimize. The Language bar docks in the taskbar at the bottom right of the screen, near the system clock.

◆ **Restore.** Right-click the Language bar, and then click Restore The Language Bar.

◆ **Display or hide option buttons.** Click the Options button (the list arrow at the right end of the toolbar), and then click an option to display or hide.

◆ **Change speech properties.** Click the Speech Tools button, and then click Options.

◆ **Change Language Bar properties.** Click the Options button (the list arrow at the right end of the toolbar), and then click Settings.

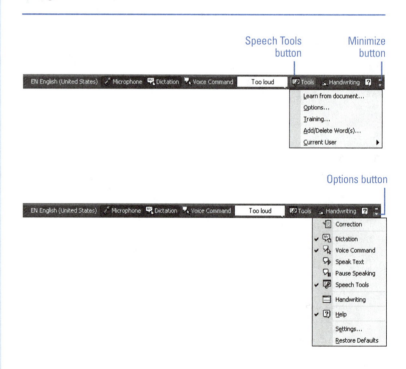

Train Your Computer to Your Voice

① Click the Speech Tools button on the Language bar, and then click Training.

② Click Next, read the instructions, ensure you are in a quiet place, and then click Next again.

③ Read the sentence provided to automatically set the proper volume of the microphone, and then click Next.

④ Read the text with hard consonants to help determine whether or not the microphone is positioned too closely to your mouth. Repeat the process until you have a clear, distinct audio playback, and then click Next.

⑤ After you are reminded to ensure that your environment is suitable for recording again, read the instructions, and then click Next.

⑥ Read the following series of dialog boxes. The words on the screen are highlighted as the computer recognizes them. As each dialog box is completed, the program will automatically move to the next one, and the process meter will update accordingly.

⑦ At the end of the training session, click Finish and your voice profile is updated and will be saved automatically.

Did You Know?

You can create additional speech profiles. Click the Speech Tools button on the Language bar, click Options, click New, and then follow the Speech Profile Wizard instructions.

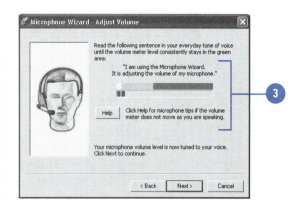

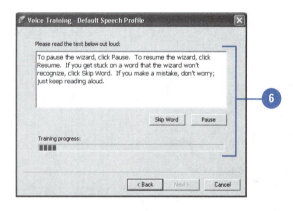

16

Executing Voice Commands

The two modes, Dictation and Voice Command, are mutually exclusive of one another. You do not want the word File typed, for example, when you are trying to open the File menu. Neither do you want the menu to open instead of the word File being typed when you are in the middle of a sentence. As such, you must manually click either mode on the Language bar to switch between them. The Voice Command mode allows you to talk your way through any sequence of menus or toolbar commands, simply by reading aloud the appropriate text instead of clicking it. For example, if you wanted to print the current page of the document you are working on, you would simply say File, Print, Current Page, OK (without saying the commas between the words as written here). You need not worry about remembering every command sequence because as you say each word in the sequence, the corresponding menu or submenu appears onscreen for your reference.

Execute Voice Commands

1 If necessary, display the Language bar.

2 Click the Microphone button on the Language bar. The toolbar expands so that the Voice Command button becomes available on the toolbar.

3 Click the Voice Command button to shift into that mode.

4 Work with your Office document normally. When you are ready to issue a command, simply speak the sequence just as you would click through it if you were using the menus or toolbar normally (i.e. with the mouse or via keyboard shortcuts).

Say "Format" to display the menu.

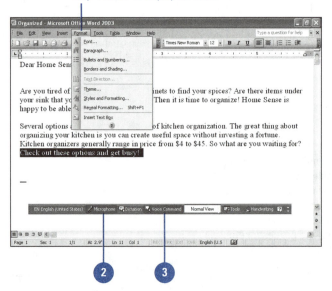

Did You Know?

You can have text read back to you. Display the Speak Text button on the Language bar. Select the text you want read back to you, and then click Speak Text.

Dictating Text

Dictating the text of a letter or other document using Office speech recognition functions may be easier for some users than typing, but don't think that it is an entirely hands free operation. For example, you must manually click the Voice Command button when you want to format anything that has been input, and then click again on Dictation to resume inputting text. Additionally, the Dictation function is not going to be 100% accurate, so you will need to clean up mistakes (such as inputting the word *Noir* when you say *or*) when they occur. Finally, although you can say punctuation marks, such as comma and period, to have them accurately reflected in the document, all periods are followed by double spaces (which may not be consistent with the document formatting you want between sentences) and issues of capitalization remain as well. Nevertheless, it is fun and freeing to be able to get the first draft of any document on paper simply by speaking it.

Dictate Text

1. If necessary, display the Language bar.

2. Click the Microphone button on the Language bar. The toolbar expands so that the Dictation button becomes available on the toolbar.

3. Click to position the insertion point inside the document where you want the dictated text to appear, and then begin speaking normally into your microphone.
    As you speak, the words will appear on the page.

4. When you have finished dictating your text, click the Microphone button again to make the speech recognition functions inactive.

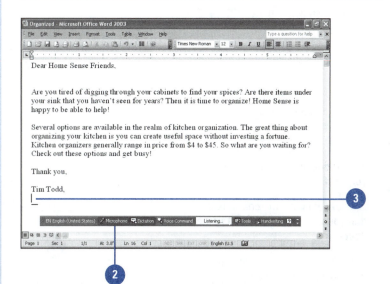

16

Recognizing Handwriting

Although entering information into an Office document through the keyboard is fast and efficient, you may find that you need to enter information in handwritten form. Office provides handwriting recognition to help you convert handwriting into text. Before you can insert handwritten text into a document, you need to have a mouse, a third party electronic stylus, an ink device, or a handwriting tablet, such as Tablet PC, attached to your computer. Although you can use the mouse, for best results you should use a handwriting input device. When you insert handwritten text into a document that already contains typed text, the handwritten text is converted to typed text and then inserted in line with the existing text at the point of the cursor. The program recognizes the handwriting when there is enough text for it to do so, when you reach the end of the line, or if you pause for approximately two seconds. In addition, the converted text will take on the same typeface attributes as the existing text.

Insert Handwritten Text into a Document

1 If necessary, display the Language bar.

2 Click the Handwriting button on the Language bar, and then click Write Anywhere.

3 Move the mouse over a blank area of your document, and then write your text.

After recognition, the characters that you write appear as text in the document.

4 Use the additional handwriting tools to move the cursor, change handwriting modes, and correct text.

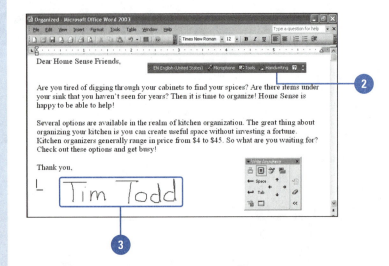

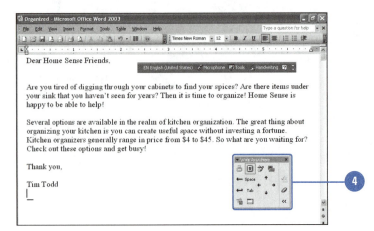

Insert Handwritten Text on a Writing Pad

1. If necessary, display the Language bar.

2. Click the Handwriting button on the Language bar, and then click Writing Pad.

3. Move the cursor over the writing area of the Writing Pad dialog box. (The cursor turns into a pen.)

4. Write your text with the pen.

   After recognition, the characters that you write appear in the document.

5. Use the additional handwriting tools to move the cursor, change handwriting modes, and correct text.

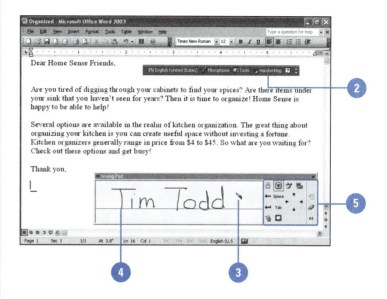

For Your Information

Using Additional Handwriting Tools

When you click the Handwriting button on the Language bar and then click the Writing Pad or Write Anywhere option, a dialog box opens on your screen with another toolbar. It has the same options that are available through the Handwriting button on the Language bar. In addition, the toolbar has the following buttons: Ink, Text, Backspace, Space, directional cursors, Enter, Tab, Recognize Now, and Write Anywhere. You use these buttons to control the input.

16

Automating Your Work with Macros

WW03E-5-1

Do you often redo many tasks that require the same, sometimes lengthy, series of steps? Rather than repeat the same actions, you can work faster by recording the entire series of keystrokes and commands in a custom command, or **macro**. A macro is a sequence of commands and entries that can be activated collectively by clicking a toolbar button, clicking a menu command, typing a key combination, or clicking the Run command in the Macros dialog box. Macros are a perfect way to speed up routine formatting, combine multiple commands, and automate complex tasks. The macro recorder archives every mouse click and key-stroke you make until you stop the recorder. Any time you want to repeat that series of actions, you "play," or run, the macro.

Record a Macro

1. Click the Tools menu, point to Macro, and then click Record New Macro.

2. Type a one word name for the macro.

3. Click the Store Macro In list arrow, and then click the template (or document) in which you want to save the macro.

4. Type a description of the macro.

5. Use one of the following methods to start recording the macro:

   ◆ If you want to assign the macro to a toolbar or shortcut key, click the Toolbars button or Keyboard button, assign the macro, and then click Close.

   ◆ If you don't want to assign the macro to a toolbar or shortcut key, click OK.

6. Perform each command or action to complete the task.

7. Click the Stop Recording button on the Stop Recording toolbar.

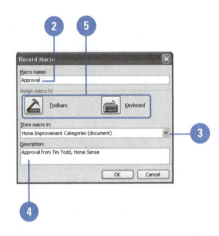

Run a Macro

① Click the Tools menu, point to Macro, and then click Macros.

② If necessary, click the Macros In list arrow, and then click the document that contains the macro you want to run.

③ Click the name of the macro you want to run.

④ Click Run.

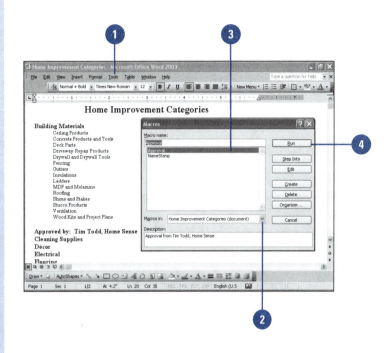

Delete a Macro

① Click the Tools menu, point to Macro, and then click Macros.

② Select the macro you want to remove.

③ Click Delete, and then click Yes to confirm the deletion.

④ Click Close.

Did You Know?

There is an appropriate location to store macros. If you want a macro to be available in all your Word documents, store it in the Normal template. If you want a macro available in all your worksheets, store it in the Personal Workbook.

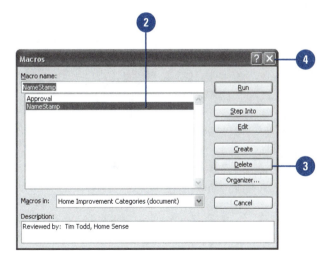

16

Modifying a Macro

WW03E-5-1

If a macro doesn't work exactly the way you want it to, you can fix the problem without re-creating the macro. Instead of recording the macro over again, Word allows you to **debug**, or repair, an existing macro so that you can change only the actions that aren't working correctly. When beginning the process, Word will step through each of the actions that you supplied when you created the macro. Look carefully for any mistakes, and then correct as necessary.

Debug a Macro Using Step Mode

1. Click the Tools menu, point to Macro, and then click Macros.

2. Click the name of the macro you want to debug.

3. Click Step Into.

4. Click the Debug menu, and then click Step Into to proceed through each action.

5. When you're done, click the File menu, and then click Close to return to your program.

6. Click OK to stop the debugger.

Module sheet

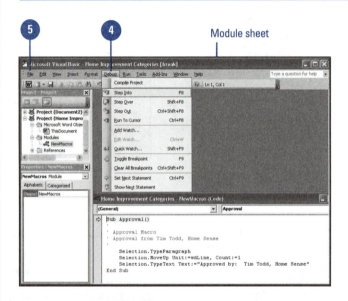

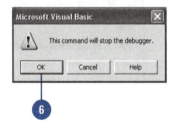

Did You Know?

You can re-record a macro. If you make a mistake as you record a macro, click the Stop Recording button on the Stop Recording toolbar, and then record the macro again using the same name. Click Yes in the dialog box to confirm that you want to replace the existing macro with the same name.

Microsoft Office Specialist

About the Microsoft Office Specialist Program

The Microsoft Office Specialist certification is the globally recognized standard for validating expertise with the Microsoft Office suite of business productivity programs. Earning an Microsoft Office Specialist certificate acknowledges you have the expertise to work with Microsoft Office programs. To earn the Microsoft Office Specialist certification, you must pass one or more certification exams for the Microsoft Office desktop applications of Microsoft Office Word, Microsoft Office Excel, Microsoft Office PowerPoint, Microsoft Office Outlook, or Microsoft Office Access. The Microsoft Office Specialist program typically offers certification exams at the "specialist" and "expert" skill levels. (The availability of Microsoft Office Specialist certification exams varies by program, program version, and language. Visit *www.microsoft.com/officespecialist* for exam availability and more information about the program.) The Microsoft Office Specialist program is the only Microsoft-approved program in the world for certifying proficiency with Microsoft Office programs.

What Does This Logo Mean?

It means this book has been approved by the Microsoft Office Specialist program to be certified courseware for learning Microsoft Office Word 2003 and preparing for the certification exam. This book will prepare you fully for the Microsoft Office Specialist exam at the specialist and expert levels for Microsoft Office Word 2003. Each certification level has a set of objectives, which are organized into broader skill sets. Throughout this book, content that pertains to a Microsoft Office Specialist objective is identified with the Microsoft Office Specialist logo and objective number below the title of the topic:

 WD03S-1-1
WD03E-2-2

Word 2003 Specialist Objectives

Objective	Skill	Page
WW03S-1	**Creating Content**	
WW03S-1-1	Insert and edit text, symbols and special characters	11, 15, 126, 194, 198-199, 291
WW03S-1-2	Insert frequently used and pre-defined text	36, 38-39, 43, 127
WW03S-1-3	Navigate to specific content	10, 18-19, 161, 192-193
WW03S-1-4	Insert, position and size graphics	99, 106
WW03S-1-5	Create and modify diagrams and charts	146-150
WW03S-1-6	Locate, select and insert supporting information	128-129
WW03S-2	**Organizing Content**	
WW03S-2-1	Insert and modify tables	68-69, 72-79, 80-82
WW03S-2-2	Create bulleted lists, numbered lists and outlines	70-71, 141
WW03S-2-3	Insert and modify hyperlinks	250-253
WW03S-3	**Formatting Content**	
WW03S-3-1	Format text	54-55, 57-58, 60-61, 92-95
WW03S-3-2	Format paragraphs	63-69
WW03S-3-3	Apply and format columns	242-243
WW03S-3-4	Insert and modify content in headers and footers	156-157, 202-203
WW03S-3-5	Modify document layout and page setup	204-205, 208-209
WW03S-4	**Collaborating**	
WW03S-4-1	Circulate documents for review	294-295, 271-272
WW03S-4-2	Compare and merge document versions	283
WW03S-4-3	Insert, view and edit comments	278-279
WW03S-4-4	Track, accept and reject proposed changes	280-281
WW03S-5	**Formatting and Managing Documents**	
WW03S-5-1	Create new documents using templates	84, 90
WW03S-5-2	Review and modify document properties	167-168
WW03S-5-3	Organize documents using file folders	20-21
WW03S-5-4	Save data in appropriate formats for different uses	258-259, 316
WW03S-5-5	Print documents, envelopes and labels	186-187, 211
WW03S-5-6	Preview documents and Web pages	210, 257
WW03S-5-7	Change and organize document views and windows	16-18, 34-35, 59, 291

Word 2003 Expert Objectives

Objective	Skill	Page
WW03E-1	**Formatting Content**	
WW03E-1-1	Create custom styles for text, tables and lists	92-95
WW03E-1-2	Control pagination	207-209
WW03E-1-3	Format, position and resize graphics using layout features	110, 112-113, 214-215, 234-235, 238-239
WW03E-1-4	Insert and modify objects	318-319
WW03E-1-5	Create and modify diagrams and charts using data from other sources	324-325
WW03E-2	**Organizing Content**	
WW03E-2-1	Sort content in lists and tables	75
WW03E-2-2	Perform calculations in tables	142-143
WW03E-2-3	Modify table formats	76-81
WW03E-2-4	Summarize document content using automated tools	166, 199
WW03E-2-5	Use automated tools for document navigation	19, 134-135
WW03E-2-6	Merge letters with other data sources	170-173, 176-177
WW03E-2-7	Merge labels with other data sources	182-183
WW03E-2-8	Structure documents using XML	322-323
WW03E-3	**Formatting Documents**	
WW03E-3-1	Create and modify forms	264, 284-285
WW03E-3-2	Create and modify document background	120-121, 256
WW03E-3-3	Create and modify document indexes and tables	137, 162-165
WW03E-3-4	Insert and modify endnotes, footnotes, captions, and cross-references	130-133, 136, 158
WW03E-3-5	Create and manage master documents and subdocuments	152-153
WW03E-4	**Collaborating**	
WW03E-4-1	Modify track changes options	282
WW03E-4-2	Publish and edit Web documents in Word	249, 254-255, 258-259
WW03E-4-3	Manage document versions	276-277
WW03E-4-4	Protect and restrict forms and documents	286-287, 290
WW03E-4-5	Attach digital signatures to documents	288
WW03E-4-6	Customize document properties	167

Word 2003 Expert Objectives *(continued)*

Objective	Skill	Page
WW03E-5	**Customizing Word**	
WW03E-5-1	Create, edit, and run macros	350-352
WW03E-5-2	Customize menus and toolbars	336-339, 341
WW03E-5-3	Modify Word default settings	200-201, 334-335

m

Preparing for a Microsoft Office Specialist Exam

Every Microsoft Office Specialist certification exam is developed from a list of objectives, which are based on studies of how Microsoft Office programs are actually used in the workplace. The list of objectives determine the scope of each exam, so they provide you with the information you need to prepare for Microsoft Office Specialist certification. Microsoft Office Specialist Approved Courseware, including the Show Me series, is reviewed and approved on the basis of its coverage of the objectives. To prepare for the certification exam, you should review and perform each task identified with a Microsoft Office Specialist objective to confirm that you can meet the requirements for the exam.

Taking a Microsoft Office Specialist Exam

The Microsoft Office Specialist certification exams are not written exams. Instead, the exams are performance-based examinations that allow you to interact with a "live" Office program as you complete a series of objective-based tasks. All the standard menus, toolbars, and keyboard shortcuts are available during the exam. Microsoft Office Specialist exams for Office 2003 programs consist of 25 to 35 questions, each of which requires you to complete one or more tasks using the Office program for which you are seeking certification. A typical exam takes from 45 to 60 minutes. Passing percentages range from 70 to 80 percent correct.

The Exam Experience

After you fill out a series of information screens, the testing software starts the exam and the Office program. The test questions appear in the exam dialog box in the lower right corner of the screen.

- The timer starts when the first question appears and displays the remaining exam time at the top of the exam dialog box. If the timer and the counter are distracting, you can click the timer to remove the display.

- The counter at the top of the exam dialog box tracks how many questions you have completed and how many remain.

- If you think you have made a mistake, you can click the Reset button to restart the question. The Reset button does not restart the entire exam or extend the exam time limit.

- When you complete a question, click the Next button to move to the next question. It is not possible to move back to a previous question on the exam.

- If the exam dialog box gets in your way, you can click the Minimize button in the upper right corner of the exam dialog box to hide it, or you can drag the title bar to another part of the screen to move it.

Tips for Taking an Exam

◆ Carefully read and follow all instructions provided in each question.

◆ Make sure all steps in a task are completed before proceeding to the next exam question.

◆ Enter requested information as it appears in the instructions without formatting unless you are explicitly requested otherwise.

◆ Close all dialog boxes before proceeding to the next exam question unless you are specifically instructed otherwise.

◆ Do not leave tables, boxes, or cells "active" unless instructed otherwise.

◆ Do not cut and paste information from the exam interface into the program.

◆ When you print a document from an Office program during the exam, nothing actually gets printed.

◆ Errant keystrokes or mouse clicks do not count against your score as long as you achieve the correct end result. You are scored based on the end result, not the method you use to achieve it. However, if a specific method is explicitly requested, you need to use it to get credit for the results.

◆ The overall exam is timed, so taking too long on individual questions may leave you without enough time to complete the entire exam.

◆ If you experience computer problems during the exam, notify a testing center administrator immediately to restart your exam where you were interrupted.

Exam Results

At the end of the exam, a score report appears indicating whether you passed or failed the exam. An official certificate is mailed to successful candidates in approximately two to three weeks.

Getting More Information

To learn more about the Microsoft Office Specialist program, read a list of frequently asked questions, and locate the nearest testing center, visit:

www.microsoft.com/officespecialist

New! Features

Microsoft Office Word 2003

Microsoft Office Word 2003 is the word processing program that makes documents easier to create, share, and read. The review and markup features have been enhanced to address the many ways that you can track changes and manage comments. Word 2003 also supports Extensible Markup Language (XML) as a file format and serves as a fully functional XML editor.

♦ **Improved readability (p. 18-19)** Word makes it easier than ever to read documents on your computer with Reading Layout view. Reading Layout view allows you to hide unnecessary toolbars, display the Document Map or the Thumbnail pane, so you can quickly jump to sections of the document, automatically scale the contents of a document to pages that fit comfortably on your screen and that are easy to browse, and highlight portions of the document and add comments or make changes.

♦ **Compare documents side by side (p. 34)** Comparing documents side by side using the Compare Side by Side With command on the Window menu allows you to determine the differences between two documents without having to merge multiple users' changes into one document. You can scroll through both documents at the same time to identify differences between the two documents.

♦ **Person Names Smart Tag menu (p. 40-41)** Quickly locate contact information, such as a person's phone number, and complete tasks, such as scheduling a meeting, using the Person Names Smart Tag menu. The menu is available using the Smart Tag Options button in Word wherever a person's name appears.

♦ **Research task pane (p. 128-129)** The Research task pane offers a wide variety of reference information and expanded resources if you have an Internet connection. You can conduct research on topics using an encyclopedia, Web search, or by accessing third-party content.

♦ **Enhanced international features (p. 176-177, 196-197)** Word provides enhanced features for creating foreign-language documents and for using documents in a multiple language setting. Mail Merge chooses the correct greeting format based on the gender of the recipient if the language requires it. Mail Merge can also format addresses based on the geographical region of the recipient. Enhancements to typography result in better display of text in more languages than ever before.

- **Enhanced document protection (p. 290-291)** Fine-tune document protection to control document formatting, content, or both. For example, you can specify that only certain styles are available to use, and those styles cannot be modified. When protecting a document for changes to content, you no longer have to apply the same restriction to everyone and to the entire document. You can selectively allow certain people to edit specified parts of the document.

- **Information Rights Management (p. 292-293)** Create or view content with restricted permission using Information Rights Management (IRM). IRM allows individual authors to specify permission for who can access and use documents or e-mail messages, and helps prevent sensitive information from being printed, forwarded, or copied by unauthorized people.

- **Document Workspaces (p. 298-311)** Create a Document Workspace to simplify the process of co-writing, editing, and reviewing documents with others in real time. A Document Workspace site is a Microsoft SharePoint Services site that is centered around one or more documents and is typically created when you use e-mail to send a document as a shared attachment.

- **Support for XML documents (p. 320-323)** Save documents in XML format to make the content of your documents available for automated data-mining and repurposing processes. You can now identify and extract specific pieces of business data from ordinary business documents. For example, an invoice that contains the name and address of a customer or a report that contains last quarter's financial results are no longer static documents. The information they contain can be passed to a database or reused elsewhere, outside of the documents.

- **Support for ink devices (p. 348-349)** If you are using a device that supports ink input, such as a Tablet PC, you can use the tablet pen to take advantage of handwriting in Word 2003. You can mark up a document with handwritten comments and annotations, incorporate handwritten content into a Word document, and send handwritten e-mail messages by using WordMail in Outlook.

LIVERPOOL LIBRARIES & INFORMATION SERVICES

Troubleshooting

Index